D. H. Lawrence:
A Bibliography
1911-1975

D. H. Lawrence:
a Bibliography
1911-1975

compiled by
John E. Stoll

Whitston Publishing Company
Troy, New York
1977

Copyright 1977
John E. Stoll

Library of Congress Catalog Card Number 73-78073

ISBN 0-87875-042-8

Printed in the United States of America

*For scholars and admirers of
Lawrence and for my friend,
Wallace Douglas.*

TABLE OF CONTENTS

Introduction

My purpose is to be useful to the general reader and to the scholar by incorporating the existing, somewhat scattered bibliographical information on D. H. Lawrence into one book, a practical guide for study and professional reference. I have not read more than a large fraction of all that has been published about D. H. Lawrence, but I have not hesitated to comment upon the content and occasionally the quality of specific works when I could. When I could not, I have sometimes made use of other sources, the *D. H. Lawrence Review* and Ronald Draper's *D. H. Lawrence: The Critical Heritage* in particular, to supply summarizing statements of fact. I have also tried to be as exhaustive as possible while knowing all along that the ultimately complete bibliography on an author who continues to be widely read and popular would be impossible.

Respecting Lawrence himself, continued interest in him seems to confirm his stature as one of the three or four critically important authors of our age, as a novelist and thinker upon whom one must take a stand in one way or another. The vast outpouring of publications on him during the last ten years, the formation of a D.H. Lawrence periodical, and the recent film adaptations of his work lend emphasis to this estimate. Not only is Lawrence in the process of seeping down into the popular consciousness (a phrase that, applied to himself at least, he would have had many, perhaps violent reservations about), but for better or worse he continues to be the subject of many doctoral dissertations, a fact that I have documented within.

As an old-fashioned Lawrence scholar, a member of the "great age" of Lawrence scholarship, the fifties and very early sixties, I have my doubts about the quality and viewpoint of much of the new work. It is incomplete, partial, and dangerously ready to commit itself unreflectingly to the Lawrentian unconscious and to the Lawrentian view of things in the guise of its interest in matters "archetypal." But the new scholarship is also vital, thorough (if too particular) in what it attempts, and passionately "involved." It has the virtue, as well, of avoiding doctrine stances and of not dividing itself up into "schools" of Lawrence criticism, the "Freudian" and "Jungian" (vitalist) syndrome of the recent past, each with its own special way of distorting the author's work by subjecting him to various kinds of a priori reasoning. The new people, many of them, seem literally hell-bent on making Lawrence "relevant" to their lives, and the not always wise old professor is put in the awkward if human position of rejecting what he would affirm.

Yet the new scholarship does show signs of "institution-alizing" itself, of becoming "respectable," and as it does so the critics tend to be more traditional in spite of themselves, if only to protect their own domains. As a result, and gradually, there will perhaps be a return to textual criticism, a process, I believe, that is already occurring. The great outpouring shows some indication of abating, and as American society returns to a more recognizable, semi-traditional cast, recent Lawrence scholarship shows signs of following the times. The task ahead is to assess its durability and value.

RELIABLE AND, FOR THE MOST PART, EASILY ACCESSIBLE PRIMARY SOURCES

D. H. Lawrence. *Aaron's Rod.* London and Toronto: William Heinemann, 1954—. The Phoenix Edition. Also, New York: Viking Press, 1961. The Compass Edition.

—. *Apocalypse.* New York: Viking Press, 1966.

—. *Art and Painting.* London: The Bureau of Current Affairs, 1951.

—. *Assorted Articles.* New York: Alfred A. Knopf, 1930.

—. *Bay.* London: Cyril W. Beaumont, 1919. Poems.

—. *The Centaur Letters.* Introduction by Edward MacDonald. Humanistic Research Center: University of Texas Press, 1971.

—. *The Collected Letters of D.H. Lawrence,* ed. Harry T. Moore. 2 vols. New York: Viking Press, 1962.

—. *The Collected Poems of D.H. Lawrence.* London: Martin Secker, 1928; New York: Jonathan Cape and Harrison Smith, 1929.

—. *Complete Plays.* New York: Viking Press, 1966. The Compass Edition.

—. *The Complete Plays.* London: William Heinemann, 1965, 1970. The Phoenix Edition.

—. *Complete Poems,* ed. Vivian de Sola Pinto and Warren Roberts. New York: Viking Press, 1964.

—. *The Complete Poems of D.H. Lawrence,* ed. Vivian de Sola Pinto and Warren Roberts. London: William Heinemann, 1957. The Phoenix Edition.

—. *The Complete Short Stories.* 3 vols. The Phoenix and Compass Editions, 1961.

—. *Eight Letters by D.H. Lawrence to Rachel Annand Taylor,* ed. Maj. Ewing. Pasadena, California: G. DAhlstrom, 1956.

—. *The Escaped Cook,* ed. Gerald M. Lacy. Los Angeles: Black Sparrow Press, 1973.

—. *Etruscan Places.* New York: Viking Press, 1963. The Compass Edition.

—. *Fire and Other Poems.* San Francisco: Grabhorn Press for the Book Club of California, 1940.

—. *The First Lady Chatterley.* Foreword by Frieda Lawrence. New York: Dial Press, 1944.

—. "Foreword," *All Things Are Possible,* Leo Shestov. Trans. S.S. Koteliansky. London: Martin Secker, 1920.

—. "Introduction," *Cavalleria Rusticana and Other Stories.* London: Jonathan Cape, 1932.

—. "Introducation," *The Grand Inquisitor,* trans. S.S. Koteliansky. London: Elkin Mathews and Marrot, 1930.

—. "Introduction," *Max Havelaar; or, The Coffee Auctions of the Dutch Trading Company,* Eduard D. Dekker. New York: London House and Maxwell, 1967.

—. "Introduction," *Mèmoirs of the Foreign Legion,* Maurice Magnus. London: Martin Secker, 1924.

—. "Introduction," *The Story of Doctor Manente,* 11 Lasca. Florence: G. Orioli, 1929; London: P.E. Grey, 1930.

—. *John Thomas and Lady Jane.* The second, unpublished version of *Lady Chatterley's Lover.* New York: Viking Press, 1972. The Compass Edition.

—. *Kangaroo.The* Phoenix Edition., 1954—. New York: Viking Press, 1968. The Compass Edition.

—. *Lady Chatterley's Lover.* Florence: G. Orioli, 1928. The third version of *Lady Chatterley's Lover.*

—. *Lady Chatterley's Lover.* Introduction by Mark Schorer. New York: Grove Press, 1959. Third version.

—. *Lady Chatterley's Lover.* London: William Heinemann, 1963. The Phoenix Edition. Third Version.

—. *D.H. Lawrence: A Critical Anthology.* Harmondsworth, Middlesex: Penguin Books, 1973. A selection of Lawrence's letters and early reviews and criticism.

—. *D.H. Lawrence and Italy: Twilight in Italy, Sea and Sardinia, Etruscan Places.* New York: Viking Press, 1972.

—. *Lawrence in Love: Letters to Louie Burrows*, ed. James T. Boulton. Nottingham, England: University of Nottingham, 1968.

—. *D.H. Lawrence on Education*, ed. Raymond and Joy Williams. Harmondsworth: Penguin Books, 1973.

—. *D.H. Lawrence's Letters to Bertrand Russell*, ed. Harry T. Moore. New York: Gotham Book Mart, 1948.

—. *D.H. Lawrence's Stories, Essays and Poems*, ed. Desmond Hawkins. London: J.M. Dent, 1974. Everyman's Library.

—. *Letters from D.H. Lawrence to Martin Secker*. Privately Published by Angelo Ravagli and C. Montague Weekly, Executors of the Estate of Frieda Lawrence Ravagli, 1970.

—. The *Letters of D.H. Lawrence*, ed. Aldous Huxley. New York: Viking Press, 1936.

—. *Life*. Marazion, Cornwall: Ark Press, 1954.

—. *The Life of J. Middleton Murry*. London: Privately Printed, 1930.

—. *The Lost Girl*. The Phoenix Edition, 1954—. The Compass Edition, 1968.

—. *The Man Who Died*. New York: Alfred A. Knopf, 1950.

—. *Mornings in Mexico and Etruscan Places*. The Phoenix Edition, 1954—.

—. Lawrence H. Davison. *Movements in European History*. London: Oxford University Press, 1921. Reissued by Oxford University Press, 1971.

—. "My Skirmish with Jolly Roger." Introduction to *Lady Chatterley's Lover*. Paris Popular Edition: Privately Printed; New York: Random House, 1929.

—. *Paintings of D.H. Lawrence*, ed. Mervyn Levy. With Essays by Harry T. Moore, Jack Lindsay, and Herbert Read. London: Cory, Adams, and Mackay; New York: Viking Press, 1964.

—. *The Paintings of D.H. Lawrence*. London: Mandrake Press, 1929.

—. *Phoenix: The Posthumous Papers of D.H. Lawrence*, ed. Edward D. MacDonald. London: William Heinemann, 1936. Reissued by Viking Press, 1968. The Compass Edition.

—. *Phoenix II: Uncollected, Unpublished, and Other Prose Works by D.H. Lawrence,* ed. Warren Roberts and Harry T. Moore. London: William Heinemann; New York: Viking Press, 1968. The Compass Edition.

—. *The Plays of D.H. Lawrence,* ed. Sylvia Sklar. New York: Barnes and Noble, 1974.

—. *The Plumed Serpent.* New York: Alfred A. Knopf, 1952.

—. *The Portable D.H. Lawrence,* ed. Diana Trilling. New York: Viking Press, 1947.

—. "The Portrait of M.M." (Maurice Magnus). In *the noble savage,* ed. Saul Bellow, Keith Botsford, and Jack Ludwig, pp. 178-253. 2d issue. New York Meridian Books, 1960.

—. *'The Princess' and Other Stories,* ed. Keith Sagar. Harmondsworth: Penguin Books, 1971. Includes "Sun," generally available for the first time.

—. *Psychoanalysis and the Unconscious; Fantasia of the Unconscious.* New York: Viking Press, 1962.

—. *The Quest for Rananim: D.H. Lawrence's Letters to S.S. Koteliansky, 1914 to 1930,* ed. George J. Zytaruk. Montreal and London: McGill-Queens University Press, 1970.

—. *The Rainbow.* The Phoenix Edition, 1954—. The Compass Edition, 1961.

—. *Reflections on the Death of a Porcupine and Other Essays.* Bloomington: Indiana University Press, 1963.

—. *Sea and Sardina.* Introduction by Richard Aldinton. New York: Viking Press, 1963. The Compass Edition.

—. *The Selected Letters of D.H. Lawrence,* ed. Diana Trilljng. New York: Ferrar, Straus & Cudahy, 1958.

—. *Selected Literary Criticism,* ed. Anthony Beal. New York: Viking Press, 1956. Reissued London: William Heinemann, 1967.

—. *Selected Poems.* Norfolk, Virgina: New Directions, 1948.

—. *Selected Poems.* New York: Viking Press, 1959.

—. *Sex, Literature and Censorship,* ed. Harry T. Moore. New York: Twayne Publishers, 1953; New York: Viking Press, 1959. The Compass Edition.

—. *Sons and Lovers.* The Phoenix Edition, 1954—. The Compass Edition, 1960.

—. *The Spirit of Place: An Anthology Made by Richard Aldington from the Prose of D.H. Lawrence.* London: William Heinemann, 1935; London: Readers Union (William Heinemann), 1944.

—. *Studies in Classic American Literature.* New York: Viking Press, 1964.

—. *Three Plays (A Collier's Friday Night, the Daughter-in-Law,* and *The Widowing of Mrs. Holroyd).* Introduction by Raymond Williams. Harmondsworth and Baltimore: Penguin Books, 1969.

—. *The Trespasser.* The Phoenix Edition, 1954—.

—. *The Triumph of the Machine.* London: Faber and Faber, 1930. Poems.

—. *Twilight in Italy.* The Phoenix Edition, 1954—. The Compass Edition, 1962.

—. *The White Peacock.* The Phoenix Edition, 1954—. Carbondale, Illinois: Southern Illinois University Press, 1966.

—. *The Widowing of Mrs. Holroyd and the Daughter-in-Law.* London: William Heinemann, 1968.

—. *Women in Love.* The Phoenix Edition, 1954—. The Compass Edition, 1960.

— and M.L. Skinner. *The Boy in the Bush.* New York: Thomas Seltzer, 1924.

—, trans. *Cavalleria Rusticana and Other Stories.* London: Jonathan Cape, 1932.

—, trans. *The Gentleman from San Francisco,* I.A. Bunin. London: Hogarth Press, 1922.

—, trans. *Little Novels of Sicily.* New York: Grove Press, 1953.

—, trans. *Mastro-Don Gesualdo,* Giovanni Verga. New York: Thomas Seltzer, 1923.

—, trans. *The Story of Doctor Manente,* 11 Lasca. Florence: G. Orioli, 1929; London: P.E. Grey, 1930.

Martin Secker. *Letters from a Publisher: Martin Secker to D.H. Lawrence and Others.* London: London: Enitharmon Press, 1970.

Reloy Garcia and James Karabatsos, ed. *A Concordance to the Poetry of D.H. Lawrence.* Lincoln: University of Nebraska Press, 1970.

—, ed. *A Concordance to the Short Fiction of D.H. Lawrence.* Lincoln: University of Nebraska Press, 1972.

Aldington, Richard. *D.H. Lawrence: A Complete List of His Works, Together with a Critical Appreciation.* London: William Heinemann, 1935.

Allendorf, Otmar. "Criticism of D.H. Lawrence in German: 1923-1970, A *Bibliography,*" *D.H. Lawrence Review,* IV (1971), 210-220.

Altenberg, Bengt. "A Checklist of D.H. Lawrence Scholarship in Scandinavia, 1934-1968," *D.H. Lawrence Review,* II (1969),275-277.

Anonymous. *A Catalogue of Valuable Books by D.H. Lawrence.* Edinburgh: Melvin Rare Books, 1950.

Beards, Richard D. "The Checklist of D.H. Lawrence Criticism and Scholarship, 1972," *D.H. Lawrence Review,* VI (1973), 100-108.

—. "The Checklist of D.H. Lawrence Criticism and Scholarship, 1972," *D.H. Lawrence Review,* VI (1973),100-108.

—. "The Checklist of D.H. Lawrence Scholarship for 1973," *D.H. Lawrence Review,* VII (1974), 89-98.

—. "The Checklist of D.H. Lawrence Criticism, 1974," *D.H. Lawrence Review,* VIII (1975), 99-105.

—. "The Checklist of D.H. Lawrence Criticism and Scholarship, 1975," *D.H. Lawrence Review,* IX (1976), 157-166.

—, assisted by Barbara Willens. "D.H. Lawrence: Criticism, 1968-1969; A Checklist," *D.H. Lawrence Review,* III (1970), 70-86.

—, with the assistance of G.B. Crump. "D.H. Lawrence: Ten Years of Criticism, 1959-1968. A Checklist," *D.H. Lawrence Review,* I (1968), 245-285.

Beebe, Maurice and Anthony Tomasic. "Criticism of D.H. Lawrence: A Selected Checklist with an Index to Studies of Separate Works," *Modern Fiction Studies,* V (1959), 83-98.

Cushman, Keith. *An Exhibition of First Editions and Manuscripts from the D.H. Lawrence Collection of John E. Baker, Jr.* Chicago: University of Chicago, 1973.

—. "A Profile of John E. Baker, Jr., and His Lawrence Collection," *D.H. Lawrence Review,* VII (1974), 83-88.

—. "A Profile of John Martin and His Lawrence Collection," *D.H. Lawrence Review,* VIII (1974), 199-205.

Edwards, Lucy I. *D.H. Lawrence: A Finding List; Holdings in the City, County and University Libaries of Nottingham.* Nottingham, England: Nottinghamshire County Library, 1968.

Fabes, Gilbert H. *D.H. Lawrence: His First Editions: Points and Values.* London: W. and G. Foyle, 1933.

Farmer, David. "A Descriptive and Analytical Catalogue of the D.H. Lawrence Collection at the University of Texas at Austin," Dissertation, University of Texas, 1970.

Ferrier, Carole. "D.H. Lawence's Pre-1920 Poetry: A Descriptive Bibliography of Manuscripts, Typescripts, and Proofs," *D.H. Lawrence Review,* VI (1973), 333-359.

Finney, Brian H. "A Profile of Mr. George Lazarus and His Lawrence Collection of Manuscripts and First Editions," *D.H. Lawrence Review,* VI (1973), 309-312.

Garmon, Gerald M. "Doctoral Dissertations on D.H. Lawrence: Bibliographical Addenda," *D.H. Lawrence Review,* V (1972), 170-173.

—, C. Howard, and Edward A. Bojarski. "Theses on D.H. Lawrence: 1931-1972: A Bibliography with Addenda of Senior Theses and Works in Progress," *D.H. Lawrence Review,* VI (1973), 217-230. Masters and Honors theses.

Heath, Alice C. "The Checklist of D.H. Lawrence Criticism and Scholarship, 1971," *D.H. Lawrence Review,* V (1972), 82-92.

Hoffman, Lois. "A Catalogue of the Frieda Lawrence Manuscripts in German at the University of Texas," *The Library Chronicle* (University of Texas), New Series, VI (1973), 87-105.

Jackson, Dennis. "Doctoral Dissertations on D.H. Lawrence: Bibliographical Addenda," *D.H. Lawrence Review,* VIII (1975), 236-241.

—. "Theses on D.H. Lawrence: Bibliographical Addenda," *D.H. Lawrence Review,* VIII (1975), 106-112.

Kai, Sadanobu, Yasuichiro Ohashi, Taiji Okada, and Toru Okumura. "A Checklist of D.H. Lawrence's Articles in Japan, 1951-1968," *D.H.Lawrence Review*, II (1969), 172-191.

Losa, Margarida and John Kennedy. "D.H. Lawrence: A Secondary Bibliography for Portugal," *D.H. Lawrence Review,* IV (1971),314-317.

MacDonald, Edward D. *Bibliography of D.H. Lawrence with Supplement,* 1925-1930. Reissued New York: Kruas Reprint Company, 1969. Replaces the earlier *Bibliography* (Philadelphia: Centaur Press, 1925) and *Supplement* (Centaur Press, 1931). Still useful, expecially for reviews, but much superseded by Warren Roberts (below).

Pinto, Vivian de Sola, ed. *D.H. Lawrence After Thirty Years, 1930-1960. Catalogue of an Exhibition Held in the Art Gallery of the University of Nottingham 17 June-30 July 1960.* Nottingham: Curwen Press, 1960.

Powell, Lawrence C. *The Manuscripts of D.H. Lawrence: A Descriptive Catalogue.* "Introduction," Aldous Huxley. Los Angeles Public Library: Ward Ritchie Press, 1937.

Roberts, F. Warren. *A Bibliography of D.H. Lawrence.* London: Repert Hart-Davis, 1963. Best source for pre-1960 editions of Lawrence, a physical description of them, and reviews of Lawrence's works.

—. "The D.H. Lawrence New Mexico Fellowship Fund Collection: A Checklist, 1950-1960," *Texas Quarterly,* III (1960), 211-216.

—. "The Manuscripts of D.H. Lawrence," *Library Chron. of the University of Texas Library,* V (1955), 36-43.

Schorer, Mark. *Lawrence in the War Years. With a Checklist of His Correspondence in the Charlotte Ashley Felton Memorial Library of the Stanford University Libraries.* Stanford: Stanford University Press, 1968.

Shirai, Toshitaka. "A Checklist of Theses on D.H. Lawrence in Japan, 1968-1973," *D.H. Lawrence Review,* VIII (1975), 233-235. Masters theses.

Silet, Charles L. "A Check-List of *The Seven Arts,*" *Serif,* IX (1972), 15-21. Includes manuscripts Lawrence published there.

Snyder, Harold J. *A Catalogue of English and American First Editions 1911-1932 of D.H. Lawrence.* New York: Privately printed, 1932.

Spilka, Mark. "Lawrence," In *The English Novel: Select Bibliographical Guides,* ed. A.E. Dyson (London: Oxford University press, 1974), 334-348.

Tannenbaum, Earl, ed. *D.H. Lawrence: An Exhibition of First Edtions, Manuscripts, Paintings, Letters, and Miscellany at Southern Illinois University Library, April, 1958.* Carbondale: Southern Illinois University Press, 1958.

Tedlock, Ernest W., Jr. *The Frieda Lawrence Collection of D.H. Lawrence Manuscripts: A Descriptive Bibliography.* Albuquerque: University of New Mexico Press, 1947.

White, William. *D.H. Lawrence: A Checklist, 1931-1949.* Detroit: Wayne State University Press, 1950.

Willison, I.R., ed. *The New Cambridge Bibliography of English Literature,* IV. Cambridge, England: Cambridge University Press, 1972. Lawrence, 482-503.

Aiken, Conrad. *A Reviewer's ABC: Collected Criticism of Conrad Aiken from 1916 to the Present*, ed. Rufus A. Blanchard. New York: Meridian Books, 1958.

—. *Skepticisms: Notes on Contemporary Poetry*. New York: Alfred A. Knopf, 1919.

Aldridge, James W., ed. *Critiques and Essays on Modern Fiction*. New York: Ronald Press, 1952.

Allen, Walter. *The English Novel: A Short Critical History*. New York: E.P. Dutton, 1957. Excellent historical account and well-written.

—. *Tradition and Dream: The English and American Novel from the Twenties to Our Time*. London: J.M. Dent & Sons, 1964. Issued in America as *The Modern Novel in Britian and the United States*. (New York: Dutton, 1964).

Alvarez, A. *The Shaping Spirit: Studies in Modern English and American Poets*. London: Chatto & Windus, 1958. The American edition (Scribners, 1958) is entitled *Stewards of Excellence*. Sections on Lawrence (140-161), Joyce, Yeats, Pound, Auden, and others.

Amis, Kingsley. *What Became of Jane Austen?*. New York: Harcourt, Brace, Jovanovich, 1971.

Asquith, Lady Cynthia. *Diaries: 1915-1918. London:* Hutchinson, 1968. References to Lawrence's responses to the war, publishing difficulties, etc.

Auden, W.H. *The Dyer's Hand and Other Essays*. New York: Random House, 1962. Excellent article on Lawrence, who was a major early influence on Auden.

Baker, Ernest A. *History of the English Novel*. London: H.F. and G. Witherby, 1939. See volume 10, 345-391, on Lawrence.

Baker, William E. *Syntax in English Poetry, 1870-1930*. Berkeley: University of California Press, 1967. References to Lawrence's use of dislocated word groups, sentence fragments, etc.

Bartlett, Phyllis. *Poems in Process*. New York: Oxford Press, 1951.

Bates, H.E. *The Modern Short Story: A Critical Survey.* New York: T. Nelson, 1943.

Beach, Joseph Warren. *The Twentieth Century Novel: Studies in Technique.* New York: The Century Company, 1932.

Bell, Quentin. *Bloomsbury.* London: Weidenfeld and Nicholson, 1968.

Bentley, Eric. *A Century of Hero Worship.* New York: Lippincott, 1944. Lawrence, 231-253.

Birnbaum, Malcolm. *The Social Context of Modern English Literature.* New York: Schocken Books, 1971. Passing references to Lawrence.

Black, Michael. *The Literature of Fidelity.* London: Chatto & Windus, 1975. A chapter on *Lady Chatterley's Lover.*

Blackmur, R.P. *Form and Value in Modern Poetry.* New York: Coubleday and Company, 1957. Anti-Lawrentian, but an excellent statement of the formalist viewpoint.

Bogan, Louise. *A Poet's Alphabet: Reflections on the Literary Art and Vocation.* New York: McGraw-Hill, 1970. Lawrence, 276-282.

Bradbury, Malcolm. *Possibilities: Essays on the State of the Novel.* New York: Oxford University Press, 1973. References to Lawrence, expecially 81-90.

—. *The Social Context of Modern English Literature.* New York: Schocken Books, 1971.

Brewster, Dorothy and Angus Burrell. *Modern Fiction.* New York: Columbia University Press, 1935. Lawrence, 137-154.

Brooks, Cleanth, John T. Purser, and Robert Penn Warren. *An Approach to Literature.* New York: Appleton-Centruy-Crofts, 1952. The formalist viewpoint.

Buckley, Jerome H. *Season of Youth: The Bildungsroman from Dickens to Golding.* Cambridge: Harvard University Press, 1974. A chapter on Lawrence.

Burke, Kenneth. *Permanence and Change: An Anatomy of Purpose.* Los Altos, California: Hermes Publications, 1957.

Canby, Henry Seidel. *Definitions: Essays in Contemporary Criticism.* Second Series. New York: Harcourt, Brace, 1924. Lawrence, 113-122.

14

Carter, Frederick. *The Dragon of Revelation.* London: Harms-worth, 1931. A "mystical" approach to Lawrence.

Channing-Pearce, Melville. *The Terrible Crystal: Studies in Kierkegaard and Modern Christianity.* New York: Oxford University Press, 1941. Lawrence, 179-189.

Charques, R.D. *Contemporary Literature and Social Revolution.* London: Martin Secker, 1933.

Chase, Richard. *The American Novel and Its Tradition.* Garden City, New York: Doubleday and Company, 1957. Collateral, but a view of the American novel essentially influenced by *Studies in American Literature.*

Clark, Colin C. *River of Dissolution: D.H. Lawrence and English Romanticism.* London: Routledge and Kegan Paul, 1969. Perhaps the best of the very recent books on Lawrence.

Collins, Joseph. *The Doctor Looks at Literature.* New York: Doran, 1923. Lawrence 256-288.

Collins, Norman. *The Facts of Fiction.* London: Gollancz, 1932. Lawrence, 237-248.

Craig, Alec. *The Banned Books of England.* London: Allen and Unwin, 1937. Includes a discussion of *Lady Chatterley's Lover.*

Craig, David. *The REal Foundations: Literature and Social Change.* New York: Oxford University Press, 1974. Chapters on Lawrence.

Cunliffe, J.W. *English Literature in the Twentieth Century.* New York: Macmillan, 1932. Lawrence, 209-228.

Dahlberg, Edward and Sir Herbert Read. *Truth is More Sacred: A Critical Exchange on Modern Literature.* New York: Horizon Press, 1961. Lawrence, 69-117.

Daiches, David. *The Novel and the Modern World.* Revised edition. Chicago: University of Chicago Press, 1960. New chapters on Lawrence by a first-rate critical mind.

De Beauvoir, Simone. *The Second Sex.* New York: Alfred A. Knopf, 1957.

Delavenay, Emile. *D.H. Lawrence and Edward Carpenter: A Study in Edwardian Transition.* New York: Taplinger Publishing Company, 1971.

Deutsch, Babette. *Poetry in Our Time.* New York: Henry Holt, 1952. Lawrence 86-91.

Dobree, Bonamy. *The Lamp and the Lute: Studies in Six Modern Authors.* Oxford: Clarendon Press, 1929. Lawrence, 86-106. Among the earliest of the established scholars to recognize Lawrence.

Donoghue, Denis. *The Ordinary Universe: Soundings in Modern Literature.* New York: Macmillan, 1968. Lawrence, 169-179.

—. *Thieves of Fire.* New York: Oxford University Press, 1974. Prometheus in Lawrenc's fiction, 111-139.

Drew, Elizabeth A. *The Modern Novel.* New York: Harcourt, Brace and Company, 1926. Still relevant, interesting, and well-written.

Durr, R.A. *Poetic Vision and the Psychedelic Experience.* Syracuse, New York: Syracuse University Press, 1970. Discussion of Lawrenc's poems throughout.

Eliot, T.S. *After Strange Gods: A Primer of Modern Heresy.* New York: Harcourt, Brace and Company, 1934. The essential conservative view of Lawrence.

Enright, D.J. *Conspirators and Poets.* London: Chatto & Windus, 1966. Lawrence, 95-101.

Fairchild, Hoxie N. *Religious Trends in English Poetry,* vol. 6. New York: Columbia University Press, 1968. References to Lawrence.

Fiedler, Leslie. *Love and Death in the American Novel.* New York: Stein and Day. Almost an application of *Studies in Classic American Literature* to the American scene by an American Lawrentian.

Friederich, Werner P. *Australia in Western Imaginative Prose Writing 1600-1960: An Anthology and a History of Literature.* Chapel Hill: University of North Carolina Press, 1967. Lawrence, 226-235.

Friedman, Alan, ed. *Forms of Modern British Fiction.* Austin and London: University of Texas Press, 1975. Six essays, Lawrence included.

Galinsky, Hans. *Deutschland in der Sicht von D.H. Lawrence und T.S. Eliot: Eine Studie zum Anglo-Amerikanischen Deutschlandsbild des 20. Jahrhunderts.* Mainz: Verlag der Akademie der Wissenschaften und der Litteratur, 1956.

Gass William H. *Fiction and the Figures of Life.* New York: Alfred A. Knopf, 1970. Review of *Phoenix II, 212-221.*

Gill, Richard. *Happy Rural Seat: The English Country House and the Literary Imagination.* New Haven: Yale University Press, 1972. References to Lawrence.

Goldknopf, David. *The Life of the Novel.* Chicago: University of Chicago Press, 1972. References to Lawrence.

Goldring, Douglas. *Reputations: Essays in Criticism.* New York: Thomas Seltzer, 1926. Contains "The Later Work of D.H. Lawrence."

Goodheart Eugene. *The Cult of the Self in Modern Literature.* Chicago: University of Chicago Press, 1968. By an author who understands Lawrence very well.

Gould, Gerald. *The English Novel of To-day.* London: John Castle, 1924.

Gray, Ronald. *The German Tradition in Literature, 1871-1945.* Cambridge, England: University Press, 1965. Influence on Lawrence, 340-354.

Grigson, Geoffrey. *The Contrary View.* Totowa, New Jersey: Rowman and Littlefield, -1974. Essays on Lawrence.

Gross, Theodore and Norman Kelvin. *An Introduction to Literature: Fiction.* New York: Random House, 1967. "Love Among the Haystacks," 205-210.

Gunn, Drewey W. *American and British Writers in Mexico, 1556-1973.* Austin: University of Texas Press, 1974.

Hall, James. *The Lunatic Giant in the Drawing Room: The British and American Novel Since 1930.* Bloomington: Indiana University Press, 1968.

Hardy, John E. *Man in the Modern Novel.* Seattle: University of Washington Press, 1964. An excellent essay on *Sons and Lovers.*

Harrison, John. *The Reactionaries: Yeats, Lewis, Pound, Eliot, Lawrence: A Study of the Anti-Democratic Intelligentsia.* New York: Schocken Books, 1967.

Hartt, Julian N. *The Lost Image of Man.* Baton Rouge: Louisiana State University Press, 1963. Lawrence, 55-60.

Hays, Peter L. *The Limping Hero: Grotesques in Literature.* New York:New York University Press, 1971.

Heilbrun, Carolyn G. *Toward a Recognition of Androgyny.* New York: Alfred A. Knopf, 1973. References to Lawrence.

Hinz, Evelyn J. *The Mirror and the Garden: Realism and Reality in the Writings of Anais Nin.* Columbus: The Ohio State University Libraries, Publications Committee, 1971. Chapter II on Nin's *D.H. Lawrence: An Unprofessional Study.*

17

Hoffman, Frederick J. *Freudianism and the Literary Mind.* Baton Rouge: Louisiana State University Press, 1945. Includes the finest analysis of Lawrence in relation to Freud that I have ever read. Historically, a basic book.

—. *The Mortal No: Death and the Modern Imagination.* Princeton:Princeton University Press, 1964. Lawrence, 406-423.

Holbrook, David. *The Quest for Love.* London: Methuen, 1964.

Hough, Graham. *Image and Experience: Reflections on a Literary Revolution.* Lincoln: University of Nebraska Press, 1960. Lawrence, 133-159.

Hughes, Glenn. *Imagism and the Imagists.* Stanford: Stanford University Press; London: Oxford University Press, 1931. Lawrence, 167-196.

Huxley, Aldous. *Music at Night and Other Essays. Lon*don: Chatto & Windus, 1932. Lawrence, 74-80, 173-183.

—. *The OliveTree.* New York: Harpers, 1937. Lawrence 203-242.

Hyman, Stanley Edgar, ed. *The Critical Performance.* New York: Vintage, 1956.

James, Henry. *Notes on Novelists.* London: J.M. Dent & Sons, 1914.

Joad, C.E.M. *Guide to Modern Thought.* London: Pan-Books, 1948. Lawrence, 238-244.

Kaplan, Harold J. *The Passive Voice: An Approach to Modern Fiction.* Athens, Ohio: Ohio University Press, 1966.

Karl, Frederick R. and Marvin Magalaner. *A Reader's Guide to Great Twentieth-Century English Novels.* New York: Noonday Press, 1959. Lawrence, 150-204.

Kazin, Alfred. *Contemporaries.* Boston: Little Brown and Company, 1962. Contains Kazin's earlier "Lady Chatterley in America," 105-112.

—. *The Inmost Leaf.* New York: Harcourt, Brace and Company, 1955. Includes an excellent appreciation, "The Painfulness of D.H. Lawrence," 98-102.

Kermode, Frank. *Romantic Image.* London: Routledge and Kegan Paul, 1957. Not about Lawrence, but helpful to an understanding of some of his imagery.

Kettle, Arnold. *An Introduction to the English Novel,* vol. 2 London: Hutchinson, 1953. Discussion of *The Rainbow,* 111-134.

Kreiger, Murray. *The Tragic Vision.* New York: Holt, Rinehart, and Winston, 1960.

Kronhaussen, Edward and Phyllis Kronhaussen. *Pornography and the Law.* New York: Ballantine Books, 1959.

Krook, Dorothea. *Three Traditions of Moral Thought.* Cambridge, England: Cambridge University Press, 1959. Lawrence, 261-292.

Lasch, Christopher. *The New Radicalism in America, 1889-1963.* New York: Alfred A. Knopf, 1964. Chapter IV, "Mabel Dodge Luhan: Sex as Politics," 104-140.

Laurensen, Diana T. and Alan Swingewood. *The Sociology of Literature.* London: Macgibbon & Kee, 1972. References to Lawrence.

Lavrin, Junko. *Aspects of Modernism, from Wilde to Pirandello.* London: Stanley Nott, 1935. Lawrence, 141-159.

Lawrence, D.H. Georgian *Poetry, 1911-1912.* London: The Poetry Bookshop, 1912.

—. *Georgian Poetry, 1913-1915.* London: The Poetry Bookshop; New York: G.P. Putnam, 1915.

—. *Imagist Anthology, 1930.* New York: Covici, Friede; London: Chatto & Windus, 1930.

—. *Some Imagist Poets.* Boston, New York: Houghton Mifflin; London: Constable, 1915.

Leavis, F.R. *New Bearings in English Poetry.* Ann Arbor: University of Michigan Press, 1960.

—. *The Common Pursuit.* London: Chatto & Windus, 1952.

Lesser, Simon. *Fiction and the Unconscious.* Boston: Beacon Press, 1957.

Lewis R.W.B. *The American Adam.* Chicago: University of Chicago Press, 1955. Again, not about Lawrence, but influenced in part by *Studies in Classic American Literature.*

Longbaum Robert. *The Modern Spirit: Essays on the Continuity of Nineteenth and Twentieth Century Literature.* New York: Oxford University Press, 1970. "Fish," 114-118; "Snake," 116.

Lowell, Amy. *Poetry and Poets.* New York: Houghton Mifflin, 1930.

Mack, Maynard and Ian Gregor, ed. *Imagined Worlds.* London: Methuen, 1968.

Macy, John. *The Critical Game.* New York: Boni and Liveright, 1922.

Maes-Jelinek, Hena. *Criticism of Society in the English Novel Between the Wars.* Paris: Societe d'Editions "Les Belles Lettres," 1970. Impact of World War I and subsequent events on Lawrence, 11-100.

Manly, J.M. and Edith Rickert. *Contemporary British Literature.* New York: Harcourt, Brace and Company, 1921.

Marble, A.R. *Study of the Modern Novel.* New York: Appleton and Company, 1928.

Marcuse, Ludwig. *Obscene: The History of an Indignation.* London: Macgibbon & Kee, 1965. Chapters on Lawrence, Henry Miller, Anthony Comstock.

Markovic, Vida. *The Changing Fact: Disintegration of Personality in the Twentieth-Century British Novel, 1900-1950.* Carbondale: Southern Illinois University Press, 1970.

Martin, E.W., ed. *The New Spirit.* London: Dennis Dobson, 1946.

Martz, Louis. *The Poem of the Mind.* New York: Oxford University Press, 1966.

Maurois, Andre. *Prophet and Poets,* trans. Hamish Hamilton. New York: Harper, 1935. Lawrence, 245-283.

McCormick, John. *Catastrophe and Imagination: A Reinterpretation of the Recent English and American Novel.* London: Longmans Green, 1957.

Meckier, Jerome. *Aldous Huxley: Satire and Structure.* London: Chatto & Windus, 1969. "Huxley's Lawrencian Interlude," 78-123.

Merivale, Patricia. *Pan the Goat-God: His Myth in Modern Times.* Cambridge: Harvard University Press, 1969. An essay on Lawrence.

Meyers, Jeffrey. *Painting and the Novel.* Manchester, England: Manchester University Press; New York: Barnes and Noble, 1975. Three chapters on Lawrence.

Milano, Paolo. *11 Letters di Professione.* Milan: Feltrinelli, n.d. Sections on Lawrence and Melville.

Miles, Rosalind. *The Fiction of Sex.* New York: Barnes and Noble, 1974. References to Lawrence and 16-21.

Miller, Henry. *The Wisdom of the Heart.* Norfolk, Virginia: New Directions, 1941.

Moore, Harry T. *Age of the Modern and Other Literary Essays.* Carbondale: Southern Illinois University Press, 1971.

Morrison, Claudia. *Freud and the Critic: The Early Use of Depth Psychology in Literary Criticism.* Chapel Hill: University of North Carolina Press, 1968. A chapter on Lawrence and American Literature.

Mosely, Edwin M. *Pseudonyms of Christ in the Modern World: Motifs and Methods.* Pittsburgh: University of Pittsburgh Press, 1963. Lawrence, 69-91.

Mueller, W.R. *Celebration of Life.* New York: Sheed and Ward, 1972. Lawrence, 144-168, "The Paradisal Quest."

Muir, Edwin. *Transition: Essays on Contemporary Literature.* New York: Viking Press, 1926. Lawrence, 49-63.

Muller, Herbert J. *Modern Fiction: A Study of Values.* New York: Funk and Wagnalls, 1937. Lawrence, 262-287.

Murray, Henry A., ed. *Myth and Mythmaking.* New York: George Braziller, 1960.

Murry, John Middleton. *Adam and Eve: An Essay Toward a New and Better Society.* London: Andrew Dakers, 1944. References to Lawrence throughout.

—. Between *Two Worlds.* London: Jonathan Cape, 1935.

—. *Love, Freedom and Society.* London: Jonathan Cape, 1957.

Nicholson, Norman. *Man and Literature.* London: S.C.M. Press, 1944. Lawrence, 62-86.

Nin, Anais. *The Novel of the Future.* New York: Macmillan, 1968. References to Lawrence.

Oates, Joyce Carol. *New Heaven, New Earth: The Visionary Experience in Literature.* New York: Vanguard, 1974. Lawrence's poetry, 37-81. Formerly a monograph of the same title published by The Black Sparrow Press, 1973.

O'Connor, Frank. *The Lonely Voice: A Study of the Short Story.* Cleveland: World Publishing Company, 1963. Lawrence, 147-155.

—. *The Mirror in the Roadway: A Study of the Modern Novel.* New York: World Publishing Company, 1963. Lawrence, 147-155.

Panichas, George A. *Adventures in Consciousness.* The Hague, London: Paris: Mouton, 1964.

Phelps, William L. *The Advance of English Poetry.* New York: Dodd, Mead and Company, 1921.

Pinto, Vivian de Sola Pinto. *Crisis in Modern Poetry.* New York: Harper and Row, 1966. A very fine appreciation of Lawrence.

Potts, Abbie F. *The Elegaic Mode.* Ithaca: Cornell University Press, 1967.

Powell, Dilys. *Descent from Parnassus.* London: The Cresset Press, 1934. New York: Macmillan, 1935. Lawrence, 1-54.

Praz, Mario. *Studi e Svaghi Inglesi.* Firenze: Sansoni, 1937.

Rabinovitz, Rubin. *The Reaction Against Experiment in the English Novel, 1950-1960.* New York: Columbia University Press, 1967. References to Lawrence.

Rahv, Philip. *Literature and the Sixth Sense.* Boston: Houghton Mifflin, 1969. Includes discussion of Lawrence and Henry Miller and Lawrence and F.R. Leavis.

Rascoe, Burton. *Prometheans: Ancient and Modern.* New York: Putnam's, 1933. Lawrence, 221-238.

Read, Herbert. *The True Voice of Feeling: Sudies in English Romanticism.* London: Faber and Faber, 1953.

Rees, Richard. *John Middleton Murry: Selected Criticism, 1916-1917.* London, New York: Oxford University Press, 1960.

Rembar, Charles. *The End of Obscenity: The Trials of Lady Chatterley, Tropic of Cancer, and Fanny Hill.* New York: Random House, 1968. Historical landmark.

Richards, I.A. *Science and Poetry.* London: Kegan Paul Trench, and Trubner; New York: Norton, 1926. Lawrence, 87-91.

Roberts, Mark. *The Tradition of Romantic Morality.* London: Macmillan, 1973. Chapter on Lawrence.

Robson, W.W. *Modern English Literature.* London: Oxford University Press, 1970. General summary of Lawrence's ideas and biography, 82-92.

Rogers, Katherine M. *The Troublesome Helpmate: A History of Misogyny in Literature.* Seattle: University of Washington Press, 1966. Lawrence, 237-247.

Rosenthal, M.L. *The Modern Poets: A Critical Introduction.* New York: Oxford University Press, 1960. Lawrence, 160-168 and in passing.

Ross, Robert H. *The Georgian Revolt.* Carbondale: Southern Illinois University Press, 1965,

Schorer, Mark, ed. *Modern British Fiction.* New York: Oxford University Press, 1961.

—. *The World We Imagined: Selected Essays.* New York: Farrar and Straus, 1968. Reprints of five earlier essays on Lawrence.

Scott, Nathan A., Jr. *Rehearsals of Discomposure: Alienation and Reconciliation in Modern Literature.* New York: King's Crown Press, 1952.

Seilliere, Ernest. *David Herbert Lawrence et les Recentes Ideologies Allemandes.* Paris: Boivin, 1936.

Shanks, Edward. *First Essays on Literature.* London: W. Collins, 1930.

Sherman, Stuart P. *Critical Woodcuts.* New York: Scribners, 1926. Lawrence, 18-31.

Slochower, Harry. *No Voice is Wholly Lost.* New York: Creative Age Press, 1945. Lawrence, 136-143.

Smith, Lewis W., ed. *Current Reviews.* New York: Henry Holt, 1926.

Sommers, Joseph. *After The Storm: Landmarks of the Modern Mexican Novel.* Alburquerque: University of New Mexico Press, 1968. Lawrence's influence on Carlos Fuentes through *The Plumed Serpent,* 128-132.

Southworth, James G. *Sowing the Spring: Studies in British Poetry from Hopkins to MacNeice.* Oxford: Basil Blackwell, 1940.

Sparrow, John. *Controversial Essays.* New York: Chilmark, 1966; paperback, 1971. References to Lawrence.

Spears, Monroe K. *Dionysus and the City: Modernism in Twentieth-Century Poetry.* London, Oxford, New York: Oxford University Press, 1970. References to Lawrence throughout.

Speirs, John. *Poetry Towards Novel.* London: Faber and Faber, 1971. Lawrence, 326-333.

Spender, Stephen. *The Creative Element: A Study of Vision, Despair and Orthodoxy among Some Modern Writers.* London: Hamish Hamilton, 1953.

—. *The Destructive Element: A Study of Modern Writers and Beliefs.* New York: Houghton Mifflin, 1936. The creative process from an anti-formalist viewpoint by a writer with a natural sympathy for Lawrence.

—. *The Struggle of the Modern.* Berkeley: University of California Press, 1963. Lawrence, 100-109 and in passing.

Springer, Mary D. *Forms of the Modern Novella.* Chicago: University of Chicago Press, 1975.

Stewart, J.I.M. *Eight Mdern Writers,* volume 12 of the *Oxford History of English Literature.* New York: Oxford University Press, 1963. Lawrence, 484-593.

Street, Brian V. *The Savage in Literature.* Boston: Routledge & Kegan Paul, 1975. References to Lawrence.

Swigg, Richard. *Lawrence, Hardy, and American Literature.* New York: Oxford University Press, 1972.

Taylor, Joshua C. *Futurism.* New York: Museum of Modern Art, 1961. The carbon.

Tindall, William York. *Forces in Modern British Literature.* New York: Alfred A. Knopf, 1947. Still a good general introduction and a good place to begin.

Turnell, Martin. *Modern Literature and Christian Faith.* Westminster, Maryland: The Newman Press, 1961. Lawrence, 25-34.

Unterecker, John. *Approaches to the Twentieth Centruy Novel.* New York: Crowell, 1965.

Van Doren, Carl. *The Roving Critic.* New York: Alfred A. Knopf, 1923.

Van Ghent, Dorothy. *The English Novel: Form and Content.* New York: Rinehart, 1953. Lawrence, 245-261, 454-462, A good defense of *Sons and Lovers.*

Various Writers. *The Borzoi, 1925.* New York: Alfred A. Knopf, 1925. Contains "A Note on D.H. Lawrence" by Brett Young.

Vickery, John B. *The Literary Impact of the Golden Bough.* Princeton: Princeton University Press, 1973.

—, ed. *Myth and Literature: Contemporary Theory and Practice.* Lincoln: University of Nebraska Press, 1966. Includes previously published essays on Lawrence.

Vivante, Leone. *A Philosophy of Potentiality.* London: Routledge and Kegan Paul, 1955. Lawrence, 77-115.

Vivas, Eliseo. *The Artistic Transaction and Essays on Theory of Literature.* Columbus: Ohio State University Press, 1963.

Wallenstein, Barry. *Visions and Revisions: An Approach to Poetry.* New York: T.Y. Crowell, 1971. "Comment," 246; "Renascence," 247; "Violets," 249; "The Piano," 253; "Man's Image," 254; "Bavarian Gentians," 255.

Walsh, William. *The Use of the Imagination: Educational Thought and the Literary Mind.* London: Chatto & Windus, 1959. Includes "The Educational Ideals of D.H. Lawrence," 199-228, and a discussion of *The Rainbow,* 163-174.

Waugh, Arthur. *Tradition and Change.* London: Chapman and Hall, 1919.

Weber, Max. *The Protestant Ethic and the Spirit of Capitalism.* New York: Scribners, 1958. The cultural background in relation to which Lawrence's social protests can perhaps be best understood.

Wickham, Harvey. *The Impuritans.* New York: Lincoln Mac-
Veagh: Dial Press, 1929.

Widmer, Kingsley, *The Literary Rebel.* Carbondale: Southern
Illinois University Press, 1965. References to Lawrence in
passing.

Williams, Raymond. *The Country and the City.* New York:
Oxford University Press, 1973. References to Lawrence.

—. *Culture and Society, 1780-1950.* New York: Columbia University Press, 1958. Lawrence, 199-215. A sane social
commentary by an author who knows Lawrence well.

Wilson, Edmund. *The Shock of Recognition.* New York: Doubleday, Doran and Company, 1943.

—. *The Shores of Light.* New York: Farrar, Straus and Young,
1952.

—, ed. *Collected Essays.* New York: Scribners, 1948.

Winegarten, Renee. *Writers and Revolution: The Fatal Lure of
Action.* New York: New Viewpoints, 1974. Lawrence,
247-260.

Woodcock, George. *Dawn and the Darkest Hour: A Study of
Aldous Huxley.* New York: Viking Press, 1972. References
to Lawrence.

BIOGRAPHICAL

Aldinton, Richard. *D.H. Lawrence: An Appreciation.* London: Chatto & Windus, 1930.

—. *D.H. Lawrence: An Indiscretion.* Seattle: University of Washington Book Store, 1927.

—. *David Herbert Lawrence in Selbstzeugnissen und Bildokumten.* Reinbek: Rowohlt, 1961.

—. *Portrait of a Genius, But . . . .* New York: Duell, Sloan & Pearce, 1950. A still relevant, interesting, and well-written critical biography.

Anonymous. *Young Bert: An Exhibition of the Early Years of D.H. Lawrence.* Nottingham, England: City of Nottingham Museum and Art Gallery, 1972.

Armitage, Merle. *Taos Quartet in Three Movements.* New York: Privately printed, 1950.

Arnold, Armin. *D.H. Lawrence.* Berlin: Verlag, 1972. A short, introductory biography.

Arrow, John. *J.C. Squire v. D.H. Lawrence.* London: E. Lahr, 1930. Blue Moon Booklet No. 4. Lawrence by a knockout.

Bedford, Sybille, *Aldous Huxley: A Biography.* Volume I, 1894-1939. London: Chatto & Windus, 1973; New York: Alfred A. Knopf, Harper and Row, 1974.

Birnbaum, Milton. *Aldous Huxley's Quest for Values.* Knoxville: University of Tennessee Press, 1971. References to Lawrence throughout.

Bowen, Elizabeth. *Collected Impression.* New York: Alfred A. Knopf, 1950.

Brett, Hon. Dorothy. *Lawrence and Brett: A Friendship.* Philadelphia: Lippincott, 1930.

Brewster, Dorothy and Angus Burrell. *Dead Reckonings.* New York and London: Longmans, Green and Company, 1924.

Brewster, Earl and Achsah Brewster. *D.H. Lawrence Reminiscences and Correspondence.* London: Martin Secker, 1934.

Bynner, Witter. *Journey with Genius: Recollections and Reflections Concerning the D.H. Lawrences.* New York: John Day Company, 1951.

Callow, Philip. *Son and Lover: The Young D.H. Lawrence.* New York: Stein and Day, 1975.

Carringotn, Dora. *Carrington: Letters and Extracts from Her Diaries,* ed. David Garnett. New York: Holt, Rinehart and Winston, 1971. References to Lawrence.

Carswell, Catherine. *D.H. Lawrence and the Press.* London: The Broadside Press, 1930.

—. *The Savage Pilgrimage: A Narrative of D.H. Lawrence.* London: Secker & Warburg, 1951.

Chambers, Jessie (E.T.). *A Personal Record,* ed. Jessie Chambers. 2d edition. New York: Barnes and Noble, 1965. In defense of "Miriam." Good background for *Sons and Lovers.*

Clark, Ronald. *The Huxleys.* New York: McGraw Hill, 1968. References to Lawrence.

Corke, Helen. *Lawrence and Apocalypse.* Reissued New York: Haskell House, 1966.

—. *D.H. Lawrence: The Croydon Years.* Austin: University of Texas Press, 1965. Illuminates a little known period of Lawrence's life.

—. *D.H. Lawrence's Princess, A memory of Jessie Chambers.* London: Merle Press, 1951.

—. *Neutral Ground.* London: Arthur Barker, 1933.

Damon, S. Foster. *Amy Lowell.* Boston, New York: Houghton Mifflin, 1935. References to Lawrence.

Darroch, Sandra J. *Ottoline.* New York: Coward, McCann & Geoghegan, 1975.

Davies, Rhys. *Print of a Hare's Foot: An Autobiographical Beginning.* New York: Dodd, Mead and Company, 1969. Includes reminiscences of Lawrence.

Delavenay, Emile. *D.H. Lawrence, The Man and His Work: The Formative Years, 1885-1919,* trans. Katharine M. Delavenay. Carbondale: Southern Illinois University Press, 1972. *D.H. Lawrence: L Homme Et La Genese de Son Oeuvre (1885-1919): Documents.* Paris: Librairie C.

Delavenay, Emile (cont.)- Klincksieck, 1969. The strength of the work is the author's ability to draw upon existing Lawrence materials to construct a loosely structured and lengthy biographical, psychological, and intellectual backdrop to the fiction and prose culminating in *Women in Love.*

Eagleton, Terry. *Exiles and Emigres: Studies in Modern Litera-Literature.* New York: Schocken Books, 1970.

Fabre-Luce, Alfred. *La Vie de D.H. Lawrence.* Paris: Grasset, 1935.

Fabricant, Noah D. *Thirteen Famous Patients.* Philadelphia: Chilton Company, 1960. Includes a study of Lawrence.

Fay, Eliot. *Lorenzo in Search of the Sun: D.H. Lawrence in Italy, Mexico, and the American Southwest.* New York: Bookman Associates, 1953; London: Vision Press, 1955.

Ford, Ford Madox. *Portraits from Life.* Boston: Houghton Mifflin, 1937. Lawrence, 70-89. A very entertaining (and true) view of one side of Lawrence.

Forster, E.M. *Maurice.* Toronto: Macmillan, 1971. Lawrence's spongy old friend of the foreign legion.

Foster, Joseph O'Kane. *D.H. Lawrence in Taos.* Alburquerque: University of New Mexico Press, 1972.

Garnett, Edward. *The Familiar Faces.* London: Chatto & Windus, 1962.

—. *The Flowers of the Forest.* London: Chatto & Windus, 1953.

—. *Friday Nights.* New York: Alfred A. Knopf, 1922.

—. *The Golden Echo.* London: Chatto & Windus, 1955.

Gathorne-Hardy, Robert. Ottoline at *Garsinton: Memories of Lady Ottoline Morrell.* London: Faber and Faber, 1974. References to Lawrence.

George, W.L. *Literary Chapters.* Boston: Little, Brown and Company, 1918.

Gilles, Daniel. *D.H. Lawrence, ou, le puritaine scandaleux.* Paris: Rene Julliard, 1964.

Glenavy. Lady Beatrice. *Today We Will Only Gossip.* London: Constable, 1964.

Goldring, Douglas. *The Nineteen Twenties: A General Survey and Some Personal Memories.* London: Nicholson and Watson, 1943.

Green, Martin. *The von Richthofen Sisters: The Triumphant and the Tragic Modes of Love, Else and Frieda von Richthofen, Otto Gross, Max Weber, and D.H. Lawrence, in the Years 1870-1970.* New York: Basic Books, 1974.

Gregory, Horace. *D.H. Lawrence: Pilgrim of the Apocalypse.* Reissued New York: Grove Press, 1957. One of the better early critical biographies.

Griffin, Ernest G. *John Middleton Murry.* New York: Twayne Publishers, 1969. "The Meaning of D.H. Lawrence," 121-140.

Hahn, Emily. *Lorenzo: D.H. Lawrence and the Women Who Loved Him.* New York: Lippincott, 1975.

Heilbrun, Carolyn G. *The Garnett Family.* New York: Macmillan, 1961. Lawrence, 142-161 and in passing.

Horsley, E.M., ed. *Lady Cynthia Asquith, Diaries 1915-1918.* New York: Alfred A. Knopf, 1969. References to Lawrence.

Huxley, Julian. *Memories.* New York: Harper and Row, 1970. Life at the Morrells', passing references to Lawrence and Frieda.

Lacon. *Lectures to Living Authors.* London: Geoffrey Bles, 1925. A short essay on Lawrence.

Lawrence, Ada and G. Stuart Gelder. *Young Lorenzo: Early Life of D.H. Lawrence.* New York: Russell and Russel, 1966.

Lawrence, Frieda. *Frieda Lawrence: Memoirs and Correspondence,* ed. E.W. Tedlock, Jr. New York: Alfred A. Knopf, 1964.

—. *Not I, But the Wind.* New York: Viking Press, 1934.

Lea, F.A. *The Life of John Middleton Murry.* London: Methuen, 1959. Includes a study of the Lawrence-Murry relationship.

Lewis, Wyndham. *Paleface.* London: Chatto & Windus, 1929.

Lowenfels, Walter. *Elegy in the Manner of a Requiem in Memory of D.H. Lawrence.* Paris: Carrefous, 1932.

Lucas, Robert. *Frieda Lawrence: The Story of Frieda von Richthofen and D.H. Lawrence,* trans. from the German by Geoffrey Skelton. Munich: Kindler Verlag Gmb. H., 1972; London: Secker and Warburg, 1973.

Luhan, Mabel Didge. *Lorenzo in Taos.* New York: Alfred A. Knopf, 1932.

Lunn, Hugh K. *The Life of D.H. Lawrence.* New York: Dodge Publishing Company, 1938. A Biography with a vengeance. Early review and defense of Lawrence by Harry T. Moore.

Mackenzie, Compton. *My Life and Times, Octave Five.* London: Chatto & Windus, 1966. References to the Lawrences and Mackenzies in Italy, etc.

Mansfield, Katherine. *Journal.* London: Constable, 1954.

—. *Letters.* London: Constable, 1928.

Marsh, Edward. *A Number of People.* London: William Heinemann, 1939.

Merrill, Knud. *A Poet and Two Painters: A Memoir of D.H. Lawrence.* London: Routledge, 1938. Reissued as *With D.H. Lawrence in New Mexico: A Memoir of D.H. Lawrence.* New York: Barnes and Noble, 1965.

Mizener, Arthur. *The Saddest Story: A Biography of Ford Madox Ford.* New York: World, 1971. References to Lawrence.

Moore, Harry T. *The Intelligent Heart: The Life of D.H. Lawrence.* New York: Farrar, Straus, and Young, 1954. Revised edition, 1962. The standard biography.

—. *The Life and Works of D.H. Lawrence.* London: George Allen and Unwin; New York: Twayne Publishers, 1951.

—. *The Priest of Love: A Life of D.H. Lawrence.* Revised edition. New York: Farrar, Straus and Giroux, 1974. Incorporates New findings since *The Intelligent Heart* and includes a more up-to-date bibliography, but otherwise substantially the same.

—. *Poste Restante: A Lawrence Travel Calendar.* introduction Mark Schorer. Berkeley: University of California Press, 1956.

—, and Warren Roberts. *D.H. Lawrence—His World.* London: Thames and Hudson, 1966. A short life with abundant and excellent photographs.

Morrell, Lady Ottoline. *Memoirs 1915-1918,* ed. Robert Gathorne-Hardy. New York: Alfred A. Knopf, 1975.

Morrill, Claire. *A Taos Mosaic: Portrait of a New Mexico Village.* Alburquerque: University of New Mexico Press, 1973. Chapters on Lawrence, Frieda, Mabel Dodge Luhan, Dorothy Brett.

—. *Ottoline, The Early Memories of Lady Ottoline Morrell,* ed. Robert Gathorne-Hardy. London: Faber and Faber, 1963.

Murry, John Middleton. *Between Two Worlds.* New York: J. Messner, 1936.

—. *D.H. Lawrence: Son of Woman.* London: Jonathan Cape, 1931. Reissued 1954. He told the truth, mainly.

—. *D.H. Lawrence: Two Essays.* Cambridge: The Minority Press, 1930.

—. *Reminiscences of D.H. Lawrence.* New York: Holt, 1933. Reissued London: Jonathan Cape, 1968.

Nardi, Piero, *La Vita di D.H. Lawrence.* Milan: Mondadori, 1947.

Nehls, Edward. *D.H. Lawrence: A Composite Biography.* 3 vols. Madison: University of Wisconsin Press, 1959. The most complete biography available. Freudian though "composite."

Nin, Anais. *A Woman Speaks,* ed. Evelyn J. Hinz. Chicago: The Swallow Press, 1975. References to Lawrence

Pinto, Vivian de Sola. *D.H. Lawrence: Prophet of the Midlands.* Nottingham: University of Nottingham, 1951.

Porter, Katherine Anne. *The Days Before.* New York: Harcourt, Brace and Company, 1952. *The Plumed Serpent,* 262-267.

Rickwood, Edgell, ed. *Scutinies,* vol. 2. London: Wishart, 1931. Includes an essay on Lawrence by Peter Quennell.

Rosenfeld, Paul. *Men Seen.* New York: Dial Press, 1925. Lawrence, 45-62.

Russell, Bertrand. *The Autobiography of Bertrand Russell, Vol. 2 1914-1944*. Boston: Little, Brown and Company, 1968. Russell and Lawrence, 10-16, 59-65 and in passing.

—. *Portraits from Memory*. London: Allen and Unwin, 1956.

Schickele, Rene. *Liebe und Argernis des D.H. Lawrence*. Amsterdam: Albert de Lange, 1934.

Schorer, Mark. *D.H. Lawrence*. New York: Dell Books, 1968. 103 pp.

Squire, J.C. *Sunday Mornings*. London: William Heinemann, 1930.

Thody, Philip. *Aldous Huxley*. New York: Scribners, 1973. References to Lawrence.

West, Rebecca. *Ending in Earnest: A Literary Log*. Garden City, New York: Doubleday, Doran, 1931. Lawrence, 122-128, 257-280.

—. *D.H. Lawrence*. Reissued Folcroft, Pa.: Folcroft Press, 1969.

Woodeson, John. *Mark Gertler*. London: Sidgwick and Jackson, 1972. Model for Loerke in *Women in Love*.

Woolf, Leonard. *Beginning Again, An Autobiography of the Years 1911-1918*. London: Hogarth Press, 1964.

—. *Downhill All the Way, An Autobiography of the Years 1919-1939*. London: Hogarth Press, 1967.

Wulfsberg, Frederick. *D.H. Lawrence fra Nottinghamshire*. Oslo, Norway: Francis Bull, 1937.

Young, Jessica B. *Francis Brett Young: A Biography*. London: William Heinemann, 1962. References to Lawrence in passing.

Adam, Michael. *D.H. Lawrence and the Way of the Dandelion.* Penzance, Cornwall: The Ark Press, 1975.

Aldritt, Keith. *The Visual Imagination of D.H. Lawrence.* London: Edward Arnold; Evanston, Illinois: Northwestern University Press, 1971.

Andrews, W.T. *Critics on D.H. Lawrence.* London: George Allen and Unwin; Coral Gables, Florida: University of Miami Press, 1971. Historical survey of criticism from 1911 to the present.

Arnold, Armin. *D.H. Lawrence and America.* New York: Philosophical Library, 1958.

—. *D.H. Lawrence and German Literature, with Two Hitherto Unknown Essays by D.H. Lawrence.* Montreal: Mansfield Book Mart (William Heinemann), 1963.

—, ed. *The Symbolic Meaning: The Uncollected Versions of Studies in Classic American Literature.* London: Centaur Press, 1962; New York: Viking Press, 1964.

Barrett, Gerald R. and Thomas L. Erskine, ed. *From Fiction to Film: D.H. Lawrence's "The Rocking-Horse Winner."* Encino and Belmont, California: Dickenson Publishing Company, 1974.

Beal, Anthony. *D.H. Lawrence.* New York: Grove Press, 1961.

Bedient, Calvin. *Architects of the Self: George Eliot, D.H. Lawrence, and E.M Forster.* Berkeley: University of California Press, 1972. A movement from the social self (Eliot) to the vital self (Lawrence) to the personal self (Forster).

Boadella, David. *The Spiral Flame: A Study in the Meaning of D.H. Lawrence.* Nottingham: Ritter, 1956.

Bredsdorff, Elias. *D.H. Lawrence. Et Forsog paa en politisk Analysis (D.H. Lawrence: An Attempt at a Political Analysis).* Copenhagen, 1937.

Brugnoli, Angelo. *Dante in Lunigiana, Bismantova, Lawrence, Luni.* Mantova: Scuola tipografica benedettina, 1968.

Carter, Frederick D. *D.H. Lawrence and the Body Mystical.* Reissued New York: Haskell House, 1966.

Cavitch, David. *D.H. Lawrence and the New World.* New York: Oxford University Press, 1969; Galaxy paperback, 1971. Repeats a well-known Freudian view of Lawrence, but is well-written and cleverly focused.

Clark, Colin C. *River of Dissolution: D.H. Lawrence and English Romanticism.* London: Routledge and Kegan Paul, 1969. Perhaps the best of the recent studies of Lawrence.

—, ed. *The Rainbow and Women in Love.* London: MacMillan, 1969. A Casebook. Essays by George H. Ford, John M. Murry, Roger Sale, Julian Moynahan, Frank Kermode, and others.

Clark, L.D. *Dark Night of the Body: D.H. Lawrence's "The Plumed Serpent."* Austin: University of Texas Press, 1964.

Cohn, Saul. *Naturalisme et Mysticisme chez D.H. Lawrence,* Paris: Libraire Lipschutz, 1932.

Consolo, Dominick P., ed. *The Rocking-Horse Winner: A Casebook.* Columbus, Ohio: Charles E. Merrill, 1969.

Cornwall, Ethel F. *The "Still Point": Theme and Variations in the Writings of T.S. Eliot, Coleridge, Yeats, Henry James, Virginia Woolf, and D.H. Lawrence.* New Brunswick, New Jersey: Rutgers University Press, 1962.

Couaillac, Maurice. *D.H. Lawrence, Essai sur la Formation et la Developpement de sa Pensee d'apres son Oeuvre en Prose.* Toulouse: Imprimerie du Commerce, 1937.

Cowan, James C. *D.H. Lawrence's American Journey: A Study in Literature and Myth.* Cleveland: Case Western Reserve University Press, 1970.

Cura-Sazdanic, Ieana. *D.H. Lawrence as Critic.* Delhi: Munshiram Manoharlal, 1969.

Daiches, David. *D.H. Lawrence.* Brighton, England: Privately printed, 1963. 24pp. pamphlet.

Daleski, H.N. *The Forked Flame: A Study of D.H. Lawrence.* Evanston, Illinois: Northwestern University Press, 1965.

Delavenay, Emile. *D.H. Lawrence and Edward Carpenter: A Study in Edwardian Transition.* New York: Taplinger Publishing Company, 1971.

—. D.H. Lawrence: *L' Homme et la genese de son oeuvre. Les annees de formation: 1885-1919.* Paris: Klincksiech, 1969. See *Biographical: The Man and His Work,* trans. Katharine Delavenay.

Drain, R.L *Traditions and D.H. Lawrence.* Groningen: J.B. Wolters, 1960. 12pp. pamphlet.

Draper, Ronald P. *D.H. Lawrence.* New York: Twayne Publishers, 1964. Reissued New York: St. Martin's Press, 1975.

—, ed. *D.H. Lawrence: The Critical Heritage.* London and Boston: Routledge and Kegan Paul; New York: Barnes and Noble, 1975. Selected reviews of Lawrence's major fiction, poetry, and prose.

Eisenstein, Samuel A. *Boarding the Ship of Death: D.H. Lawrence's Quester Heroes.* The Hague, Paris: Mouton, 1974.

Ellis, Charles R. and E.D. Hubbar, ed. *Sons and Lovers: A Critical Commentary.* New York: American R.D.M. Corporation, 1964.

Farr, Judith, ed. *Twentieth Century Interpretations of Sons and Lovers: A Collection of Critical Essays.* Englewood Cliffs, New Jersey: Prentice-Hall, 1970.

Fedder, Norman J. *The Influence of D.H. Lawrence on Tennessee Williams.* The Hague: Mouton, 1966.

Ford, George H. *Double Measure: A Study of the Novels and Stories of D.H. Lawrence.* New York: Holt, Rinehart and Winston, 1965. The comparisons with Dickens sometimes get in the way of Lawrence.

Freeman, Mary. *D.H. Lawrence: A Basic Study of His Ideas.* Gainesville: University of Florida Press, 1955. The first systematic presentation of Lawrence's thought and a book written with courage.

Friedman, Alan. *The Turn of the Novel.* New York: Oxford University Press, 1966. Hardy, Conrad, Forster, Joyce, and Lawrence.

Garrett, Peter K. *Scene and Symbol from George Eliot to James Joyce: Studies in Changing Fictional Mode.* New Haven: Yale University Press, 1969. Lawrence, 181-213.

Gilbert, Sandra M. *Acts of Attention: The Poems of D.H. Lawrence.* Ithaca: Cornell University Press, 1972. A finely written, interesting, and sensitive study that, however, misapplies Jung to Lawrence.

Gomes, Eugenio. *D.H. Lawrence e Outros.* Porto Alegre, Brazil: Globo, 1937.

Goodheart, Eugene. *The Utopian Vision of D.H. Lawrence.* Chicago: University of Chicago Press, 1963. An excellent discussion of Lawrence, anarchism, and nihilism.

Goodman, Richard. *Footnote to Lawrence.* London: White Owl Press, 1932. pamphlet.

Gordon, David J. *D.H. Lawrence as a Literary Critic.* New Haven: Yale University Press, 1966.

Gottwald, Johannes. *Die Erzahlformen der Romane von Aldous Huxley und David Herbert Lawrence.* Munich, 1964.

Hamalian, Leo, ed. *D.H. Lawrence: A Collection of Critical Essays.* New York: McGraw-Hill paperback, 1973. An attempt at a new modern criticism of Lawrence that overreaches itself. Essays by Hamalian, Beal, Cavitch, Clark, Engel, Hough, Kazin, Jacobson, D.H. Lawrence, Frieda Lawrence, Anais Nin, Rexroth, Sagar, and Yudistar.

Hamill, Elizabeth. *Three Modern Writers.* Melbourne: Georgian House, 1946. Lawrence, 86-99.

Handley, Graham. *Notes on D.H. Lawrence: Sons and Lovers.* Bath, England: James Brodie Ltd., 1967.

Harrison, John. *The Reactionaries: Yeats, Lewis, Pound, Eliot, Lawrence: A Study of the Anti-Democratic Intelligentsia.* "Introduction" William Empson. New York: Schocken Books, 1967.

Hess, Elizabeth. *Die Naturbetrachtung im Prosawerk von D.H. Lawrence.* Bern, Switzerland: Francke, 1957.

Hochman, Baruch (Barry Hojman). *Another Ego: The Changing View of Self and Society in the Work of D.H. Lawrence.* Columbia: University of South Carolina Press, 1970.

Hoffman, Frederick J. and Harry T. Moore, ed. *The Achievement of D.H. Lawrence.* Norman: University of Oklahoma Press, 1953. An excellent collection of representative (fifties, early sixties) essays presenting traditional viewpoints.

Honig, Edwin. *Dark Conceit: The Making of Allegory.* Evanston, Illinois: Northwestern University Press, 1959. Sections on Lawrence, Melville, Hawthorne, Kafka, and Joyce.

Hough, Graham. *The Dark Sun: A Study of D.H. Lawrence.* New York: Macmillan, 1957. With that of Leavis, the best work on Lawrence by an English scholar.

—. *Two Exiles: Lord Byron and D.H. Lawrence.* Nottingham. Byron Foundation Lectures (University of Nottingham), 1956. A brief booklet. Included in Hough's *Image and Experience* (Lincoln: University of Nebraska Press, 1960).

Hsia, Adrian. *D.H. Lawrence: die Charakters in der Handlung und Spannung Seiner Kurzgeschichten.* Bonn: H. Bouvier, 1968.

Innis, Kenneth. *D.H. Lawrence's Bestiary: A Study of His Use of Animal Trope and Symbol.* The Hague: Mouton, 1971; New York: Humanities Press, 1972.

Jaensson, Knut. *D.H. Lawrence.* Stockholm: Tidens, 1934.

Jennings, Elizabeth. *Reaching Into Silence: A Study of Eight Twentieth-Century Visionaries.* New York: Barnes and Noble, 1974. Lawrence included.

Johnsson, Melker. *D.H. Lawrence. Ett modernt tankeaventyr (D.H. Lawrence: A Modern Thought-Adventurer).* Stockholm: Albert Bonniers, 1939.

Joost, Nicholas and Alvin Sullivan. *D.H. Lawrence and The Dial.* Carbondale: Southern Illinois University Press; London and Amsterdam: Feffer and Simmons, 1970.

Kenmare, Dallas. *Fire-bird: A Study of D.H. Lawrence.* New York: Philosophical Library, 1951.

Kermode, Frank. *d. h. lawerence.* New York: Viking Press, 1973. Modern Masters Series. Too derivative and slick.

Kinkaid-Weekes, Mark, ed. *Twentieth-Century Interpretations of The Rainbow.* Englewood Cliffs, New Jersey: Prentice-Hall, 1971.

Leavis, F.R. *D.H. Lawrence.* Cambridge, England: The Minority Press, 1930.

—. *D.H. Lawrence, Novelist.* New York: Alfred A. Knopf, 1956; paperback: Simon and Schuster (New York), 1970. Lawrence and the Evangelical Tradition of George Eliot. An

—.(cont.)- author taken to heart by the vitalist (Jungian) critics of Lawrence.

Lerner, Laurence. *The Truthtellers: Jane Austen, George Eliot, D.H. Lawrence.* New York: Schocken Books, 1967.

Lucia, Dino. *"A Proposito di L'Amanti di Lady Chatterley" di D.H. Lawrence.* Matera: Motemurro, 1951.

Marshall, Tom. *The Psychic Mariner: A Reading of the Poems of D.H. Lawrence.* New York: Viking Press, 1970. Marshall makes abundant use of direct quotation, and the book seems to be well-researched.

Megroz, L.R. *Five Novelist Poets of Today.* London: Joiner and Steele, 1933. Lawrence one of the five.

Miko, Stephen J. *Toward Women in Love: The Emergence of a Laurentian Aesthetic.* New Haven: Yale University Press, 1971. Concentrates upon the imagery and asserts that the body-mind duality in the early Lawrence is overcome in *Women in Love* through a religious reconciliation of opposites.

—, ed. *Twentieth Century Interpretations of Women in Love: A Collection of Critical Essays.* Englewood Cliffs, New Jersey: Prentice-Hall, 1969.

Miles, Kathleen. *The Hellish Meaning: The Demonic Motif in the Works of D.H. Lawrence.* Carbondale: Southern Illinois University Press, 1969. Southern Illinois Monographs, Humanistic Series 2.

Miller, James E., Jr., Karl Shapiro, and Bernice Slote. *Start with the Sun: Studies in Cosmic Poetry.* Lincoln: University of Nebraska Press, 1960. The Whitman Tradition in Lawrence, Hart Crane, Dylan Thomas.

Moore, Harry T. *D.H. Lawrence, His Life, and Works.* New York: Twayne Publishers, 1964.

—, ed. *A D.H. Lawrence Miscellany.* Carbondale: Southern Illinois University Press, 1959. Not quite up to the quality of *The Achievement of D.H. Lawrence,* but still an excellent collection of representative essays.

— and Warren Roberts. *D.H. Lawrence and His World.* London: Thames and Hudson, 1966.

Moore, Olive, *Further Reflections on the Death of a Porcupine.* London: Blue Moon Press, 1932. A brief pamphlet re-printed in her *The Apple is Bitten Again* (New York: E.P. Dutton, 1935), 146-167.

Mori, Haruhide, ed. *A Conversation with D.H. Lawrence.* Los Angeles: Friends of the UCLA Library, 46 pp., 1974.

Moynahan, Julian. *The Deed of Life: The Novels and Tales of D.H. Lawrence.* Princeton: Princeton University Press, 1965. A sensitive, well-written book in the tradition of vitalist (Jungian) criticism that takes the Freudian view seriously into account.

—, ed. *Sons and Lovers: Text, Background, and Criticism.* New York: Viking Press, 1968. A casebook.

Nahal, Chaman. *D.H. Lawrence: An Eastern View.* Cranbury, New Jersey: A.S. Barnes and Company, 1970. Parallels between Oriental and Lawrentian ideas.

Napolitano, Giovanni. *"L'Amante de Lady Chatterley" o del Pudore.* Naples: Miccoli, 1948.

Negrioli, Claude. *La Symbolique de D.H. Lawrence.* Paris: Presses Universitaires de France, 1970.

Nin, Anais. *D.H. Lawrence: An Unporfessional Study.* London: E.W. Titmus, 1932. Reissued Denver: A. Swallow, 1964.

Nojima, Hidekatsu. *Exiles' Literature: A STudy of James Joyce, D.H. Lawrence, and T.S. Eliot.* Tokyo: Nanundo, 1964.

Oates, Joyce Carol. *The Hostile Sun: The Poetry of D.H. Lawrence.* Los Angeles: Black Sparrow Press, 1973.

Obler, Paul C. *D.H. Lawrence's World of The Rainbow.* Madison, New Jersey: Drew University Studies No. 8, 1955. A Monograph.

Panichas, George A. *Adventures in Consciousness: The Meaning of D.H. Lawrence's Religious Quest.* The Hague: Mouton, 1964.

—. *The Reverent Discipline: Essays in Literary Criticism and Culture.* Knoxville, Tennessee: University of Tennessee Press, 1974. Five chapters on Lawrence, and Lawrence and Eliot, Forster, Dostoevsky, and the Ancient Greeks.

Paterson, John. *The Novel as Faith: The Gospel According to James, Hardy, Conrad, Joyce, Lawrence, and Virginia Woolf.* Boston: Gambit, Inc., 1973.

Peyre, Henri. *Hommes et Oeuvres du XX Siecle.* Paris: R.A. Correa, 1938.

Poole, Roger H. *Lawrence and Education.* Nottingham: University of Nottingham, 1968.

Potter, Stephen. *D.H. Lawrence: A First Study.* London: Jonathan Cape, 1930.

Pritchard, Ronald E. *D.H. Lawrence: Body of Darkness.* London: Hutchinson, 1971: Pittsburgh: University of Pittsburgh Paperback Series, 1971. New insights into Lawrence's imagery, but very reductive and unnecessarily Freudian.

Rashin, Jonah. *The Mythology of Imperialism: Rudyard Kipling, Joseph Conrad, E.M Forster, D.H. Lawrence, and Joyce Cary.* New York: Random House, 1971.

Rees, Richard. *Brave Men: A Study of D.H. Lawrence and Simone Weil.* London: Gollancz, 1958; Southern Illinois University Press, 1959.

Reul, Paul de. *L'Oeuvre de D.H. Lawrence.* Paris: Urin, 1937.

Reuter, Irmgard. *Studien uber die Personlichkeit und die Kunstsform von D.H. Lawrence.* Marburg: Heinrich Poppinghaus, 1934.

Rolph, C.H., ed. *The Trial of Lady Chatterley.* Baltimore: Penguin Books, 1961.

Sagar, Keith M. *The Art of D.H. Lawrence.* Cambridge, England: University Press, 1966.

Sale, Roger. *Modern Heroism: Essays on D.H. Lawrence, Wiliam Empsom, and J.R. Tolkien.* Berkeley: University of California Press, 1973. Chapter II, "D.H. Lawrence, 1910-1916," 16-106.

Salgado, Gamini, ed. *D.H. Lawrence: Sons and Lovers: A Casebook.* London: Macmillian, 1969.

Sanders, Scott. *D.H. Lawrence: The World of the Five Major Novels.* New York: Viking Press, 1973. Lawrence as a negative cultural manifestation, laboring class, and "personal" without being proletarian and "social."

Seilliere, Ernest. *David Herbert Lawrence Et Les Recentes Ideologies Allemande.* Paris: Boivin, 1936.

Seligman, Herbert J. *D.H. Lawrence: An American Interpretation.* New York: Thomas Seltzer, 1924. Reissued Freeport, New York: Books for Libraries Press, 1971.

Sinzelle, Claude M. *The Geographical Background of the Early Works of D.H. Lawrence.* Paris: Didier, 1964.

Sitesh, Aruna. *D.H. Lawrence: The Crusader as Critic.* Delhi, Bombay, Calcutta, Madras: Macmillan, 1975.

Slade, Tony. *D.H. Lawrence.* London: Evans Bros., 1969.

Smailes, T.H. *Some Comments on the Verse of D.H. Lawrence.* Port Elizabeth, South Africa: University of Port Elizabeth, 1970.

Smith, Frank G. *D.H. Lawrence: The Rainbow. Studies in English Literature,* no. 46. London: Arnold, 1971.

Spender, Stephen, ed. *D.H. Lawrence: Novelist, Poet, Prophet.* New York: Harper and Row; London: Weidenfeld and Nicholson, 1973. A tasteful collection of essays by various hands generously interspersed with photographs, perhaps for the book trade and collectors.

Spilka, Mark. *The Love Ethic of D.H. Lawrence.* Bloomington: Indiana University Press, 1955. The beginning, or almost, and in many respects the fullest statement of vitalist criticism.

—, ed. *D.H. Lawrence: A Collection of Critical Essays.* Englewood Cliffs, New Jersey: Prentice-Hall, 1963.

Stewart, J.I.M. *Eight Modern Writers.* Oxford: Clarendon Press, 1963. Section on Lawrence, 483-593.

Stoll, John E. *D.H. Lawrence's Son and Lovers: Self-Encounter and the Unknown Self,* Muncie, Indiana: *Ball State University Monograph Series, Number 11,* 1968. An examination of previous criticism and a new departure.

—. *The Novels of D.H. Lawrence: A Search for Integration.* Columbia: University of Missouri Press, 1971. A study of Lawrence's imagery, the theories informing it, and the bases of previous criticism.

Swigg, Richard. *Lawrence, Hardy, and American Literature.* London and New York: Oxford University Press, 1972.

Talon, Henri-A. *D.H. Lawrence. Sons and Lovers, les aspects sociaux, la vision de l'artiste.* Paris: Lettres Modernes, 1965.

Tedlock, Ernest W., Jr. *D.H. Lawrence, Artist and Rebel.* Albuquerque: University of New Mexico Press, 1963. A book that stands by itself, independent of "schools" of criticism. Explores the works and their psychological implications.

—, ed. *D.H. Lawrence and Sons and Lovers: Sources and Criticism.* New York: New York University Press, 1965.

Tindall, William York. *D.H. Lawrence and Susan His Cow.* New York: Columbia University Press, 1939. Still enjoyable and shocking in its way.

—, ed. *The Later D.H. Lawrence.* New York: Alfred A. Knopf, 1952.

Tiverton, Father William (Martin Jarrett-Kerr). *D.H. Lawrence and Human Existence.* New York: Philosophical Library, 1951. A noble but foredoomed attempt to bring Lawrence within the Christian scheme of things.

Trease, Geoffrey. *D.H. Lawrence: The Phoenix and the Flame.* London and New York: Macmillan, 1973.

Vickery, John B. *The Literary Impact of the Golden Bough.* Princeton: Princeton University Press, 1973. Five chapters on Lawrence.

Vivas, Eliseo. *D.H. Lawrence: The Failure and the triumph of Art.* A book questionable in its methods of literary analysis but persuasive in its conclusions. Quintessentially moralistic.

Weidner, Ingeborg. *Botschaftverkungdigung und Selbstrausdruck im Prosawerk von D.H. Lawrence ("Meaning and Expression in the Porse of D.H. Lawrence").* Berlin: Forst, 1938.

Weiss, Daniel A. *Oedipus in Nottingham: D.H. Lawrence.* Seattle: University of Washington Press, 1963. An eager book about *Sons and Lovers* from a Freudian viewpoint, but one that makes Lawrence's achievement in the work almost diametrically opposed to his purpose.

West, Anthony. *D.H. Lawrence.* London: Arthur Barker, 1950.

Wickramasinge, Martin. *The Mysticism of D.H. Lawrence.* Colombo, Ceylon: M.D. Gunasena and Company, 1951.

Widmer, Kingsley. *The Art of Perversity: D.H. Lawrence's Shorter Fiction.* Seattle: University of Washington Press, 1962. A seminal work on Lawrence and an excellent application of the theme to the art.

Williams, Raymond. *The English Novel; From Dickens to Lawrence.* New York: Oxford University Press, 1970.

Young, Kenneth. *D.H. Lawrence.* London and New York: Longmans, Green, 1952. Bibliographical Series of Supplements to *British Book News,* No. 31.

Yudhistar, M. *Conflict in the Novels of D.H. Lawrence.* Edinburgh: Oliver and Boyd, 1969.

Zytaruk, George J. *D.H. Lawrence's Response to Russian Literature.* The Hague: Mouton, 1971.

ARTICLES

Abel, Patricia and Robert Hogan. "D.H. Lawrence's Singing Birds," In *A D.H. Lawrence Miscellany*, ed. Harry T. Moore (Carbondale: Southern Illinois University Press, 1959), 204-214.

Abolin, Nancy. "Lawrence's 'The Blind Man': The Reality of Touch," In *A D.H. Lawrence Miscellany*, ed. Harry T. Moore, 215-220.

Abraham, Adolfine. "Die Kunst form von D.H. Lawrence's Versdichtungen: Eine Psychological-Untersuching," Dissertation, Vienna, 1932.

Adam, Ian. "Lawrence's Anti-Symbol: The Ending of *The Rainbow*," *Journal of Narrative Technique*, III (1973), 77-84.

Adamowski, T.H. "Being Perfect: Lawrence, Sartre, and *Women in Love*," *Critical Inquiry*, II (1975), 345-368.

—. "Character and Consciousness: D.H. Lawrence, Wilhelm Reich, and Jean-Paul Sartre," *University of Toronto Quarterly*, XLIII (1974), 311-334.

—. "*The Rainbow* and Otherness," *D.H. Lawrence Review*, VII (1974), 58-77.

Adams, Elsie B. "Lawrence Among the Christians: MLA, 1968," *D.H. Lawrence Review*, II (1969), 168-171.

—. "A 'Lawrentian' Novel by Bernard Shaw," *D.H. Lawrence Review*, II (1969), 245-253.

Adelman, Gary. "Beyond the Pleasure Principle: An Analysis of D.H. Lawrence's 'The Prussian Officer,'" *Studies in Short Fiction*, I (1963), 8-15.

—. "Lawrence's *Rainbow*," *Dissertation Abstracts*, XXIV (1963), 5402-5403 (Columbia).

Aiken, Conrad. "The Melodic Line," *Dial*, LXVII (August 9, 1919), 97-100. Review of *Look! We Have Come Through!*, but also an analysis of Lawrence's metrics and his relation to modern poetry.

Alanei, Tamara. "Imagery and Meaning in D.H. Lawrence's *The Rainbow*," *Yearbook of English Studies*, II (1972), 205-211.

—. "Three Times Morel: Recurrent Structure in *Sons and Lovers,*" *Dutch Quarterly Review,* V (1975), 39-53.

Alcorn, John M. "Hardy to Lawrence: A Study in Naturism," *Dissertation Abstracts,* XXIX (1968), 251A-252A (New York University).

Aldinton, Richard. "The Composite Biography as Biography," In *A D.H. Lawrence Miscellany,* ed. Harry T. Moore, 144-153.

—. "Introduction," *St. Mawr and The Virgin and the Gypsy* (Baltimore: Penguin Books, 1950).

—. "Introduction," *Women in Love* (Phoenix Edition).

—. "Note" to *Last Poems, Complete Poems* (Phoenix Edition).

Alexander Edward. "Lawrence and Huxley," *Queen's Quarterly,* XLII (1935), 96-108.

—. "Thomas Carlyle and D.H. Lawrence: A Parallel," *University of Toronto Quarterly,* XXXVII (1968), 248-267.

Alexander, John C. "D.H. Lawrence and Teilhard de Chardin: A Study in Agreements," *D.H. Lawrence Review,* II (1969), 138-156.

—. "D.H. Lawrence's *Kangaroo:* Fantasy, Fact, or Fiction," *Mean jin Quarterly,* XXIV (1965), 179-197.

Allen, Walter, "Lawrence in Perspective," *Penguin New Writing,* No. 29 (1947), 104-115.

Allendorf, Otmar. "Die Bedeutung Thomas Hardy fur das Fruhwerk von D.H. Lawrence," Dissertation, Marburg: Lahn, 1969.

—. "The Origin of Lawrence's *Study of Thomas Hardy,*" *Notes & Queries,* XVII (1970), 466-467.

Allott, Kenneth and Miriam Allott. "D.H. Lawrence and Blanche Jennings," *Review of English Literature* (Leeds), I (1960), 57-76.

Alvarez, A. "D.H Lawrence: The Single State of Man," In *A D.H. Lawrence Miscellany,* ed. Harry T. Moore, 342-359.

Alves, Leonard. "The Relevance of D.H. Lawrence," *English Literature and Language,* X (1973), 83-108.

Amon, Frank. "D.H. Lawrence and the Short Story," *In The Achievement of D.H. Lawrence,* ed. Frederick J. Hoffman and Harry T. Moore (Norman: University of Oklahoma Press, 1953), 222-234.

Anderson, Sherwood. " A Man's Mind," *New Republic,* LXIII (May 21, 1930), 22-23.

—. "A Man's Song of Life," *Virginia Quarterly Review,* IX (1933), 108-114.

Ando, Yukio. "Lawrence Hihyo o Megutte" ("Around the Criticisms on Lawrence"), *Journal of the Department of Literature* (Rissho University), XII (February, 1960), 37-57.

Andrews, W.T. "Laurentian Indiffernece," *Notes & Queries,* XVI (1969), 260-261.

—. "D.H. Lawrence's Favorite Jargon," *Notes & Queries,* XIII (1966), 97-98.

—. "D.H. Lawrence's Novels as Irritants," *Notes & Queries,* XIII (1966), 418-419.

—. "Silence in D.H. Lawrence," *Notes & Queries,* XIV (1967), 252-253.

Anonymous. "Lady Chatterley at Last," *Meanjin Quarterly* (Melbourne), XVIII (1959), 450-455.

Anon. "Lady Chatterley in Ottowa," *Canadian Forum,* XLII (April, 1962), 11-13.

Anon "D.H. Lawrence in Taos," *Listener,* LXXXII (1969), 336-339.

Anon. "The Rainbow. Destruction of a Novel Ordered," *The Times,* November 15, 1915, 3. Account of the seizure.

Anon. "The Three Lady Chatterley's," *Essays and Reviews from the Times Literary Supplement,* XII (1974), 103-114.

Aoyoma, Seiko. "Ikiku no Ka' ni Okeru Lawrence Bungaku no Haga" ("D.H. Lawrence's Genius in 'Odour of Chrysanthemums'"), *Essays* (Tokyo University), No. 21 (May, 1967), 59-72.

—. *"The Virgin and The Gypsy* ni Tsuite (Lawrence no Tanpen-Shose- Tsu ni Okeru Semimeishugi no Keifu)" ("A Study of *The Virgin and The Gypsy"), Collected Essays* (Kyoritsu Women's Junior College), No. 9 (December, 1965), 83-101.

Appel, George Fowler. "Modern Masters and Archaic Motifs of the Animal Poem," Dissertation, University of Minnesota, 1973.

Appleman, Philip. "D.H. Lawrence and the Intrusive Knock," *Modern Fiction Studies*, III (1957), 328-332.

—. "One of D.H. Lawrence's 'Autobiographical' Characters," *Modern Fiction Studies*, IV (1958), 237-238.

Armytage, W.H. "The Disenchanted Mechanophobes in Twentieth Century England," *Extrapolation*, IX (1968). 33-60. Lawrence, Orwell, Huxley, and Auden.

—. "Superman and the System," *Riverside Quarterly*, III (1967), 44-51.

Arnold, Armin. "Genius with a Dictionary: Reevaluating D.H. Lawrence's Translation," *Comparative Literature Studies*, V (1968), 389-401.

—. " The German Letters of D.H. Lawrence," *Comparative Literature Studies, III (1966), 285-298.*

—. "In the Footsteps of D.H. Lawrence in Switzerland: Some New Biographical Material," *Texas Studies in Literature and Language*, III (1961), 184-188.

—. "D.H. Lawrence and Thomas Mann," *Comparative Literature*, XIII (1961), 33-38.

—. "D.H. Lawrence, the Russians, and Giovanni Verga," *Comparative Literature Studies*, II (1965), 249-257.

—. "D.H. Lawrence's First Critical Essays: Two Anonymous Reviews Identified," *Publications of the Modern Language Association*, LXXIX (1964), 185-188.

—. "The Transcendental Element in American Literature," *Midway*, No. 12 (1962), 28-33. On *Studies in Classic American Literature.*

—. "The Transcendental Element in American Literature: Some Unpublished D.H. Lawrence Manuscripts," *Modern Philology*, LX (1962), 41-46.

—, ed. "Three Unknown Letters from Frieda Lawrence to Bertrand Russell," *D.H. Lawrence Review*, II (1969), 157-161.

Asakawa, Jun. "Oboegaki Lawrence (1)" ("A Note on D.H. Lawrence (1)": *Sons and Lovers). English Language and*

English and American Literature (Chuo University), I (1960), 1-9.

—. "Oboegaki Lawrence (II)" *(On Symbol), English Language and English and American Literature*, II (1961), 21-28.

—. "Oboegaki Lawrence (III)" (On Symbol), *English Language and English and American Literature*, III (1962), 84-94.

—. "Oboegaki Lawrence (IV)" (On The *Ladybird*), *English Language and English and American Literature*, IV (1963), 33-40.

Atkinson, Curtis. "Was There Fact in D. H. Lawrence's *Kangaroo?*," *Meanjin Quarterly* (Melbourne), XXIV (1965), 358-359.

Auden, W.H. "Heretics," In *Literary Opinion in America*, ed. Morton Zabel (New York: Harpers, 1951), 256-259.

—. "Some Notes on D.H. Lawrence," *The Nation*, CLXIV (1947), 482-484.

Austin, Allan E. "D.H. Lawrence's Shorter Fiction: The Question of Chronology," *Dissertation Abstracts*, XXV (1964), 2976 (University of Rochester).

Baim, Joseph. "D.H. Lawrence's Social Vison," *In Honor of Austin Wright, Carnegie Series in English*, No. 12 (Pittsburgh: Carnegie-Mellon University, 1972), 1-9.

—. "Past and Present in D.H. Lawrence's 'A Fragment of Stained Glass,'" *Studies in Short Fiction*, VIII (1971), 323-326.

—. "The Second Coming of Pan: A Note on D.H. Lawrence's 'The Last Laugh,'" *Studies in Short Fiction*, VI (1968), 98-100.

—. "Structure in the Short Stories of D.H. Lawrence," *Dissertation Abstracts*, XXVIII (1967), 462A (Syracuse University).

Bair, Hebe. "Lawrence as Poet," *D.H. Lawrence Review*, VI (1973), 313-325.

Baisch, Dorothy R. "London Literary Circles, 1910-1920, with Special Reference to Ford Madox Ford, Ezra Pound, D.H. Lawrence, and Virginia Woolf," *Doctoral Dissertations*, XVII (1950), 197 (Cornell University).

Baker, James R. "Lawrence as Prophetic Poet," *Journal of Modern Literature*, III (1974), 1219-1238.

Baker, James R. " Lawrence as Prophetic Poet," *Journal of Modern Literature,* III (1974), 1219-1238.

Baker, Paul. "A Critical Examination of D.H. Lawrence's *Aaron's Rod,"* Dissertation, University of Toronto, 1974.

Balakian, Nona. "The Prophetic Vogue of the Anti-heroine," *Southwest Review,* XLVII (1962), 134-141. On Lady Chatterley.

Balbert, Peter H. "D.H. Lawrence and the Psychology of Rhythm: The Meaning of Form in *The Rainbow," Dissertation Abstracts International* XXX (1969), 3934A (Cornell University).

Baldanza, Frank. "D.H. Lawrence's Song of Songs," *Modern Fiction Studies,* VII (1962), 106-114.

—. *"Sons and Lovers:* Novel to Film as a Record of Cultural Growth," *Literature/Film Quarterly,* I (1973), 64-70.

Baldeshwiler, Eileen. "The Lyric Short Story: The Sketch of a History," *Studies in Short Fiction,* VI (1969), 443-453. Includes "The Blind Man" and "The Christening."

Baldwin, Alice. "The Structure of the Coatly Symbol in *The Plumed Serpent,"Style,* V (1971), 138-150.

Ballin, Michael. "D.H. Lawrence and William Blake: A Comparative and Critical Study," Dissertation, University of Toronto, 1972.

Bantock, G.H. "D.H. Lawrence and the Nature of Freedom," In *Freedom and Authority in Education* (London: Faber and Faber, 1952), 133-181.

Barber, David S. "Can a Radical Interpretation of *Women in Love* Be Adequate?," *D.H. Lawrence Review,* III (1970), 168-174.

—. "Community in *Women in Love," Novel,* V (1971), 32-41.

Barber, Janet. "Mexican Machismo in Novels by Lawrence, Sendu, Fuentes," Dissertation, University of Southern California, 1972.

Bareiss, Dieter. "Die Vierpersonenkonstellation im Rome: Strukturuntersuchungen Zur Personenfuhrung. Dargestellt an N. Hawthornes "The Blithedale Romance," G. Eliots "Daniel Deronda," H. James "The Golden Bowl," und D.H. Lawrence "Women in Love, ""' Dissertation, Erlangen-Nurnberg, 1969.

Baron, Carl E. "D.H. Lawrence's Early Paintings," In *Young Bert: An Exhibition of the Early Years of D.H. Lawrence* (Nottingham, 1972), 32-40.

—. "The Nottingham Festival D.H. Lawrence Exhibition, 1972," *D.H. Lawrence Review,* VII (1974), 19-57.

—. "Two Hitherto Unknown Pieces by D.H. Lawrence," *Encounter,* XXXIII (1969), 293-303. Lawrence's first critical review of Bithell's *Contemporary German Poetry* and an essay entitled "With the Guns."

Barr, Barbara. "I Look Back," *Twentieth Century,* CLXV (1959), 254-261.

—. "Memoir of D.H. Lawrence," In *D.H. Lawrence: Novelist, Poet, Prophet,* ed. Stephen Spender, 8-36.

Barr, William. "The Metaphor of Apocalypse in the Novels of D.H. Lawrence," Dissertation, University of Michigan, 1973.

Barriere, Francoise. *"Women in Love* ou le roman de l'antagonisme," *Les Langues Modernes,* LXIII (1969), 293-303.

Barry, J. "Lswald Spengler and D.H. Lawrence," *English Studies in Africa,* XII (1969), 151-161.

Barry, Sandra. "Singurlarity of Two: The Plurality of One," *Paunch,* No. 26 (1966), 34-39. On *Aaron's Rod.*

Bartlett, Norman. "Aldous Huxley and D.H. Lawrence," *Australian Quarterly,* XXXVI (1964), 76-84.

Bartlett, Phyllis. "Lawrence's *Collected Poems:* The Demon Takes Over," *Publications of the Modern Language* Association, LXVI (1951), 583-593. On Lawrence's revisions.

Barzun, Jacques. "Lawrence in Life and Letters," *The Griffin,* VII (1958), 4-11.

Beach, Joseph Warren. "Impressionism: Lawrence," In *The Twentieth Century Novel: Studies in Technique* (New York: Appleton, 1932), 366-384.

Beal, Anthony. "Introduction," In *D.H. Lawrence and Italy: Twilight in Italy, Sea and Sardinia, Etruscan Places* (New York: Viking Press, 1972).

Beards, Richard. "D.H. Lawrence and the *Study of Thomas Hardy,* His Victorian Predecessor," *D.H. Lawrence Review,* II (1969), 210-229.

—. "Lawrence Now," *Journal of Modern Literature*, I(1969), 434-438. Review of Cavitch's *D.H. Lawrence and the New World*, Clark's *River of Dissolution*, and Yudhistar's *Conflicts in the Novels of D.H. Lawrence*.

—. "The Novels of Thomas Hardy and D.H. Lawrence: A Comparative Study," *Dissertation Abstracts*, XXVI (1965), 2743 (University of Washington).

—. "*Sons and Lovers* as Bildungsroman," *College Literature*, I (1974), 204-217.

Beatty, C.J.P. "Konrad Lorenz and D.H. Lawrence," *Notes and Queries*, XIX (1972), 54.

Beauchamp, Gorman. "Lawrence's 'The Rocking-Horse Winner,'" *Explicator*, XLI (January, 1973), 32.

Becker, Henry, III. "'The Rocking-Horse Winner': Film as Parable," *Literature/Film Quarterly*, I (1973), 55-63.

Beckham, Richard Hamilton. "The Ritual of Love: A Study of Symbolic Technique in D.H. Lawrence's Shorter Fiction," Dissertation, Kent State University, 1969.

Bedford, Sybille. "The Last Trial of Lady Chatterley," *Esquire*, XLV (1961), 132-136, 138, 141-155.

Bedient, Calvin B. "The Fate of the Self: Self and Society in the Novels of George Eliot, D.H. Lawrence, and E.M. Forster," *Dissertation Abstracts*, XXV (1964), 1187 (University of Washington).

—. "The Radicalness of *Lady Chatterley's Lover*," *Hudson Review*, XIX (1966), 407-416.

Beebe, Maurice. "Lawrence's Sacred Fount: The Artist's Theme of *Sons and Lovers*," *Texas Studies in Literature and Language*, IV (1962), 539-552. One of the best defenses of the artistic wholeness of Sons *and Lovers* written.

Beharriel, Frederick J. "Freud and Literature," *Queen's Quarterly*, LXV (1958), 118-125. Review article.

Beirne, Raymond M. "Lawrence's Night-Letter on Censorship and Obscenity," *D.H. Lawrence Review*, VII (1974), 321-322.

Beker, Miroslav. "'The Crown,' 'The Reality of Peace,' and *Women in Love*," *D.H. Lawrence Review*, II (1969), 254-264.

Bell, Michael. "The Shift from a Romantic to a Primitive View of Life in D.H. Lawrence, with Particular Reference to Defferences in the Language of *The Rainbow, Women in Love,* and *The Plumed Serpent,"* Dissertation, University of London, 1970.

Bennett, James R. "The Novel, Truth, and Community," *D.H. Lawrence Review,* IV (1971), 74-89. Review of Garrett's *Scene and Symbol,* Lerner's *The Truthtellers,* Williams's *The English Novel from Dickens to Lawrence.*

Benstock, Bernard. "The Present Recaptured: D.H. Lawrence and Others," *Southern Review,* IV (1968), 802-816. Review of books on Lawrence by Harry T. Moore and Warren Roberts, David J. Gordon, H.M. Daleski, and Keith Sagar.

Bentley, Joseph. "Huxley's Ambivalent Response to the Ideas of D.H. Lawrence," *Twentieth Century Literature,* XIII (1967), 139-153.

Bergler, Edmund, M.D. "D.H. Lawrence's 'The Fox' and the Psychoanalytic Theory on Lesbianism," In *A D.H. Lawrence Miscellany,* ed. Harry T. Moore, 49-55.

Bersani, Leo. "Lawrentian Stillness," *Yale Review,* LXV (1975), 38-60. On *Women in Love.*

Bertoci, Angelo. "Symbolism in *Women in Love,"* In *A D.H. Lawrence Miscellany,* ed. Harry T. Moore, 83-102. An early and perceptive examination.

Betsky, Sarah Z. "America, American Literature, and D.H. Lawrence: A Study in Reciprocity," *Dissertation Abstracts,* XVII (1956), 2265-2266 (New York University).

Betsky, Seymour. "Rhythm and Theme: D.H. Lawrence's *Sons and Lovers,"* In *The Acievement of D.H. Lawrence,* ed. Frederick J. Hoffman and Harry T. Moore, 138-151.

Beutmann, Margarete. "Die Bildungswelt D.H. Lawrences," Dissertation, Freiburg: Breisgau Universitat, 1940.

Bhalla, Brij Mohan. "The Mutual Flame: The Quest for Selfhood in Relation to Form in the Later Novels of D.H. Lawrence," Dissertation, University of Wisconsin, 1971.

Bhat, Vishnu. "D.H. Lawrence's Sexual Ideal," *Literary Half-Yearly,* X (1969), 68-73.

Bickerton, Derek. "The Language of *Women in Love*," *Review of English Literature*, VIII (1967), 56-67.

Bickley, Francis. "Some Tendencies in Contemporary Poetry," In *New Paths*, ed. C.W. Beaumont and M.T. Ladler (London: C.W. Beaumont, 1918).

Biles, Jack I. "An Interview in London with Angus Wilson," *Studies in the Novel*, II (1970), 76-87. Lawrence's depersonalization of love through ritualization.

Birrell, T.H. "Where the Rainbow ends: A Study of D.H. Lawrence," *Downside Review*, LXIX (1959), 453-467.

Bishop, John P. "Distrust of Ideas," In *Collected Essays*, ed. Edmund Wilson (New York: Scribners, 1948), 233-237.

Bjorkman, Edwin. "Introduction," *The Widowing of Mrs. Hol royd* (New York: Mitchell Kennerley, 1914).

Black, Michael. "Sexuality in Literature: *Lady Chatterley's Lover*," In *The Literarure of Fidelity* (New York: Barnes and Noble, 1975), 184-198.

Blackmur, R.P. "D.H. Lawrence and Expressive Form," In *Language as Gesture* (New York: Harcourt, Brace and Company, 1952), 286-300. The classic formalist statement on Lawrence.

Blanchard, Lydia. "Love and Power: A Reconsideration of Sexual Politics in Lawrence," *Modern Fiction Studies*, XXI (1975), 431-443.

Blanchard, Margaret. "Men in Charge: A Review of *Women in Love*," *A Journal of Liberation*, fall 1970, 31-32. Women's liberation and the film version.

Bleich, David. "The Determination of Literary Value," *Literature and Psychology*, XVII (1967), 19-30. Analysis of the Poem, "Piano," in response to I.A. Richards.

Blissett, William. "D.H. Lawrence, D'Annunzio, Wagner," *Wisconsin Studies in Contemporary Literature*, VII (1966), 21-46.

Blitzer, Gerhard. "D.H. Lawrence und das nachchristliche Suchen nach einer Religion," Dissertation, University of Heidelburg, 1960.

Blomberg, Erik. "D.H. Lawrence dikter" (On Lawrence's Poems), Lyrikvannen (Stockholm), IV, iii (1957), 12-24.

Bloom, Harold. "Lawrence, Blackmur, Eliot, and the Tortoise," In *A D.H. Lawrence Miscellany*, ed. Harry T. Moore, 360-369.

Bobbitt, Joan. "Lawrence and Bloomsbury: The Myth of a Relationship," *Essays in Literature* (University of Denver), I (1973), 31-42.

Bogan, Louise. "The Poet Lawrence," In *Selected Criticism: Prose and Poetry* (New York: Noonday Press, 1955), 346-349.

Bolsterli, Margaret. "Studies in Context: The Homosexual Ambience in Twentieth Century Literary Culture," *D.H. Lawrence Review*, VI (1973), 71-85.

Bordinat, Philips. "The Poetic Images in D.H. Lawrence's 'The Captain's Doll,'" *West Virginia University Bulletin: Philological Papers*, XIX (1972), 45-49.

Boren, James L. "Commitment and Futility in 'The Fox,'" *University Review* (Kansas City), XXXI (1965), 301-304.

Boulton, James T. "'D.H. Lawrence: Study of a Free Spirit in Literature,' A Note on an Uncollected Article," *Renaissance and Modern Studies*, XVIII (1974), 5-16.

—. "D.H. Lawrence's *Odour of Chrysanthemums*: An Early Version," *Renaissance and Modern Studies*, XIII (1969), 5-48.

Brady, Emily K. "The Literary Faulkner: His Indebtedness to Conrad, Lawrence, Hemingway, and Other Modern Novelists," *Dissertation Abstracts*, XXIII (1962), 2131-2132 (Brown University).

Bramley, J.A. "The Challenge of D.H. Lawrence," *Hilbert Journal*, LVIII (1960), 281-287.

—. "D.H. Lawrence and Miriam," *Cornhill Magazine*, CLXXI (1960), 241-249.

—. "D.H. Lawrence's Sternest Critic," *Hilbert Journal*, LXIII (165), 109-111. On Jessie Chambers.

—. "The Significance of D.H. Lawrence," *Contemporary Review*, No. 1121 (1959), 304-307.

Branda, Eldon S. "Textual Changes in *Women in Love*," *Texas Studies in Literature and Language*, VI (1964), 306-322.

Brandabur, A.M. "The Ritual Corn Harvest Scene in *The Rainbow*," *D.H. Lawrence Review*, VI (1973), 284-302.

Brashear, Lucy M. "Lawrence's Companion Poems: 'Snake' and *Tortoises*," *D.H. Lawrence Review*, V (1972), 54-62.

Braysfield, Peggy. "Lawrence's 'Male and Female Principles' and the Symbolism of 'The Fox,'" *Mosaic*, IV (1971), 41-51.

Briscoe, Mary L. and Martha Vicinus. "Lawrence Among the Radicals: MLA, 1969: An Exchange," *D.H. Lawrence Review*, III (1970), 63-69.

Broembsen, Francesca von. "Moses off the Mountain: Readings in Paul Valery and D.H. Lawrence," Dissertation, Harvard University, 1972.

—. "Mythic Identification and Spatial Inscendence: The Cosmic Vision of D.H. Lawrence," *Western Humanities Review*, XXIX (1975), 137-154.

Brookesmith, Peter. "The Future of the Individual," *Human World*, No. 10 (February 1973), 42-65. On Ursula.

Brotherston, J.G. "Revolution and the Ancient Literature of Mexico, for D.H.Lawrence and Antonin Certaud," *Twentieth Century Literature*, XVIII (1972), 181-189.

Brown, Homer O. "The Passionate Struggle into Conscious Being: D.H. Lawrence's *The Rainbow*," *D.H. Lawrence Review*, VII (1974), 275-290.

Bryan, Frederick. "Court Opinion on the Postal Ban of *Lady Chatterley's Lover*," *Evergreen Review*, IX (1959), 37-68.

Buckley, Jerome H. "D.H. Lawrence: The Burden of Apology," In *Seasons of Youth: The Bildungsroman from Dickens to Golding* (Cambridge: Harvard University Press, 1974), 204-224.

Burke, Kenneth. "In Qualified defense of Lawrence," In *Permanence and Change: An Anatomy of Purpose* (Los Altos, California: Hermes Publications, 1957), 250-254.

Burns, Robert. "The Novel as a Metaphysical Statement: Lawrence's *The Rainbow*," *Southern Review*, IV (1970), 139-160.

Burns, Wayne. "*Lady Chatterley's Lover: A Pilgrim's Progress for Our Time*," *Paunch*, No. 26 (April, 1966), 16-33.

Burwell, Rose Marie. "A Catalogue of D.H. Lawrence's Reading from Early Childhood," *D.H. Lawrence Reveiw,* III (1970), 193-330.

—. "A Catalogue of D.H. Lawrence's Reading from Early Childhood: Addenda," *D.H. Lawrence Review,* VI (1973), 86-99.

—. "Schopenhauer, Hardy, and Lawrence: Toward a New Understanding of *Sons and Lovers,"* Western Humanities Review, XXVIII (1974), 105-117.

Busch, Gunther. "Kritische These uber D.H. Lawrence," *Wort in der Zeit* (Vienna), VIII (1962), 44-48.

Butler, Joseph. *"The Rainbow* and D.H. Lawrence's Repudiation of Sex Tragedy," Dissertation, University of Washington, 1969.

Byngham, Dion. "D.H. Lawrence," In *Modern British Writing,* ed. Denys Val Baker (New York: Vanguard, 1947), 326-331.

Cameron, Mary C. "The Reputation of D.H. Lawrence: 1912-1960," *Dissertation Abstracts,* XXVII (1966), 176A (Yale).

Capitanchik, Maurice. "D.H. Lawrence: The Sexual Impasse," *Books and Bookmen,* XVIII (November 1972), 28-31. Review article on the English edition of Emile Delavenay's *The Man and His Work.*

Carey, John "D.H. Lawrence's Doctrine," In *D.H. Lawrence: Novelist, Poet, Prophet,* ed. Stephen Spender, 122-134. Agrees with Lawrence's view of the unconscious.

Carroll, La Von B. "Syzgy: A Study of the Light-Dark Imagery in Five of the Novels of D.H. Lawrence," *Proceedings of the Utah Academy of Sciences, Arts, and Letters,* XLIV (1967), 139-149.

Carstarphen, Sally S. "The Divided Sympathetic Bond: A Study of D.H. Lawrence's Drama," Dissertation, University of North Carolina, Greensboro, 1974.

Casey, Paul C. "The Casey Judgment," *Tamarack Review,* No. 21 (Autumn 1961), 58-70. Judge Casey's opinion regarding *Lady Chatterley's Lover.*

Caudwell, Christopher. "D.H. Lawrence: A Study of the Bourgeios Artist," In *The Critical Performance,* ed. Stanley Edgar Hyman (New York: Vintage, 1956), 153-173.

Cavitch, David B. "D.H. Lawrence and the New World," *Dissertation Abstracts,* XXVII (1966), 1052A (University of California, Berkeley).

—. "Merging—with Fish and Others," *D.H. Lawrence Review,* VII (1974), 172-178.

—. "Solipsism and Death in D.H. Lawrence's Late Works," *Massachusetts Review,* VII (1966), 495-508.

Cecchetti, Giovanni. "Verga and D.H. Lawrence's Translations," *Comparative Literature,* IX (1957), 333-344.

Chamberlain, Robert L. "Pussum, Minette, and the Africo-Nordic Symbol in Lawrence's *Women in Love,*" *Publications of the Modern Language Association,* LXXVIII (1963), 407-416. An excellent discussion of some of the major symbolism, its significance, and its all-pervasiveness.

Chambers, Jessie. "D.H. Lawrence's Literary Debut," *European Quarterly,* November, 1934.

—. "D.H. Lawrence's Student Days," *European Quarterly,* August, 1934.

—. "The Literary Formation of D.H. Lawrence," *European Quarterly,* May, 1934.

Chambers, Jonathan D. "Memories of D.H. Lawrence," *Renaissance and Modern Studies,* XVI (1972), 5-16.

Chambers, Mary C. "Afternoon in Italy with D.H Lawrence," *Texas Quarterly,* VII (1964), 114-120.

Chapman, R.T. "Lawrence, Lewis and the Comedy of Literary Reputations," *Studies in the Twentieth Century,* VI (1970), 85-95.

Chauchan, Praydunma. "D.H. Lawrence and the Making of an American Myth," Dissertation, Duke University, 1971.

Chavis, Geraldine B. "Ursula Brangwen: Toward Self and Selflessness," *Thoth,* XII (1971), 18-28.

Christian, Moe. "Playwright Lawrence Takes the Stage in London," *D.H Lawrence Review,* II (1969), 93-97.

Church, Richard. "Three Established Poets," *Spectator,* August 3, 1929, 164-165.

Cipolla, Elizabeth. "The *Last Poems* of D.H. Lawrence," *D.H. Lawrence Review,* II (1969), 103-119.

Clancy, Jack. "The Film and the Book: D.H. Lawrence and Joseph Heller on the Screen," *Meanjin*, XXX (1971), 96-101. *The Virgin and the Gypsy* and *Women in Love.*

Clark, L.D. "The Apocalypse of Lorenzo," *D.H. Lawrence Review*, III (1970), 141-160.

—. "The D.H. Lawrence Festival: Kiowa Ranch, New Mexico, September 30-October 4, 1970." *D.H. Lawrence Review*, IV (1971), 44-60.

—. "Lawrence, *Women in Love:* The Contravened Knot," In *Approaches to the Twentieth Century Novel*, ed. John Unterecker (New York: Crowell, 1965), 51-78.

—. "D.H. Lawrence's 'The Plumed Serpent,'" *Dissertation Abstracts*, XXIV (1963), 5405 (Columbia).

Clarke, Richard. "Autobiography, Doctrine, and Genre Comparison in the Plays of D.H. Lawrence," Dissertation, Florida State University, 1974.

Clements, A.L. "The Quest for Self: D.H. Lawrence's *The Rainbow*," *Thoth* (Syracuse), III (1962), 90-100.

Cline, C.L. "A Visit to Frieda," *Library Chronicle* (University of Texas), New Series, VII (1974), 37-41.

Clor, Harry M. "The Law and the Obscene," *Denver Quarterly*, III (1968), 1-24.

Clupper, Beatrice B. "The Male Principle in D.H. Lawrence's Fiction," Dissertation, University of Illinois, 1971.

Cobau, William W. "A View from Eastwood: Conversation with Mrs. O.L. Hopkin." *D.H. Lawrence Review*, IX (1976), 126-136.

Cohen, Judith D. "The Violation or Fulfillment of Individuality in Marriage, as Seen in Selected Works of D.H. Lawrence, Dissertation, University of Pennsylvania, 1970.

Cohn, Dorritt. "Narrative Monologue: Definition of a Fictional Style," *Comparative Literature*, XVIII (1966), 97-112.

Colacurcio, Michael J. "The Symbolic and the Symptomatic: D.H. Lawrence in Recent American Criticism," *American Quarterly*, XXVIII (1975), 486-501.

Collier, Peter. "The Man Who Died," *Ramparts*, VI (1968), 12-14.

Collis, J. S. "An Inevitable Prophet," In *Farewell to Argument* (London: Cassell, 1935), 156-195.

Conti, Giuseppe G. "Una lettera inedita di D.H. Lawrence," *English Miscellany*, XIX (1968), 335-338.

Coolidge, Theresa. "D.H. Lawrence to His Agent," *More Books*, XXIII (1948), 23-24. Three unpublished letters.

Coombes, H. "D.H. Lawrence Placed," *Scrutiny*, March, 1949.

—. "The Paintings of D.H. Lawrence," *Gemini*, II (1959), 56-59.

Cooney, Seamus. "The First Edition of Lawrence's Foreword to *Women in Love*," Library Chronicle (University of Texas), New Series VII (1974), 71-79.

—. "Reply to Ian Gregor," *Essays in Criticism*, IX (1959), 451-453.

Corbin, Richard J. "Unity and Meaning in D.H. Lawrence's *Birds, Beasts and Flowers*, Dissertation, Tulane University, 1973.

Corke, Helen. "Beyond the Gentility Principle," In *The New Poetry* (Baltimore: Penguin Books, 1962).

—. "Concerning *The White Peacock*," *Texas Quarterly*, II (1959), 186-190.

—. "D.H. Lawrence as I Saw Him," *Renaissance and Modern Studies*, IV (1960), 5-13.

—. "D.H. Lawrence: The Early Stage," *D.H. Lawrence Review*, IV (1971), 111-121.

—. "Portrait of D.H. Lawrence, 1909-1910," *Texas Quarterly*, V (1962), 169-177.

—. "The Writing of *The Trespasser*," *D.H. Lawrence Review*, VII (1974), 227-239.

Corsani, Mary, "D.H. Lawrence tradrettore dall'italiano," *English Miscellany*, XVII (1966), 249-278.

Couaillac, Maurice. "D.H. Lawrence, Essai sur la Formation et le Developpement da sa pensee apres son oeuvre en prose," Dissertation, University of Toulouse, 1937.

Cowan, James C. "The Function of Allusions and Symbols in Lawrence's *The Man Who Died*," *American Imago*, XVII (1960), 241-253,

—. "Lawrence in Old and New Mexico: The Quest and the Art," *Dissertation Abstracts,* XXV (1964), 3567 (University of Oklahoma).

—. "Lawrence's Criticism of Melville," *Extracts* (University of Pennsylvania), XIX (1969), 6-9.

—. "D.H. Lawrence's Dualism: The Apollonian-Dionysian Polarity and *The Ladybird,"* In *Forms of Modern British Fiction,* ed. Alan Friedman, 73-99.

—. "Lawrence's *Phoenix:* An Introduction," *D.H. Lawrence Review,* V (1972), 187-199.

—. "Lawrence's *The Princess* as Ironic Romance," *Studies in Short Fiction,* IV (1967), 245-251.

—. "D.H. Lawrence's Quarrel with Christianity," *University of Tulsa Department of English Monographs, No. 7: Literature and Theology* (1966), 32-43.

—. "Lawrence's Romantic Values: *Studies in Classic American Literature,"* Forum (Ball State), VIII (1967), 30-35.

—. "The Symbolic Structure in *The Plumed Serpent,"* Tulane *Studies in English,* XIV (1965), 75-96.

Cowan, S.A. "Lawrence's 'The Rocking-Horse Winner,'" *Explicator,* XXVII (1968), item 9.

Cowell, Catherine R. "The Laurentian Philosophy of Communication: An Analysis of Selected Essays of D.H. Lawrence," Dissertation, University of Denver, 1972.

Cox, C.B., *et al.* "Symposium: Pornography and Obscenity," *Critical Quarterly,* III (1961), 99-122.

Coze, Paul. "The Phoenix Bird," *Arizona Highways,* XXXIX (1963), 1-13.

Craig, David. "Fiction and the Rising Industrial Classes," *Essays in Criticism,* XVII (1967), 258-281. *Women in Love* does not embody industrial reality accurately.

—. "Lawrence and Democracy," In *The Real Foundations: Literature and Social Change* (New York: Oxford University Press, 1974), 143-167.

—. "Shakespeare, Lawrence, and Sexual Freedom," In *The Real Foundations,* 17-38.

—, Mark Roberts, and T.W. Thomas. "Community," *Essays in Criticism,* V (1955), 64-80. On Robert Liddell's "Lawrence and Dr. Leavis: The Case of St. Mawr."

Craig, G. Armour. "D.H. Lawrence on Thinghood and Selfhood," *Massachusetts Review*, I (1959), 59-60.

Crehan, Hubert. "Lady Chatterley's Painter: The Banned Pictures of D.H. Lawrence," *Art News*, LV (1957), 38-41, 63-66.

Crump, G.B. "Gopher Prairie or Papplewick?: *The Virgin and The Gypsy* as Film" *D.H. Lawrence Review*, IV (1971), 142-153.

—. "Lawrence and the Literature/Film Quarterly," *D.H. Lawrence Review*, VI (1973), 326-332.

—. *"Women in Love:* Novel and Film," *D.H. Lawrence Review*, IV (1971), 28-41.

Cunliffe, J.W. "Georgian Novelists," In *English Literature in the Twentieth Century* (New York: Macmillan, 1933), 201-258.

Cunningham, J.S. "Lady Chatterley's Husband," *Litterary Half-Yearly*, III (1962), 20-27.

Cura-Sazdanic, I. "D.H. Lawrence as Critic," *Index to Theses*, XV (1965), 16 (University of Exeter).

Cushman, Keith. "'A Bastard Begot': The Origin of D.H. Lawrence's 'The Christening,'" *Modern Philology*, LXX (1972) 146-148.

—. "D.H. Lawrence and Nancy Henry: Two Unpublished Letters and a Lost Relationship," *D.H. Lawrence Review*, VI (1973), 21-32.

—. "D.H. Lawrence at Work: The Making of 'Odour of Chrysanthemums,'" *Journal of Modern Literature*, II (1972), 367-392.

-. " D.H. Lawrence at Work: The Making of *The Prussian Officer and Other Stories,"* Dissertation, Princeton University, 1969.

—. "D.H. Lawrence at Work: 'The Shadow in the Rose Garden," *D.H. Lawrence Review*, VIII (1975), 31-46.

—. "Lawrence's Use of Hardy in 'The Shades of Spring,'" *Studies in Short Fiction*, IX (1972), 402-404.

—. "The Making of D.H. Lawrence's 'The White Stocking,'" *Studies in Short Fiction*, X (1973), 51-65.

—. "The Making of 'The Prussian Officer': A Correction," D.H. *Lawrence Review*, IV (1971), 263-273.

—. *"The Prussian Officer* and *The Rainbow,"* D.H. *Lawrence Review*, VIII (1975), 175-197.

—. "Putting Lawrence in His Place: Recent Studies in Modern Literature and Culture," *D.H. Lawrence Review*, V (1972), 158-169.

—. "Some Varieties of D.H. Lawrence Criticism," *Modern Philology*, LXIX (1971), 152-158. Review of books by Cavitch, Hochman, and Joost and Sullivan.

Dahlberg, Edward and Herbert Read. "A Literary Correspondence," *Sewanee Review*, LXVII (1959), 177-203, 422-445.

Daiches, David. "Georgian Poetry," In *Poetry and the Modern World* (Chicago: University of Chicago Press, 1960), 38-60.

Daleski, H. N. "The Duality of Lawrence," *Modern Fiction Studies*, V (1959), 3-18.

—. "The First and Second Generation," In *Twentieth Century Interpretations* of *The Rainbow*, ed. Mark Kinkaid-Weekes, 33-57.

Dalton, Jack P. "A Note on D.H. Lawrence," *Papers of the Bibliographic Society of America*, LXI (1967), 269.

Dalton, Robert O. *"Snake:* A Moment of Consciousness," *Brigham Young University Studies*, IV (1962), 243-253.

Danby, John F. "D.H. Lawrence," *Cambridge Journal*, IV (1951), 273-289.

Daniel, John. "D.H. Lawrence: His Reputation Today," *London Review*, VI (1969-1970), 25-33.

Daniel, John T. "The Influence of the English Class Structure on the Work of D.H. Lawrence,," Dissertation, University of Minnesota, 1973.

Dataller, Roger. "Eastwood in Taos," *Adelphi*, XXVIII (1952), 673-681.

—. "Elements of D.H. Lawrence's Prose Style," *Essays in Criticisim*, III (1953), 413-424.

—. "Mr. Lawrence and Mrs. Woolf," *Essays in Criticism*, VIII (1958), 48-59.

Davidson, Eugene. "The Symbol and the Poets," *Yale Review*, XXIII (1933), 178-182. Includes a review of *Last Poems*.

Davie, Donald. "On Sincerity: From Wordsworth to Ginsburg," *Encounter*, XXXI (1968), 61-66.

—. "A Doggy Demos: Hardy and Lawrence," In *British Poetry* (New York: Oxford University Press, 1972), 130-151.

Davis, Herbert. "The Poetic Genius of D.H. Lawrence," *University of Toronto Quarterly*, III (1934), 439-453.

—. *"Women in Love:* A Corrected Typescript," *University of Toronto Quarterly*, XXVII (1957), 34-53.

Davis, Patricia C. "Chicken Queen's Delight: D.H. Lawrence's 'The Fox,'" *Modern Fiction Studies*, XIX (1973-1974), 565-571.

Dawson, Eugene W. "D.H. Lawrence and Trigant Burrow: Pollyanalytics and Phylobioloby," *Dissertation Abstracts*, XXIV (1963), 2906-2907 (University of Washington).

—. "Lawrence's Pollyanalytic Esthetic for the Novel," *Paunch*, No. 26 (1966), 60-68.

—. "Love Among the Mannikins: *The Captains Doll*," *D.H. Lawrence Review*, I (1968), 137-148.

Deakin, William. "D.H. Lawrence's Attack on Proust and Joyce," *Essays in Criticsim*, VII (1957), 383-403.

Dehring, Erna. "Das Tier bei D.H. Lawrence," Dissertation, University of Gottingen, 1961.

Dekker, George. "Lilies that Fester," *New Left Review*, No. 28 (November 1964), 75-84. "The Woman Who Rode Away," *The Last of the Mohicans*, and the WASPS.

Delany, Paul. "D.H. Lawrence: The Man and His Work," *New York Times Book Review*, December 10, 1972, 4. Review of Delavenay's *The Man and His Work*.

—. "Lawrence and E.M Forster: Two Rainbows," *D.H. Lawrence Review*, VIII (1975), 54-62.

—, ed. "D.H. Lawrence: Twelve Letters," *D.H. Lawrence Review,* II (1969), 195-209.

Delavenay, Emile. "D.H. Lawrence and Sacher-Masock," *D.H. Lawrence Review,* VI (1973), 119-148.

—. "D.H. Lawrence entre six femmes et entre deux cultures,'. *Etudes Anglaises,* XXII (1969), 152-158.

—. "D.H. Lawrence's Letters to Catherine Carswell," *Yale University Library Gazette,* XLIX (1975), 253-260.

—. "Making Another Lawrence: Frieda and the Lawrence Legend," *D.H. Lawrence Review,* VIII (1975), 80-98. Review-article of Harry Moore's *The Priest of Love,* Robert Lucas's *Frieda Lawrence,* and Martin Green's *The von Richthofen Sisters.*

—. "Le Phenix et ses cendres," *Etudes Anglaises,* XXI (1968), 373-380.

— and W.J. Keith. "Mr. Rolf Gardiner, 'The English Nazi': An Exchange," *D.H. Lawrence Review,* VII (1974), 291-294.

De Michelis, Eurialo. "Lawrence in versi," *Letterature moderne,* XI (1961), 232-244.

DeNitto, Dennis. "Modern Literary Primitivism in the Writings of D.H. Lawrence and Other British Novelists," *Dissertation Abstracts,* XXVII (1966), 3867A (Columbia University).

Denny, N. "The Ladybird," *Theoria* (South Africa), No. 11 (1958), 17-28.

Derrick, John B. "Wildershins: Reversed Parental Identification and Narrative Point of View in the Work of D.H. Lawrence," Dissertation, University of California, Berkeley, 1973.

Diaz de Leon, Martha. "El Mexico Visits por D.H. Lawrence," *Cuadernos Americanos,* XXIV (1965), 262-283.

DiMaggio, Richard. "A Note on *Sons and Lovers* and Emerson's 'Experience,'" *D.H. Lawrence Review,* VI (1973), 214-216.

Ditsky, John M. "Darker, Darker than Fire: Thematic Parallels in Lawrence and Faulkner," *Southern Humanities Review,* VIII (1974), 497-505.

Dobrowolny, Welleda. "D.H. Lawrence and Italy," Dissertation, University of Trieste, 1974.

Doheny, John. "Lady Chatterley and Her Lover," *West Coast Review,* VIII (1974), 51-56. Review article of *John Thomas and Lady Jane.*

—. "The Novel as the Book: Illustration of Argument or Insight into Experience," Dissertation, University of Washington, 1972.

—. "The Novel as the Book: D.H. Lawrence and a Revised Version of Polymorphous Perversity," *Paunch,* No. 26 (April 1966), 40-59. On *Sons and Lovers.*

Donald, D.R. "The First and Final Versions of *Lady Chatterley's Lover,*" *Theoria* (South Africa), No. 22 (1964), 85-97.

Donnelly, J.B. "Cultural Consolations During the Great War," *Topic* XII (1972), 22-34. Lawrence included.

Donnerstag, Jurgen. "Die Stilentwicklung von D.H. Lawrence," Dissertation, University of Cologne, 1969.

Donoghue, Denis. "Action is Eloquence," *Lugano Review* (Japan), I (1965), 147-154. On "Odour of Chrysanthemums."

—. "Melville," *Lugano Review,* I (1965), 67-82. Compares Lawrence, Hardy, Melville.

—. "Prometheus in Straits," *Times Literary Supplement,* November 10, 1972, 1371-1373. Lawrence as Prometheus and his quarrel with Eliot.

—. "'Till the Fight is Finished': D.H. Lawrence in His Letters," In *D.H. Lawrence,* ed. Stephen Spender, 197-209.

Dorner, Marjorie L. "The *Blutbruderschaft* Theme in the Fiction of D.H. Lawrence," Dissertation, Purdue University, 1972.

Douglas, Norman. "D.H. Lawrence and Maurice Magnus: A Plea for Better Manners," In *Experiments* (London: Chapman and Hall, 1925).

Drain, R.L. "Formative Influences on the Work of D.H. Lawrence," *Index to Theses,* XII (1962), 11 (Cambridge University).

Draper, Ronald P. "Authority and the Individual: A Study of D.H. Lawrence's *Kangaroo, Critical Quarterly,* I (1959) 208-215.

—. "The Defeat of Feminism: D.H. Lawrence's *The Fox* and 'The Woman Who Rode Away,'" *Studies in Short Fiction,* III (1966), 186-198.

—. "Form and Tone in the Poetry of D.H. Lawrence," *English Studies,* XLIX (1968), 498-508.

—. "D.H. Lawrence," *Time and Tide* (January 30,1963), 23-24.

—. "Lawrence on Mother-Love," *Essays in Criticism,* VIII (1958), 285-289.

—. "Satire as a Form of Sympathy: D.H. Lawrence as a Satirist," In *Renaissance and Modern Essays,* ed. G.R. Hibbard (London: Routledge and Kegan Paul, 1966), 189-197.

—. "The Sense of Reality in the Work of D.H. Lawrence," *Revue des Langues Vivantes,* XXXIII (1967), 461-470.

Duncan, Iris J. "The Theme of the Artist's Isolation in Works by Three Modern British Novelists," *Dissertation Abstracts,* XXVI (1965), 3332 (University of Oklahoma). On Joyce, Lawrence, and Orwell.

Durham, John. "D.H. Lawrence: Outline for a Psychology of Being," Dissertation, Occidental College, 1967.

Durrell, Lawrence. "Preface," *Lady Chatterley's Lover* (New York: Bantam Books, 1968), vii-xi.

Eastman, Donald Roger, III. "The Concept of Character in the Major Novels of D.H. Lawrence," Dissertation, University of Florida, 1971.

Efron, Arthur. "Lady Chatterley's Lecher?," *Paunch,* No. 26 (April, 1966). Attacks Eliseo Vivas's view of the novel's sexuality in *The Failure and the triumph of Art.*

Egashira, Teruo. "Ikoisuru Onnatachi no Shudai" ("The Theme of *Women in Love"*), *Humane Studies* (Kanagawa University) No. 32 (February, 1966), 33-63.

Ehrstine, John W. "The Dialectic in D.H. Lawrence," *Research Studies* (Washington State University), XXXIII (1965), 11-26.

Eichrodt, John M. "Doctrine and Dogma in *Sons and Lovers,*" *Connecticut Review,* IV (1970), 18-32.

—. "D.H. Lawrence and the Protestant Crisis," *Dissertation Abstracts,* XXV (1964), 4144 (Columbia).

Eisenstein, Samuel A. "The Quester Hero: A Study of Creative Evolution in the Fiction of D.H. Lawrence," *Dissertation Abstracts,* XXVI (1965), 3950 (University of California, Los Angeles).

—. "' The Woman Who Rode Away,'" *Kyushu American Literature* (Fukuoka, Japan), No. 9 (1965) 1-18.

Elder, John. "The Treatment of Nature in D.H. Lawrence, William Faulkner, and Thomas Mann: Three Essays," Dissertation, Yale University, 1973.

Eliot, T.S. "Introduction," *Revelation,* ed. John Baillie and Hugh Martin (London: Faber and Faber, 1937).

—. "The Victim and the Sacrificial Knife," *Criterion,* X (July, 1931), 768-774. Lawrence as victim and Murry's *Son of Woman.*

Elliott, John R., ed. "'The Man Who Was Through with the World': An Unfinished Story by D.H. Lawrence," *Essays in Criticism,* IX (1959), 213-221.

Ellmann, Richard. "Barbed Wire and Coming Through," In *The Achievement of D.H. Lawrence,* ed. Frederick J. Hoffman and Harry T. Moore, 253-267. A slight but pointed essay on Lawrence's poetry.

Elsbree, Langdon. "The Breaking Chain: A Study of the Dance in the Novels of Jane Austen, George Eliot, Thomas Hardy, and D.H. Lawrence," *Dissertation Abstracts,* XXIV (1963) 2476 (Claremont Graduate School).

—. "D.H. Lawrence, *Homo Ludens,* and the Dance," *D.H. Lawrence Review,* I (1968), 1-30.

—. "On the Teaching of D.H. Lawrence: A Forum," *D.H. Lawrence Review,* VIII (1975), 63-79. Joanne Trautman, Sanford Pinsker, William R. Lowry, James Cox, and Elsbree.

—. "The Purest and Most Perfect Form of Play: Some Novelists and the Dance," *Criticism,* XIV (1963), 361-372.

—. "The Writer as Professional," *D.H. Lawrence Review,* IV (1971), 197-209. Review article of Bell, *Bloomsbury;* Griffin, *John Middleton Murry;* Reese, ed., *Poets, Critics, Mystics;* Joost and Sullivan, *D.H. Lawrence and the Dial.*

Emmett, V.J., Jr. "Structural Irony in D.H. Lawrence's 'The Rocking-Horse Winner,'" *Connecticut Review*, V (1972), 5-10.

Empson, William "Lady Chatterley Again," *Essays in Criticism*, XIII (1963), 101-104.

Engel, Monroe. "The Continuity of Lawrence's Short Novels," *Hudson Review*, XI (1958), 210-219.

—. "Lawrence's Short Novels," *Hudson Review*, XI (1958), 201-209.

Engleberg, Edward. "Escape from the Circle of Experience: D.H. Lawrence's *The Rainbow* as a Modern Bildungsroman," *Publications of the Modern Language Association*, LXVIII (1963), 103-113. An account of the underlying continuity of the various Brangwan generations that also explains the ambivalent conclusion of *The Rainbow*, a bone of contention among Lawrence critics.

Engelborghs, Maurits. "De reputatie van D.H. Lawrence," *Dietsche Warande en Belfort*, CVII (1962), 726-736.

Englander, Ann. "D.H. Lawrence: Technique as Evasion," *Dissertation Abstracts*, XXVII (1966), 252A (Northwestern University).

—. "'The Prussian Officer': The Self-Divided," *Sewanee Review*, LXXI (1963), 605-619.

Enright, D.J. "A Haste for Wisdom: The Poetry of D.H. Lawrence," In *Conspirators and Poets* (London: Chatto & Windus, 1966).

Erlich, Richard D. "Catastrophism and Coition: Universal and Individual Development in *Women in Love*," *Texas Studies in Literature and Language*, IX (1967), 117-128.

Every, George. "D.H. Lawrence," In *The New Spirit*, ed. E.W. Martin (London: Dennis Dobson, 1946), 58-65.

Faas, Egbert. "Charles Olson and D.H. Lawrence: Aesthetics of the 'Primitive Abstract,'" *Boundary*, II (1973-1974), 113-126.

Fadiman, Regina. "The Poet as Choreographer: Lawrence's 'The Blind Man,'" *Journal of Narrative Technique*, II (1972), 60-67.

Fahey, William A. "Lawrence's San Gaudenzio Revisited," *D.H. Lawrence Review*, I (1968), 51-59. *Twilight in Italy*.

—. "Lawrence's *The White Peacock,*" *Explicator,* XVII (1958), item 17.

—. "The Travel Books of D.H. Lawrence: Records of a Spiritual Pilgrimage," *Dissertation Abstracts,* XXV (1964), 5927-5928 (New York University).

Fairbanks, N. David. "Strength Through Joy in the Novels of D.H. Lawrence," *Literature and Ideology,* VIII (1971), 67-78.

Farjeon, Eleanor. "Springtime with D.H. Lawrence," *London Magazine,* II (April 4, 1955.).

Farmer, David. "D.H. Lawrence's "The Turning Back": The Text and Its Genesis in Correspondence," *D.H. Lawrence Review,* V (1972), 121-131.

—. "Textual Alterations in *Not I But the Wind . . . .,*" *Notes and Queries,* XIX (1972), 336.

—. "An Unpublished Version of D.H. Lawrence's Introduction to *Pansies,*" *Review of English Studies,* XXI (1970), 181-184.

Fedder, Norman J. "The Influence of D.H. Lawrence on Tennessee Williams," *Dissertation Abstracts,* XXIV (1963), 742-743 (New York University).

Fergusson, Francis. "D.H. Lawrence's Sensibility," *Hound and Horn,* VI (1933), 447-463. See also *Critiques and Essays on Modern Literature,* ed. James W. Aldridge (New York: Ronald Press, 1952), 328-339. An aestheitc appreciation of the first order.

Ferrier, Carole. "The Earlier Poetry of D.H. Lawrence: A Variorum Text, to 1920," Dissertation, University of Auckland (New Zealand), 1971.

—. "D.H. Lawrence: An Ibsen Reference," *Notes and Queries,* XIX (1972), 335-336. In Lawrence's poem, "Nils Lykke."

— and Egon Tiedje. "D.H. Lawrence's Pre-1920's Poetry: The Textual Approach: An Exchange," *D.H. Lawrence Review,* V (1972), 149-157.

Fiderer, Gerald. "D.H. Lawrence's *The Man Who Died:* The Phallic Christ," *American Imago,* XXV (1968), 91-96.

Fiedler, Leslie A. "The Literati of the Four-Letter Word," *Playboy,* VIII (1965), 85,125-128.

Fifield, William. "Joyce's Brother, Lawrence's Wife, Wolfe's Mother, Twain's Daughter," *Texas Quarterly*, X (1967), 69-97.

Finney, Brian H. "Additional Bibliographical Information on Some D.H. Lawrence Stories," *Notes and Queries*, XIX (1972), 337.

—. "The Artistic Development of D.H. Lawrence as a Writer of Short Stories," Dissertation, London University, 1973.

—. "The Hitherto Unknown Publication of Some of D.H. Lawrence's Short Stories," *Notes and Queries*, XIX (1972), 55-56. Early and unrecorded publications of "The Fox," "The Blue Moccasins," "Smiles," "In Love," And "The Rocking-Horse Winner."

—. "D.H. Lawrence's Progress to Maturity: From Holograph Manuscript to Final Publication of 'The Prussian Officer and Other Stories,'" *Studies in Bibliography* (University of Virginia), XXVIII (1975), 321-332.

—. "A Newly Discovered Text of D.H. Lawrence's 'The Lovely Lady,'" *Yale University Library Gazette*, XLIX (1975), 245-252.

—. "Two Missing Pages from 'The Ladybird,'" *Review of English Studies*, XXIV (1973), 191-192.

— and Michael L. Ross. "Two Versions of 'Sun': An Exchange," *D.H. Lawrence Review*, VIII (1975), 371-374.

Fisher, William J. "Peace and Passivity: The Poetry of D.H. Lawrence," *South Atlantic Quarterly*, LV (1956), 337-348.

Fitz, L.T. "'The Rocking-Horse Winner' and *The Golden Bough*," *Studies in Short Fiction*, XI (1974), 199-200.

Fleissner, Robert F. "Reacting to *The Reactionaries*: Libertarian Views," *Journal of Human Relations*, XVII (1969), 138-145. A response to John Harrison's *The Reactionaries: Yeats, Lewis, Pound, Eliot, Lawrence: A Study of the Anti-Democratic Intelligentsia.*

Fletcher, John Gould. "A Modern Evangelist," *Poetry*, XII (1918), 269-274.

Fogel, Stanley. "'And All the Little Typtopies': Notes on Language Theory in the Contemporary Experimental Novel," *Modern Fiction Studies*, XX (1974), 328-336. References to Lawrence.

Fois, Franca. "D.H. Lawrence Traduttore Di Verga," Dissertation, Bologna University, 1973.

Ford, Ford Madox. "D.H. Lawrence," *American Mercury,* XXXVIII (1936), 167-179.

Ford, George H. "An Introductory Note to D.H. Lawrence's 'Prologue' to *Women in Love,*" *Texas Quarterly,* VI (1963), 92-97. The unpublished draft follows (98-111) and offers basic evidence respecting Lawrence's view of the Birkin-Gerald relationship.

—. "Jessie Chambers' Last Tape on D.H. Lawrence, *Mosaic,* VI (1973), 1-12.

—. "Shelley or Schiller?: A Note on D.H. Lawrence at Work," *Texas Studies in Literature and Language,* IV (1962), 154-156. On a passage in Women in Love.

—, ed. "The Wedding Chapter of D.H. Lawrence's *Women in Love,*" *Texas Studies in Literature and Language,* VI (1963), 134-147. Another illuminating unpublished draft.

Ford, George M. "The Rainbow and the Bible," *Twentieth Century Interpretations* of *The Rainbow,* ed. Mark Kinkaid-Weekes, 73-82.

—, Frank Kermode, Colin Clark, and Mark Spilka. "Critical Exchange," *Novel,* V (1971), 54-70.

Forster, E.M. "On Lawrence's Art and Ideas," *The Listener,* III (April 30, 1930), 753-754.

Foster, D.W. "Lawrence, Sex and Religion," *Theology,* LXIV (1961), 8-13.

Foster, Joseph. "First Winter," *South Dakota Review,* IV (1966), 29-34. Memoir of Lawrence in Taos, 1922-1923.

Foster, Richard. "Criticism as Rage: D.H. Lawrence," In *A D.H. Lawrence Miscellany,* ed. Harry T. Moore, 312-325. On *Studies in Classic American Literature.*

Fotheringham, Richard. "Expatriate Publishing: P.R. Stephensen and the Mandrake Press," *Meanjin,* XXXI (1972), 183-188. A short history of the Mandrake Press *(Paintings of D.H. Lawrence).*

Fox, Carol L. "The Artistic and Critical Significance of D.H. Lawrence's *Studies in Classic American Literature,* Dissertation, Case Western Reserve University, 1972.

Fraenkel, Michael. "The Otherness of D.H. Lawrence," In *Death is Not Enough* (London: Daniel, 1939), 73-108.

Fraiberg, Louis. "The Unattainable Self; D.H. Lawrence's Sons *and Lovers,*" In *Twelve Original Essays on Great American Novels,* ed. Charles Shapiro (Detroit: Wayne State University Press, 1960), 175-201. A Freudian viewpoint that illumines the work.

Fraiberg, Selma. "Two Modern Incest Heroes," *Partisan Review,* XXVIII (1940), 646-661.

Freeman, Mary. "D.H. Lawrence in Valhalla?," *New Mexico Quarterly,* X(1940), 211-224.

Friedland, Ronald L. "The Craft of D.H. Lawrence's Short Stories: A Study of Five Early Tales," *Dissertation Abstracts,* XXVIII (1967), 1075A (Columbia).

Friedman, Alan. "The Other Lawrence," *Partisan Review,* XXXVII (1970), 239-253.. Lawrence's artistic devices in relation to his true subject, the unconscious self.

—. "The Turn of the Novel: Changes in the Pattern of English Fiction since 1890 in Hardy, Conrad, Forster, and Lawrence," *Dissertation Abstracts,* XXV (1964), 6622 University of California, Berkeley).

Friedman, Norman. "Point of View in Fiction: The Development of a Critical Concept," *Publications of the Modern Language Association,* LXX (1955), 1160-1184. Includes a brief discussion of *Sons and Lovers.*

Fu, Shaw-Shien. "Death in Lawrence's Last Poems," *Tamkang Review,* I (1970), 79-91.

—. "Imagery as Related to Theme in D.H. Lawrence's Poetry," *Dissertation Abstracts,* XXVIII (1967), 1075A (University of Wisconsin).

Fujii, Kazumi. "Musuko Tachi to Koi Bito Tachi' o Toshite Mita D.H. Lawrence" ("D.H. Lawrence and *Sons and Lovers*"), *Seiji-Keizai Ronso* (Seikei University), V (1955), 116-132.

—. "1910-Mendai no D.H. Lawrence" ("D.H. Lawrence in the 1910's"), *Ippan Kenkyu Hokoku* (Seikei University), IV (1967), 59-74.

Fulmer, O. Bryan. "The Significance of the Death of the Fox in D.H. Lawrence's 'The Fox,'" *Studies in Short Fiction,* V (1968), 275-282.

Gajdusek, Robert E. "A Reading of 'A Poem of Friendship':
A Chapter in Lawrence's *The White Peacock*," *D.H.
Lawrence Review*, III (1970), 47-62.

—. "A Reading of *The White Peacock*," In *A.D.H. Lawrence
Miscellany*, ed. Harry T. Moore, 182-203. For some a
seminal essay and a close reading of the major character
relationships and symbolism.

Gallo, Rose. "Mythic Concepts in D.H. Lawrence," Dissertation,
Rutgers University, 1974.

Gamache, Laurence B. "Brangwen Men in *The Rainbow:* A
Study of the Function of Two Male Characters," Dissertation, University of Ottowa, 1969.

Garcia, Reloy. "Adam in Nottingham: Literary Archetypes in
the Novels of D.H. Lawrence," *Dissertation Abstracts
International*, XXX (1969), 720A (Kent State University).

—. "The Quest for Paradise in the Novels of D.H. Lawrence,"
D.H. Lawrence Review, III (1970), 93-114.

—. "Steinbeck and D.H. Lawrence: Fictive Voices and the Ethical Imperative," *Steinbeck Monograph Series* No. 2, 1972,
1-35.

Garlington, Jack. "Lawrence—With Misgivings," *South Atlantic
Quarterly*, LIX (1960), 404-408.

Garnett, David. "Frieda and Lawrence," In *D.H. Lawrence:
Novelist, Poet, Prophet*, ed. Stephen Spender, 37-41.

Garnett, Edward. "D.H. Lawrence and the Moralists," In *Friday
Nights* (London: Jonathan Cape, 1929), 117-128. See also
Dial, LXI (1916), 377-381. In defense of Lawrence after
the suppression of *The Rainbow*.

Garrett, Peter. "Scene and Symbol: Changing Mode in the
English Novel from George Eliot to Joyce," *Dissertation
Abstracts*, XXVII (1967), 4251A (Yale University).

Gatti, Hilary. "D.H. Lawrence and the Idea of Education," *English Miscellany*, XXI (1970), 209-231. Lawrence's own
teaching values, Ursula and Birkin as teachers, and Lawrence's essay, "Education of the People."

Geracimos, Ann. "In D.H. Lawrence Country They Still Hold the
Grudge," *New York Times*, June 6, 1971, section 10,
35, 48-49. Visit to Nottingham and the neighbors.

Gerard, David E. "Glossary of Eastwood Dialect Words Used by
D.H. Lawrence in His Poems, Plays, and Fiction," *D.H.
Lawrence Review*, I (1968), 215-237.

Gerber, Philip L. and Robert J. Gemmett, ed. "The Dream of Logic: A Conversation with Ihab Hassan," *University of Windsor Review*, V (1969), 27-37. Urges a return to the impressionistic criticism of Lawrence.

Gerber, Stephen. "Character, Language, and Experience in 'Water Party,'" *Paunch*, Nos. 36-37 (April, 1973), 3-29. On *Women in Love*.

Ghiselin, Brewster. "D.H. Lawrence and a New World," *Western Review*, XI (1947), 150-159.

—. "D.H. Lawrence and the Peacocks of Atrani," *Michigan Quarterly Review*, XIV (1975), 119-134. Peacocks and Lawrence's phoenix.

—. "D.H. Lawrence in Bandol," *London Magazine*, V (1958), 13-22.

—. "D.H. Lawrence in Bandol: A Memoir," *Western Humanities Review*, XII (1958), 293-305.

Gidley, Mick. "D.H. Lawrence's *St. Mawr*," *Ariel*, V (January, 1974), 25-41.

Gifford, Henry. "Anna, Lawrence, and 'The Law,'" *Critical Quarterly*, I (1959), 203-206. Tolstoy, Lawrence, and morality.

Gilbert, Sandra M. "Acts of Attention: The Major Poems of D.H. Lawrence," *Dissertation Abstracts International*, XXX (1969), 721A-722A (Columbia).

Gill, Stephen. "The Composite World: Two Versions of *Lady Chatterley's Lover*," *Essays in Criticism*, XXI (1971), 347-364.

Gilles, Daniel. "D.H. Lawrence ou la poesie immediate," *Revue Generale Belge*, No. 1 (1963), 43-59.

Gillis, James M. "Novelists and Sexual Perversion," In *This Our Day: Approvals and Disapprovals* (New York: Paulist Press, 1933), 32-37.

Gindin, James. "Society and Compassion in the Novels of D.H. Lawrence," *Centennial Review*, XII (1968), 355-374. Reprinted in Gindin's *Harvest of a Quiet Eye* (Bloomington: Indiana University Press, 1971), 205-221.

Gindre, J.M. "Points de vue sur D.H. Lawrence," *Etudes Anglaises*, XI (1958), 229-239.

Girard, Denis. "John Middleton Murry, D.H. Lawrence, and Albert Schweitzer," *Etudes Anglaises,* XII (1959), 212-221.

Glicksberg, Charles I. "D.H. Lawrence and Science," *Scientific Monthly,* LXXIII (August, 1951), 99-104.

—. "D.H. Lawrence: The Prophet of Surrealism" *Nineteenth Century,* CXLII (April, 1948), 229-237.

—. "The Poetry of D.H. Lawrence," *New Mexico Quarterly,* XVIII (1948), 289-303.

Goldberg, Michael K. "Dickens and Lawrence: More on Rocking Horses," *Modern Fiction Studies,* XVII (1972), 574-575.

—. "Lawrence's 'The Rocking-Horse Winner': A Dickensian Fable," *Modern Fiction Studies,* XV (1969), 525-536.

Goldberg, S.L. *"The Rainbow:* Fiddle-Bow and Sand," *Essays in Criticism,* XI (1961), 418-434.

Goldknopf, David. "Realism in the Novel," *Yale Review,* LX (1970), 69-84.

Goldring, Douglas. From "The Later Work of D.H. Lawrence," In *Reputations* (London: Chapman and Hall, 1920), 67-78. Lawrence's lonely genius.

Goodheart, Eugene. "Freud and Lawrence," *Psychoanalysis and the Psychoanalytic Review,* XLVII (1960), 56-64.

—. "Lawrence and Christ," *Partisan Review,* XXI (1964), 42-59.

—. "Lawrence and His Critics," *Chicago Review,* XVI (1963), 127-137.

—. "The Utopian Vision of D.H. Lawrence," *Dissertation Abstracts,* XXII (1961), 4015-4016 (Columbia).

Goodman, Richard. "Footnote to Lawrence," In *Contemporary Essays, 1933,* ed. Sylva Norman (London: Matthews and Marrot, 1933), 51-63.

Gordon, David J. "D.H. Lawrence's Quarrel with Tragedy," *Perspective,* XIII (1964), 135-150.

—. "Two Anti-Puritans: Bernard Shaw and D.H. Lawrence," *Yale Review,* LVI (1966), 76-90.

Gose, Eliott B., Jr. "An Expense of Spirit," *New Mexico Quarterly,* XXV (1956), 358-363. On *Sons and Lovers.*

76

Gottwald, Johannes. "Die Erzahlformen der Romane von Aldous Huxley und David Herbert Lawrence," Dissertation, University of Munich, 1964.

Gouirand, Jacqueline. "Sur Trois Manuscrits de D.H. Lawrence: *The White Peacock, The Trespasser, The Rainbow.* Contribution a l'etude de la Creation litterairs," Dissertation, University of Nice, 1974.

Grandsen, K.W. "The S.S. Koteliansky Bequest," *British Museum Quarterly,* XX (1956), 83-84.

—. "Rananim: D.H. Lawrence's Letters to S.S. Koteliansky," *Twentieth Century,* CLIX (1956), 22-32.

Grant, Douglas. "England's Phoenix," *University of Toronto Quarterly,* XXVII (1958), 216-225. Review including Nehls, *Composite Biography,* and Beal, ed., *Selected Literary Criticism.*

—. "Hands Up, America!," *Review of English Literature* (Leeds), IV (1963), 11-17.

Green, Eleanor H. "Blueprints for Utopia: The Political Ideas of Nietzsche and D.H. Lawrence," *Renaissance and Modern Studies,* XVIII (1974), 141-161.

—. "Schopenhauer and D.H. Lawrence on Sex and Love," *D.H. Lawrence Review,* VIII (1975), 329-345.

—. "The Works of D.H. Lawrence in Relation to the Ideas of Schopenhauer and Nietzsche," Dissertation, University of Nottingham, 1973.

Green, Martin. "British Decency," *Kenyon Review,* XXI (1959), 505-532.

—. "The *Composite Biography* as Composition Text," In *A D.H. Lawrence Miscellany,* ed. Harry T. Moore, 154-167. On Nehls's work.

—. "Cottage Realism," *Month,* IV (September, 1971), 85-88. Rural values.

—. "Old Flames at the Ranch," *London Magazine,* X (March, 1971), 69-83. The D.H. Lawrence Festival, Taos.

—. "The Reputation of D.H. Lawrence in America," *Dissertation Abstracts,* XIX (1958), 138-139 (University of Michigan).

Greene, Thomas. "Lawrence and the Quixotic Hero," *Sewanee Review,* LIX (1951), 559-573.

Gregor, Ian. "'The Fox': A Caveat," *Essays in Criticism,* IX (1959), 10-21.

—. "Towards a Christian Literary Criticism," *Month,* XXXIII (1965), 239-249. On *Women in Love* and Iris Murdoch's *A Severed Head.*

— and Brian Nicholas. "The Novel as Prophecy: *Lady Chatterley's Lover,"* In *The Moral and the Story* (London: Faber and Faber, 1962), 217-248.

Gregory, Horace. "On D.H. Lawrence and His Posthumous Reputation," In *The Shield of Achilles: Essays on Belief in Poetry* (New York: Harcourt, Brace and Company, 1944), 156-164.

Greiff, Louis K. "The Rhythm of Perfection: A Study and Reappraisal of D.H. Lawrence's 'Leadership Novels'— *Aaron's Rod, Kangaroo, and The Plumed Serpent,"* Dissertation, Syracuse University, 1973.

Grey, Anthony. "Up the Rough Deserted Pasture . . . the Country of My Heart," *In Britain* (April, 1974), 15-19. A travel sketch of Eastwood and local attitudes toward Lawrence.

Griffin, Ernest G. "The Circular and the Linear: The Middleton Murry—D.H. Lawrence Affair," *D.H. Lawrence Review,* II (1969), 76-92.

Grigson, Geoffrey. "The Poet in D.H. Lawrence," *London Magazine,* V (May, 1958), 66-69.

Gross, Anna. "Die Farbadjektiva in den Romanen und Kurgeschichten von David Herbert Lawrence," Dissertation, Graz University, 1943.

Gullason, Thomas A. "Revelation and Evolution: A Neglected Dimension of the Short Story," *Studies in Short Fiction,* X (1973), 347-356. "The Horse-Dealer's Daughter."

Gurko, Jane. "The Flesh Made Word: A Study of Narrative and Stylistic Techniques in Five Novels by D.H. Lawrence," Dissertation, University of California, Berkeley, 1971.

Gurko, Leo. *"Kangaroo:* D.H. Lawrence in Transit," *Modern Fiction Studies,* X (1965), 349-358.

—. "D.H. Lawrence's Greatest Collection of Short Stories- What Holds It Together," *Modern Fiction Studies,* XVIII (1972), 173-182. "The Ladybird," "The Fox," And "The Captain's Doll."

—. "'The Lost Girl': D.H. Lawrence as a 'Dickens of the Midlands,'" *Publications of the Modern Language Association,* LXXVIII (1963), 601-605.

—. *"The Trespasser:* D.H. Lawrence's Neglected Novel," *College English,* XXIV (1962), 29-35.

Gurling, Freda E. "D.H. Lawrence's Apology for the Artist," *London Mercury,* XXXIII (April, 1936), 596-603.

Gurtoff, Stanley A. "The Impact of D.H. Lawrence on His Contemporaries," *Dissertation Abstracts,* XXVI (1965), 5412-5413 (University of Minnesota).

Gutierrez, Donald. "Circles and Arcs: The Rhythm of Circularity and Centrifugality in D.H. Lawrence's *Last Poems," D.H. Lawrence Review,* IV (1971), 291-300.

—. "Lawrence's *The Virgin and the Gypsy* as Ironic Comedy," *English Quarterly* (Waterloo, Canada), V (197301974).

—. "The Pressure of Love: Kinesthetic Action in an Early Lawrence Poem," *Contemporary Poetry* (Fairleigh Dickinson), I (1973), 6-20. Lawrence's "Lightning."

Guttmann, Allen. "D.H. Lawrence: The Politics of Irrationality," *Wisconsin Studies in Contemporary Literature,* V (1964), 151-163.

Haegert, Jonathan. "D.H. Lawrence and the Idea of the Erotic," Dissertation, University of Chicago, 1972.

Hafley, James. "The Lost Girl: Lawrence Really Real," *Arizona Quarterly,* X (1954), 312-322.

Hall, Roland. "D.H. Lawrence and A.N Whitehead," *Notes and Queries,* IX (1962), 188.

Hall, Stuart. *"Lady Chatterley's Lover:* The Novel and Its Relationship to Lawrence's Work" *New Left Review,* No. 6 (December, 1960), 32-35.

Hall, William F. "The Image of the Wolf in Chapter XXX of D.H. Lawrence's *Women in Love," D.H. Lawrence Review,* II (1969), 272-274.

Halperin, Irving. "Unity in *St. Mawr," South Dakota Review,* IV (1966), 58-60.

Hamalian, Leo. "The Lady Chatterley Spectacle," *Columbia University Forum,* III (1960), 8-13. On the trial.

Hardy, Barbara. "Women in D.H. Lawrence's Works," In *D.H. Lawrence: Novelist, Poet, Prophet,* ed. Stephen Spender, 90-121.

Harkin, M. "'For the Public Good': A Summary of the *Lady Chatterley's Lover* Controversy," *Manchester Review,* IX (1960), 91-93.

Harper, Howard M., Jr. "Fantasia and the Psychodynamics of *Women in Love,*" In *The Classic British Novel,* ed. Harper and Charles Edge (Athens: University of Georgia Press, 1972), 202-219.

Harpham, Geoffrey. "Degeneration and the Grotesque in Wells, London, and Lawrence," Dissertation, University of Caolifornia, Los Angeles, 1973.

Harris, Janice H. "D.H. Lawrence and Kate Millett," *Massachusetts Review,* XV (1974), 522-529.

—. "Mode and Development in D.H. Lawrence's Tales," Dissertation, Brown University, 1973.

Harris, Wilson. "A Comment on *A Passage to India,*" *Literary Half-Yearly,* X (July 1959), 35-39. Conrad, Lawrence, and *A Passage to India.*

Hartoge, Renatus M. "Intercourse with Lady Chatterley," In *Four Letter Word Games: The Psychology of Obscenity* (New York: M. Evans and Company, 1967), 11-24.

Harvey, R.W. "On Lawrence's 'Bavarian Gentians,'" *Wascana Review,* I (1966), 74-86.

Hasegawa, Toshimitsu. "D.H. Lawrence no *Women in Love* (On *Women in Love), Ritsumeikan Bungaku* (Ritsumeikan University), No. 208 (October, 1962), 23-44.

Hashimoto, Hiroshi. *"Lady Chatterley's Lover Josetus"* ("Introduction *to Lady Chatterley's Lover"), Scientific Researches* (Waseda University), VIII (1959), 59-70.

—. "D.H. Lawrence ni Okeru Ai" ("D.H. Lawrence's Love Ethic"), *Scientific Researches,* X (1961), 43-52.

Hassall, Christopher. "Black Flowers: A New Light on the Poetics of D.H. Lawrence," In *A D.H. Lawrence Miscellany,* ed. Harry T. Moore, 370-377.

—. "D.H. Lawrence and the Etruscans," *Essays by Divers Hands,* XXXI (1962), 61-78.

Hawkins, Desmond. "Introduction," *Stories, Essays and Poems* (London: J.M Dent, 1939).

Haya, Ken-ichi. "D.H. Lawrence ni Okeru Shokai-Ishiki" ("The Social Awareness of D.H. Lawrence"), *Thought Currents in English Literature* (Aoyama Gakuin University), XXIX (January, 1959), 217-249.

Heilbut, Anthony O. "The Prose of D.H. Lawrence," Dissertation, Harvard University, 1966.

Heilman, Robert B. "Nomad, Monads, and the Mystique of the Soma," *Sewanee Review*, LXVIII (1960), 635-659.
Review, criticism, and discussion of Vivas's *D.H. Lawrence: The Failure and the triumph of Art.*

Heldt, Lucia H. "Lawrence on Love: The Courtship and Marriage of Tom Brangwen and Lydia Lensky," *D.H. Lawrence Review*, VIII (1975), 358-370.

Hendrick, George. "Jesus and the Osiris-Isis Myth: Lawrence's *The Man Who Died* and Williams' *The Night of the Iguana,'* *Anglia* (Tubingen), Band 84, Heft 3-4 (1966), 398-406.

—. "'10' and the Phoenix," *D.H. Lawrence Review*, II (1969), 162-167.

Henig, Suzanne. "D.H. Lawrence and Virginia Woolf," *D.H. Lawrence Review*, II (1969), 665-671.

Henry, G.B. "Carrying On: *Lady Chatterley's Lover,"* *Critical Review* (Melbourne), X (1967), 46-62.

Hepburn, James G. "Disarming and Uncanny Visions: Freud's 'The Uncanny' with Regard to Form and Content in Stories by Sherwood Anderson and D.H. Lawrence," *Literature and Psychology*, IX (1959), 9-12.

—. "D.H. Lawrence's Plays: An Annotated Bibliography," *Book Collector*, XIV (1965), 78-81.

Heppenstall, Rayner. "Outsiders and Others," *Twentieth Century*, CLVIII (1955), 453-459.

Herrick, Jeffrey. "Visionary Sequences: D.H. Lawrence's Major Poetry," Dissertation, University of Chicago, 1974.

Hess, Elizabeth. "Die Naturbetrachtung im Prosawerk von D.H. Lawrence," Dissertation, Bern Switzerland, 1957. Published as *Swiss Studies in English,* vol. 44, Bern, 1957, 115

Heuzenroeder, John. "D.H. Lawrence's Australia," *Australian Literary Studies* (University of Tasmania), IV (1970), 319-333. On *Kangaroo, The Boy in the Bush*, and the Australian background.

Heywood, C. "D.H. Lawrence's *The Lost Girl* and Its Antecedents by George Moore and Arnold Bennett," *English Studies*, XLVII (1966), 131-134.

Hidalgo, Pilar. "Frank Kermode, Lawrence," *Filogia Moderna* (Madrid), (1974), 50-51.

Highet, Gilbert. "Lawrence in America," In *People, Places, and Books* (New York: Oxford Press 1953), 37-44,

Hill, Ordelle G. and Potter Woodbury. "Ursula Brangwen of *The Rainbow:* Christian Saint or Pagan Goddess," *D.H. Lawrence Review*, IV (1971), 274-279.

Hinz, Evelyn J. "The Beginning and the End: D.H. Lawrence's 'Psychoanalysis' and 'Fantasia,'" *Dalhousie Review*, LII (1972), 251-265.

—. "Juno and *The White Peacock:* Lawrence's English Epic," *D.H. Lawrence Review*, III (1970), 115-135.

—. "D.H. Lawrence and 'Something Called "Canada",' " *Dalhousie Review*, LIV (1974), 240-250.

—. "Lawrence at the MLA, 1974: A Critique," *D.H. Lawrence Review*, VIII (1975), 213-219.

—. "D.H. Lawrence's Clothes Metaphor," *D.H. Lawrence Review*, I (1968), 87-113.

—. "Lorenzo Mythistoricus: Studies in the Archetypal Imagination of D.H. Lawrence," Dissertation, University of Massachusetts, 1973.

—. "*Sons and Lovers:* The Archetypal Dimensions of Lawrence's Oedipal Tragedy," *D.H. Lawrence Review*, V (1972), 26-53.

—. "*The Trespasser:* Lawrence's Wagnerian Tragedy and Divine Comedy," *D.H. Lawrence Review*, IV (1971), 123-141.

Hirashima, Junko. "Guwa (D.H. Lawrence—'The Man Who Loved Islands' no Sekai)" ("On "The Man Who Loved Islands"), *Baika Joshidaigaku Bungaku Kiyo* (Baika Joshidaigaku),I (December, 1964), 49-72.

—. "Inochi no Nagara (D.H. Lawrence: Sun no Buntai)" (On D. H. Lawrence's "Sun'), *Baika Tankidaigaku Kenkyu Kiyo* (Baika Tankidaigaku), IX (December, 1960), 13-34.

—. "Ishikika no Sekai (D.H. Lawrence: The Fox no Buntai)" (On *The Fox*), *Baika Tankidaigaku Kenkyu Kiyo*, XII (1963), 44-58.

—. "Jiyu to Sokubaku (D.H. Lawrence: *The Thorn in the Flesh* no Sekai)" *Baika Tankidaigaku Kenkyu Kiyo*, XII (1963), 44-58.

—. "D.H. Lawrence: *The Man Who Died,"* *Baika Joshidaigaku Bungakuku Kiyo* (Baika Joshidaigaku), II (1965), 105-130.

—. "D.H. Lawrence: *The Rainbow* no Buntai," *Baika Joshidaigaku Bungakuku Kiyo*, III (1966), 103-138.

Hirata, Atsushi. "Brangwen Saga ni Tsuite" (On the Brangwen Saga of *The Rainbow), Journal of Literature and Linguistics of Toyama University*, VIII (1958), 27-41.

—. "*Sons and Lovers* ni Tsuite," *Journal of Literature and Linguistics*, VIII(1957), 57-71.

Hoare, Dorothy M. "The Novels of D.H. Lawrence," In *Some Studies in the Modern Novel* (London: Chatto & Windus, 1938), 97-112.

Hochman, Baruch. "'Another Ego': The Changing View of Self and Society in the Work of D.H. Lawrence," *Dissertation Abstracts*, XXV (1964), 7269 (Columbia).

Hoffman, Frederick J. "Freudianism: A Study of Influence and Reactions, Especially as Revealed in the Fiction of James Joyce, D.H. Lawrence, Sherwood Anderson, and Waldo Frank. *Dissertation Abstracts*, XLI (1943), 81-88 (Ohio State University).

—. "From Surrealism to the Apocalypse: A Development in Twentieth Century Irrationalism," *Journal of English Literary History*, XV (1948), 147-165.

—. "Lawrence's Quarrel with Freud," In *Freudianism and the Literary Mind* (Baton Rouge: Louisiana State University Press, 1945), 149-185. As previously stated, the best essay I have read on the relation of Lawrence to Freud.

Hogan, Robert. 'The Amorous Whale: A Study in the Symbolism of D.H. Lawrence," *Modern Fiction Studies*, V (1959), 39-46.

—. "D.H. Lawrence and His Critics," *Essays in Criticism,* IX (1959), 381-387.

—. "Lawrence's 'Song of a Man Who Came Through,'" *Explicator,* XVII (1959), item 51.

Hoggart, Richard. "A Question of Tone: Some Problems in Autobiographical Writing," *Essays by Divers Hands,* XXXIII (1965), 18-38.

Holtgen, K.J. "D.H. Lawrence's Poem 'Masses and Classes,'" *Notes and Queries,* IX (1962), 153-168.

Honig, Edwin. "The Ideal in Symbolic Fictions," *New Mexico Quarterly,* XXIII (1953), 153-168.

Horney, Larry J. "The Emerging Woman of the Twentieth-Century: A Study of the Women in D.H. Lawrence's NovelsThe *Rainbow* and *Women in Love,*" Dissertation, Ball State University, 1972.

Howarth, Herbert. "Impersonal Aphrodite," *Mosaic,* I (1968), 74-86. On Lawrence, Yeats, Conrad, Forster, Durrell, George Moore, etc.

—. "D.H. Lawrence's from Island to Glacier," *University of Toronto Quarterly,* XXXVII (1968), 215-229. On *The Trespasser.*

Howe, Irving. "Sherwood Anderson and D.H. Lawrence," *Furioso,* V (1950), 21-33.

Howe, Marguerite B. "D.H. Lawrence as Ego Psychologist: Self and Being in the Novels," Dissertation, Columbia University, 1973.

Hoyles, John. "D.H. Lawrence and the Counter-Revolution," *D.H. Lawrence Review,* VI (1973), 173-200.

Hoyt, C.A. "D.H. Lawrence: The Courage of Human Contact," *The English Record,* XIV (1964), 8-15.

Hoyt, William R., III' "Re: 'D.H. Lawrence's Appraisal of Jesus,' (A Response to William E. Phipps)," *The Christian Century,* LXXXVIII (July 14, 1971), 861-862.

Hsia, Adrian. "Die Kurzgeschichten von D.H. Lawrence," Dissertation, Berlin, 1966. Published as Adrian Hsia, "D.H. Lawrence: Die Charaktere seiner Kurzgeschichten in Handlung und Spannung." Abhandlungen Zur Kunst—, Musik—und Literaturwissenschaft, Vol. 56, Bonn, 1968, 132.

Hudspeth, Robert N. "Duality as Theme and Technique in D.H. Lawrence's 'The Border Line,'" *Studies in Short Fiction,* IV (1966), 51-56.

—. "Lawrence's 'Odour of Chrysanthemums': Isolation and Paradox," *Studies in Short Fiction,* VI (1969), 630-636.

Hugger, Ann-Grete. "The Dichotomy Between Private and Public Spheres: Sex Roles in D.H. Lawrence's Novels," *Language and Literature,* II (1973), 127-136.

Hulley, Kathleen. "Disintegration: A Symbol of Community. A Study of *The Rainbow, Women in Love, Light in August, Prisoner of Grace, Except the Lord, Not Honour More,*" Dissertation, University of California, Davis, 1973.

Humma, John B. "From Transcendental to Descendental: The Romantic Thought of Blake, Nietzsche, and Lawrence," *Dissertation Abstracts International,* XXX (1969), 4454A (Southern Illinois University).

—. "D.H. Lawrence as Friedrich Nietzsche," *Philological Quarterly,* LIII (1974), 110-120.

—. "Melville's *Billy Budd* and Lawrence's 'The Prussian Officer': Old Adams and New," *Essays in Literature* (Western Illinois University), I (1974), 83-88.

Huveröd, Susel H' "Eyvind Johnson i Lawrencsk belysning," *Ord och Bild,* LXIX (1960), 46-50.

Huxley, Aldous. "D.H. Lawrence," In *The Achievement of D.H. Lawrence,* ed. Frederick J. Hoffman and Harry T. Moore, 63-87.

—. "To the Puritans All Things Are Impure," In *Music at Night and Other Essays* (New York: Doubleday, Doran, (1931), 153-162.

Hyde, G.M. "D.H. Lawrence as a Translator," *Delos: A Journal on and of Translation,* IV (1970), 146-174.

Hyde, Virginia Mae. "The Artist-Priest and the Cosmic Land—scape: D.H. Lawrence's Debt to Medieval and Renaissance Graphic Arts," Dissertation, University of Wisconsin, 1971.

—. "Will Brangwen and Paradisal Vision in *The Rainbow* and *Women in Love,*" *D.H. Lawrence Review,* VIII (1975), 346-357.

Idema, James M. "The Hawk and the Plover: The Polarity of Life in the 'Jungle Aviary' of D.H. Lawrence's Mind in *Sons and Lovers* and *The Rainbow,*" *Forum* (Houston), III (1961),11-14.

Iida, Kosaku. "Bannen no D.H. Lawrence" ("D.H. Lawrence in sity), No. 8 (winter, 1956), 61-82.

—. "D.H. Lawrence ni Okeru Teikyoku no Kwannen" ("The Idea of Polarity in D.H. Lawrence"), *Study of Humanities*, No. 3 (June 1955), 31-43.

—. "D.H. Lawrence Sonzai to Ai" ("D.H. Lawrence: Existence and Love"), *Collected Treatises for the 35th Anniversary of Kanagawa University* (1963), 663-677.

—."D.H. Lawrence to Hyohaku" ("The Wandering of D.H. Lawrence"), *Sylvan* (Tohoku University), II (1956), 17-27.

IIjima, Yoshida. "Sojosaku Jidai no Lawrence" ("The Background of Sons *and Lovers*"), *Rikkyo Review* (Rikkyo University), No. 14 (June, 1952), 17-55.

Imanishi, Motoshige. "Lawrence to Butler no Seimei-Shugi" ("Vitalism in Lawrence and Butler"), *English Literature-Study and Appreciation* (Waseda University), No. 8 (December, 1953), 71-79.

Innis, Kenneth B. "D.H. Lawrence's Bestiary: A Study of His Use of Animal Trope and Symbol," *Dissertation Abstracts*, XXVI (1965), 3340 (University of Kansas).

Irie, Takanori. "D.H. Lawrence no Shisoteki Igi" ("D.H. Lawrence as a Thinker"), *Metropolitan* (Tokyo Metropolitan University), X (1965), 1-17.

—. "Lawrence to Rilke-Shi no Mondai o Megutte" ("Lawrence and Rilke on the Problem of Death"), *Metropolitan*, XI (1966), 12-23.

Irvine, Peter L. and Anne Kiley. "D.H. Lawrence: Letters to Goedon and Beatrice Campbell," *D.H. Lawrence Review*, VI (1973), 1-20.

— and Anne Kiley, ed. "D.H. Lawrence and Frieda Lawrence: Letters to Dorothy Brett," *D.H. Lawrence Review*, IX (1976), 1-116.

Irwin, W.R. "The Survival of Pan," *Publications of the Modern Language Association*, LXXVI (1961), 159-167. Lawrence's use of the Pan myth.

Isaacs, Neil D. "The Autoerotic Metaphor in Joyce, Sterne, Lawrence, Stevens, and Whitman," *Literature and Psychology*, XV (1965), 92-106.

Ishihara, Fumio. "Lawrence Bungaku no Jigen (I)" ("The Dimensions of Lawrencean Literature (I): Introduction"), *Bulletin: Faculty of Foreign Languages* (Kitakyushu University), No. 1 (March, 1958), 47-63.

—. "Lawrence Bungaku no Jigen (II)," *Bulletin: Faculty of Foreign Languages*, No. 3 (October, 1959), 31-49.

—. "Lawrence Bungaku no Jigen (IV)" ("An Approach to Lawrence's View of Life: Resistance and Human Alienation (IV)"), *Bulletin: Faculty of Foreign Languages*, No. 11 (November, 1965), 1-16.

—. "Lawrence Bungaku no Jigen (V)" ("Comparison with Poe: Closed Form and Open Form in Literature"), *Bulletin: Faculty of Foreign Languages*, No. 14 (September, 1967), 1-23.

Ishikawa, Masafumi. "D.H. Lawrence Keknyu Shojosaku 'Shirokujaku' ni Tsuite" *Kyushu Sangyo Daigaku Kyoyobu Kiyo* (Kyushu Sangyu University), III (1966), 69-82.

Ito, Hidekazu. "Death-Drift karano Dasshutsu (Lawrence no Shoki Shosetsu ni Tsuite)" ("An Escape from Death-Drift: D.H. Lawrence's Early Novels"), *Studies in Langugage and Literature* (Science University of Tokyo), No. 2 (March, 1968), 20-50.

—. "D.H. Lawrence to Koku" ("Solitude in D.H. Lawrence"), *Studies in Language and Literature,* No. 1 (December, 1960), 67-88.

Iwata, Katsuyi. "D.H. Lawrence no *Apocalypse* ni Tsuite" (On *Apocalypse), Studies in British and American Literature* (The University of Osaka Prefecture), No. 1 (July, 1954), 15-20.

Iwata, Noboru. *"The Fox* ni Tsuite" ("On *The Fox"), Literary Symposium* (Aichi University), No. 21 (February, 1961), 183-202.

—. "Hans to Dobutsu *(Sons and Lovers* no Baii).. ("Flowers and Animals in *Sons and Lovers"), Literary Symposium* (Aichi University), No. 29 (February, 1965), 99-126.

—. *"St. Mawr* no Hyoka" ("An Evaluation of *St. Mawr"), Literary Symposium,* No. 24 (February, 1963), 105-129.

—. *"St. Mawr* Sairon (II)," *Bulletin of the Faculty of Literature* (Aichi Prefectural University), No. 17 (December, 1966), 39-58.

Jacobson,Sibyl. "The Paradox of Fulfilment: A Discussion of *Women in Love," Journal of Narrative Technique,* III (1973), 53-65.

James, Clive. "D.H. Lawrence in Transit," *D.H. Lawrence, ed.* Stephen Spender, 159-169.

James, Stuart B.   "Western American Space and the Human Imagination," *Western Humanities Review,* XXIV (1970), 147-155.

Janik, Del Ivan. "D.H. Lawrence: The Poetry of Intuition," Dissertation, Northwestern University, 1971.

—. "D.H. Lawrence's 'Future Religion': The Unity of *Last Poems," Texas Studies in Literature and Language,* XVI (1974), 739-754.

—. "Toward 'Thingness': Cezanne's Painting and Lawrence's Poetry," *Twentieth Century Literature,* XIX (1973), 119-127.

—. "The Two Infinites: D.H. Lawrence's *Twilight in Italy, D.H. Lawrence Review,* VII (1974), 179-198.

Jarrett, James L. "D.H. Lawrence and Bertrand Russell," In *A D.H. Lawrence Miscellany,* ed. Harry T. Moore, 186-187.

Jarv, Harry. "D.H. Lawrence—'var tids Skapande Geni'" ("D.H. Lawrence: The Creative Genius of Our Time"), *Horisont* (Stockholm), VIII (1961), 16-19.

Jarvis, F.P. "A Textual Comparison of the First British and American Editions of D.H. Lawrence's *Kangaroo," Papers of the Bibliographic Society of America,* LIX (1965), 400-424.

Jauch, Cleveland E., Jr. "D.H. Lawrence: A Critical Reappraisal," *Doctoral Dissertations,* XXII (1955), 257 (Yale).

Jeffers, Robinson. "Foreword," *Fire and Other Poems* (San Francisco: Grabhorn Press, 1940).

Jeffries, C. "Metaphor in *Sons and Lovers," The Personalist,* XXIX (1948), 287-292.

Johnson, Dale S. "The Development of the Non-Formalistic Modern English Novel and Its Realtion to D.H. Lawrence's *Sons and Lovers*," *Dissertation Abstracts International,* XXX (1969), 726A (University of Michigan).

Johnsson, Melker. "Helgon och Livsdyrkare" ("Saint and Worshipper of Life"), In *En Klosterresa. Farder och Fragor* (Stockholm: Natur och Kultur, 1960), 100-115.

—. "Historien om D.H. Lawrence" ("The Story of D.H. Lawrence"), In *En Klosterresa. Farder och Fragor* (Stockholm: Natur och Kultur, 1960), 90-96.

—. "Introduktion till D.H. Lawrence," *Bonniers Litterara Magasin,* VII (1938), 442-449.

—. "D.H. Lawrence i Narbild" ("A Close-up of D.H. Lawrence"), *Tiden,* XLVII (1955), 418-424.

—. "D.H. Lawrence och Hans Stad" ("D.H. Lawrence and His Town"), *Vi* (Stockholm), XLIV (1957), 16-17.

—. "D.H. Lawrençe och Mexico," *Ord och Bild* (Stockholm), XLVIII (1939), 31-38.

—. "Livsdyrkaren och Doden" ("Death and the Worshipper of Life"), In *En Klosterresa. Farder och Fragor* (Stockholm: Natur och Kultur, 1960), 97-103.

—. "Sunpuntker pa D.H. Lawrence" ("Views on D.H. Lawrence"), *Tiden,* XLIV (1952), 418-425.

Johnston, Walter E. "The Shepherdess in the City," *Comparative Literature,* XXVI (1974), 124-141. References to Lawrence.

Jones, Keith. "Two Morning Starts," *Western Review,* XVII (1952), 15-25.

Jones, William M. "Growth of a Symbol: The Sun in Lawrence and Eudora Welty," *University of Kansas City Review,* XXXVI (1959), 68-73.

Junkins, Donald. "D.H. Lawrence's 'The Horse-Dealer's Daughter,'" *Studies in Short Fiction,* VI (1969), 210-212.

—. "'The Rocking-Horse Winner': A Modern Myth," *Studies in Short Fiction,* II (1964), 87-89.

Juta, Jan. "Portrait in Shadow: D.H. Lawrence," *Columbia Literary Columns,* XVIII (1969), 2-16.

Kai, Sadanobu. "Juzika no Genso Teki Ningenzo" ("A Vision of the Crucifixion: A Self-Portrait by D.H. Lawrence"), *Studies and Essays by the Faculty of Law and Literature* (Kanazawa University), No. 5 (January, 1957), 140-152.

—. "Kyobo na Junreiko no Ato o Otte-Cornwall" ("After the Savage Pilgrimage of D.H. Lawrence: Cornwall"), *Studies in Foreign Literatures* (Ritsumeikan University), No. 12 (May , 1966), 1-11.

—. "Kyobo na Janreiko no Ato o Otto - Sicily," *Studies in Foreign Literature*, No. 15 (January, 1968), 63-79.

—. "Lawrence Bungaku no Haigo ni Aru Mono" ("Behind D.H. Lawrence: His Contact Motif"), *Kanazawa English Studies*, No. 2 (December, 1955), 45-52.

—. "D.H. Lawrence ni Okeru Shi to Fukkatsu 'Shinda Otoko' no Daimei o Megutte" ("Death and Resurrection in D.H. Lawrence with Special Reference to *The Man Who Died*"), *Studies in Foreign Literatures*, No. 4 (December, 1961), 13-24.

—. "D.H. Lawrence ni Okeru to Fukkatsu -Shocho to Shiteno Fushicho ni Tsuite" ("On Death and Resurrection in D.H. Lawrence: Phoenix as His Personal Symbol"), *Studies in Foreign Literatures*, No. 5 (December, 1962), 50-72.

—. "D.H. Lawrence no Nostalgia," *Studies and Essays by the Faculty of Law and Literature*, No. 1 (January, 1953), 154-166.

—. "Tensai no Me (Lawrence Bungaku no Himitsu)" ("The Dark Eyes in *Sons and Lovers*"), *Studies in Foreign Literatures*, No. 2 (December, 1959), 46-63.

Kalnins, Mara. "A Study of Style: The Development of D.H. Lawrence's Style in *The Prussian Officer Tales*," Dissertation, Edinburgh University, 1972.

Kamei, Shunsuke. "Whitman to Lawrence," *Eigo Seinen*, CXIV (1968), 430-432.

Kamimura, Tetsuhiko. "'Hokkyosen' to D.H. Lawrence" ("'The Border Line' and D.H. Lawrence"), *English Literature Review* (Kyoto Women's University), X (February, 1966), 11-27.

—. "Sei no Heisoku -'Shima o Aishita Otoko' Kara" ("The Blockaded Sex -from 'The Man Who Loved Islands'"), *English Literature Review*, XI (November, 1967), 44-61.

—. "Yamaaraski no Shi ni Omou Kora" ("On *Reflections on the Death of a Porcupine"), English Literature Review,* VIII (March, 1965), 55-70.

Kanzaki, Daigoro. "D.H. Lawrence no Kirisuto-Kyo-Kan ni Tsuite" ("D.H. Lawrence's View of Christianity"), *Critical Essays on English Literature* (Kyoto Industrial University), I (January, 1968), 51-65.

Karl, Frederick R. "Lawrence's 'The Man Who Loved Islands': The Crusoe Who Failed," In *A D.H. Lawrence Miscellany,* ed. Harry T. Moore, 265-279.

Karr, Harold S. "Samuel Butler: His Influence on Shaw, Forster, and Lawrence," *Dissertation Abstracts,* XIII (1953), 551 (Michigan State University).

Kato, Muneyuki. "'Musuko to Koibitotachi' o Chushin to Shite Mita Lawrence no Ai to Jitsuzon to Sogai to Jyutai" ("Love, Real Existence, Alienation, and Bond Themes Seen Mainly Through *Sons and Lovers"), Treatises in Commemoration of the 15th Anniversary of the Foundation of Kitakyusha University,* December, 1961, 97-155.

Katsumata, Kikuo. "Shosetsu 'Niji' ni Okeru Ursula no Seicho" ("Ursula's Growth in *The Rainbow"), Kyushu Sangyo Daigaku Kyoyobu Kiyo* (Kyushu Sangyo University), III (1967), 43-57.

Kauffman, Stanley. *"Women in Love:* A Textual Note," *Notes and Queries,* XVII (1970), 466.

Kawabata, Takashi. "D.H. Lawrence (Atara Shii Sekai no Kokai) " ("D.H. Lawrence: His Voyage of Discovery to the New World"), *English Literature in Hokkaido* (Hokkaido University), No. 9 (January, 1964), 50-57.

—. "The Cortege of Dionysus: Lawrence and Giono," *Southern Quarterly,* IV (1966), 159-171.

Kay, Wallace G. "The Cortege of Dionysus: Lawrence and Giono," *Southern Quarterly,* IV (1966), 159-171.

—. "The Cortege of Dionysus: A Study of the Fiction of D.H. Lawrence and Jean Giono," *Dissertation Abstracts,* XXVII (1966), 208A (Emory University).

—. "Lawrence and *The Rainbow:* Apollo and Dionysus in Conflict," *Southern Quarterly,* X (1972), 209-222.

—. *"Women in Love* and *The Man Who Died:* Resolving Apollo and Dionysus," *Southern Quarterly,* X (1972), 325-339.

Kazin, Alfred. "Lady Chatterley in America," *Atlantic Monthly,* CCIV (July, 1959), 33-36. See also *Contemporaries* (Boston: Little Brown and Company, 1962), 105-112.

—. "The Painfulness of D.H. Lawrence," In *The Inmost Leaf* (New York: Harcourt, Brace and Company, 1955), 98-102 A very fine appreciation.

—. "Psychoanalysis and Contemporary Literary Culture," *Psychoanalysis and the Psychoanalytic Review,* XLV (1958), 41-51.

—. "Sons, Lovers, and Mothers," *Partisan Review,* XXIX (1962), 373-385.

—. "The Writer as Political Crazy," *Playboy,* June, 1973. Lawrence included.

Keith, W.J. "D.H. Lawrence's *The White Peacock:* An Essay in Criticism," *University of Toronto Quarterly,* XXXVII (1968), 230-247.

—. "The Spirit of Place and Genius Loci: D.H. Lawrence and Rolf Gardiner," *D.H. Lawrence Review,* VII (1974), 127-138.

Kendle, Burton S. "D.H. Lawrence: The Man Who Misunderstood Gulliver," *English Language Notes,* II (1964), 42-46.

Kenmare, Dallas. "Voice in the Wilderness: The Unacknowledged Lawrence." *Poetry Review,* May-June, 1943, 145-148.

Kermode, Frank. "Lawrence and the Apocalyptic Types," *Critical Quarterly,* X (1968), 14-38. Kermode has keen insight into the apocalyptic tendencies of some modern literature, and Lawrence does bear a relation to this "movement."

—. "The Novels of D.H. Lawrence," *D.H. Lawrence,* ed. Stephen Spender, 78-89. A very compact review of the major novels.

—. "Spenser and the Allegorists," *Proceedings of the British Academy,* XLVIII (1962), 261-279. Lawrence and *The Fairie Queene.*

Kessler, Jascha F. "Ashes on the Phoenix: A Study of Primitivism and Myth-mkaing in D.H. Lawrence's *The Plumed Serpent,*" *Dissertation Abstracts,* XVII (1956), 143-144 (University of Michigan).

—. "Descent in Darkness: The Myth of *The Plumed Serpent,*" In *A D.H. Lawrence Miscellany,* ed. Harry T. Moore, 238-261. Creative and critical.

—. "D.H. Lawrence's Primitivism," *Texas Studies in Literature and Language,* V (1964), 467-488. An exact definition and application of the word.

Ketters, David. "New Worlds for Old: The Apocalyptic Imagination, Science Fiction, and American Literature," *Mosaic,* V (1971), 37-57. Lawrence included.

Kettle, Arnold. "D.H. Lawrence — Some New Letters," *Mosaic: A Journal for the Comparative Study of Literature and Ideas,* IV (1970), 123-126.

Kimpel, Ben D. "One Lawrence from Two Viewpoints," *D.H. Lawrence Review,* IV (1971), 301-313. Review of Nahal's *D.H. Lawrence: An Eastern View* and Delavenay's *D.H. Lawrence and Edward Carpenter.*

Kinkaid-Weekes, Mark. "Introduction," *Twentieth Century Interpretations of The Rainbow* (Englewood Cliffs, New Jersey: Prentice-Hall, 1971), ed. Mark Kinkaid-Weekes, 1-10.

—. "The Marble and the Statue," *Twentieth Century Interpretations of The Rainbow,* 96-120.

King, Nancy. "D.H. Lawrence and German Expressionism," Dissertation, McGill University, 1975.

Kirkham, Michael. "D.H. Lawrence's *Last Poems,*" *D.H. Lawrence Review,* V (1972), 97-120.

Kissane, Leedice. "D.H. Lawrence, Ruth Suckow, and 'Modern Marriage,'" *Rendezvous,* IV (1969), 39-45.

Kistel, Paul D. "Nature in the Poetry of D.H. Lawrence," Dissertation, University of California at Los Angeles, 1970.

Kitawa, Yoshiro. "D.H. Lawrence no Kaikyukan (Dai Ikki no Baii)" ("D.H. Lawrence and Class-Consciousness"), *Preliminary Essay* (Tohoku University), No. 5 (March, 1963), 31-36.

—. "D.H. Lawrence no Saku Hia ni Arawareta Shokubutsu to Sono Giho ni Tsuite" ("Plants in D.H. Lawrence's Work and His Treatment of Them"), *Sylvan* (Tohoku University), VI (May, 1965), 23-35.

Kitchin, Laurence. "Colliers," *Listener,* LXXV (April 28, 1966), 617-618. *Sons and Lovers* and *Lady Chatterley's Lover* as collier novels of class.

—. "The Zombie's Lair," *Listener,* LXXIV (November 4, 1965), 701-702. Lawrence's treatment of industrialism in *Women in Love* and *Lady Chatterley's Lover.*

Klein, Robert C. "I, Thou and You in Three Lawrencian Relationships," *Paunch,* No. 31 (April, 1968), 52-70.

Kleinbard, David J. "The Invisible Man Made Visible: Representation of the Unconscious in the Writings of D.H. Lawrence," *Dissertation Abstracts,* XXX (1969), 727A-728A (Yale).

—. "Laing, Lawrence, and the Maternal Cannibal," *The Psychoanalytic Review,* LVIII (1971), 5-13. Analysis of *Sons and Lovers, The Rainbow,* and *Women in Love.*

—. "D.H. Lawrence and Ontological Insecurity," *Publications of the Modern Language Association,* LXXXIX (1974), 154-163.

Klingopulus, G.D. "Lawrence's Criticism," *Essays in Criticism,* VII (1957), 294-303. Review of *Selected Literary Criticism,* ed. Anthony Beal.

Knight, G. Wilson, "Lawrence, Joyce, and Powys," *Essays in Criticism,* XI (1961), 403-417. With John Sparrow's "Regina v. Penguin Books," the best of the "buggery" analyses of *Lady Chatterley's Lover.*

Knoepflmacher, U.C. "The Rival Ladies: Mrs. Ward's *Lady Connie* and Lawrence's *Lady Chatterley's Lover,*" *Victorian Studies,* IV (1960), 141-158.

Knoll, Robert F. *"Women in Love,"* Film Heritage, VI (1971), 1-6.

Knutzen, J. "Den Moderne Livsdyrkelse" ("The Modern Worship of Life"), *God's Danske Magasin* (Copenhagen), XXX (1938), 278-285.

Koga, Masakazu. "Lawrence no Motometa Mono Shi to Yami no Sekai" ("About Lawrence's Death and Darkness"), *Critical Essays on English Literature* (Kyoto University), I (January, 1968), 66-79.

Kohler, Dayton. "D.H. Lawrence" *Sewanee Review,* XXXIX (1931), 25-38.

Krieger, Robert N. "D.H. Lawrence's Eclectic Symbolism: The Erotic Design to *Look! We Have Come Through*," Dissertation, University of Washington, 1971.

Krishnaumurtly, M.G. "D.H. Lawrence's 'The Woman Who Rode Away,'" *Literary Criterion* (India), summer, 1960.

Kuczkowski, Richard. "Lawrence's 'Esoteric' Psychology: *Psychoanalysis and the Unconscious* and *Fantasia of the Unconscious*," Dissertation, Columbia University, 1973.

Kuo, Carol H. "Lawrence's *The Rainbow*," *Explicator*, XIX (1961), item 60.

Kuramochi, Saburo. "D.H. Lawrence no Sekai" ("D.H. Lawrence's World"), *Ronshu* (Senshu University), No. 31 (December, 1962), 33-41.

—. "D.H. Lawrence to Shoki no Shosetsu" ("D.H. Lawrence's Early Novels"), *Kenkyu Hokoku* (Kagawa University), No. 13 (August, 1960), 53-85.

—. "'Niji' no Ursula" ("Ursula in *The Rainbow*)))*, *Ronshu*, No. 14 (September, 1961), 19-50.

—. "Personification and De-personification in D.H. Lawrence's Poetry," *Otsuka Review* (Tokyo University of Education), I (June, 1964), 49-58.

—. "Shosetsu wa Ika ni Owaru Ka?: D.H. Lawrence no Shosetsu to Kaishin," *Eigo Seinen* (The Rising Generation), No. 115 (1969), 224-226.

Kurono, Yutaka. *"The Lost Girl* Shiron — Shudai to Giho Oyobi Hyoka ni Tsuite" ("An Essay on *The Lost Girl:* Theme, Technique, and Evaluation"), *Okayama University: Faculty of Letters*, No. 26 (March, 1967), 27-44.

—. *"The Rainbow* ni Okeru Byoshaho (D.H. Lawrence no Gengo ni Taisuru Shisei)" ("Descriptions in *The Rainbow:* D.H. Lawrence's Attitude Toward the Efficacy of Words"), *SPES* (Okayama University), No. 1 (July, 1966), 19-30.

Kuttner, Alfred B. *"Sons and Lovers:* A Freudian Appreciation," *Psychoanalytic Review,* II (1916), 295-317.

Kuwayama, Taisuke. "D.H. Lawrence no *The Forsyte Saga* no Hihyo" ("D.H. Lawrence's Critical Essay on *The Forsyte Saga*"), *Studies in Cultural Science*, No. 8 (March, 1967), 56-60.

—. "D.H. Lawrence no John Galsworthy," *Studies in Cultural Science* (Nihon University), No. 9 (March, 1968), 40-44.

Lacy, Gerald M. "An Analytical Calendar of the Letters of D.H. Lawrence" Dissertation, University of Texas, 1971.

Lagercrantz, Olof. "D.H. Lawrence Lady Chatterley's Alskare," *Forbjudna Bocker,* ed. Karl-Erik Lundevall (Stockholm: Wahlstrom and Widstrand, 1958), 113-125.

Lainoff, Seymour. *"The Rainbow:* The Shaping of Modern Man,"Modern *Fiction Studies,* I (1955), 23-37.

—. "The Wartime Setting of Lawrence's 'Tickets, Please,'" *Studies in Short Fiction,* VII (1970), 649-651.

Lambert, J.W. "Plays in Performance," *Drama,* LXXXIX (1968), 19-30. Lawrence included.

Langbaum, Robert. "Lords of Life, Kings in Exile: Idnetity and Sexuality in D.H. Lawrence," *American Scholar,* XLV (1975), 807-815.

Langman, F.H. *"Women in Lvoe,"* Essays in Criticism, XVII (1967), 183-206.

Latta, William. "Lawrence's Debt to Rudolph, Baron von Hube," *D.H. Lawrence Review,* I (1968), 60-62.

—. "The Theme of Spiritual Death and Rebirth in the Novels of D.H. Lawrence," *Dissertation Abstracts,* XXVI (1965), 5439 (University of Nebraska).

Laurent, C. "E.M Forster et D.H. Lawrence," *Les Langues Modernes,* LXIV (1970), 281-288.

Lauter, Paul. "Lady Chatterley with Love and Money," *New Leader,* XLII (1959), 23-24.

Lawrence, D.H. *"The Merry-go-round,"* Virginia Quarterly, XVII (1940), Supplement to issue No. 1. A five act play.

Lawrence, Frieda. "Introduction," *The First Lady Chatterley* (New York: Dial Press, 1944).

—. "A Small View of D.H. Lawrence," *Virginia Quarterly,* XVI (1940), 127-129.

Lea, F.A. "Murry and Marriage," *D.H. Lawrence Review,* II (1969), 1-21. Includes Murry's relation to Lawrence.

Leaver, Florence. "The Man-Nature Relationship of D.H. Lawrence's Novels," *University of Kansas City Review*, XIX (1953), 241-248.

Leavis, F.R. "Anna Karenina," *Cambridge Quarterly*, I (1965), 5-27. Lawrence's view and his oversimplification of Tolstoy.

—. "Lawrence and Class," *Sewanee Review*, LXII (1954), 535-562.

—. "D.H. Lawrence and Professor Irving Babbitt," In *For Continuity* (Cambridge: Heffer, 1933), 149-159.

—. "Lawrence Scholarship and Lawrence," *Sewanee Review*, LXXI (1963), 25-35.

—. "The New Orthodoxy," *Spectator*, February 17, 1961, 229-230. Review of *The Trial of Lady Chatterley*, ed. C.H. Rolph (London: Penguin Books, 1961). The novel is a failure and the case for it silly.

—. "The Novel as Dramatic Poem (IV): *St. Mawr*," *Scrutiny*, XVII (1950-1951), 38-53. The *Scrutiny* articles are incorporated into Leavis's major work, *D.H. Lawernce, Novelist*

—. "The Novel as Dramatic Poem (V): *Women in Love* (I):" *Scrutiny*, XVII (1950-1951), 203-220.

—. "The Novel as Dramatic Poem (V): *Women in Love* (II)," *Scrutiny*, XVII (1950-1951), 318-330.

—. "The Novel as Dramatic Poem (VI): *Women in Love* (III)," *Scrutiny*, XVIII (1951-1952), 18-31.

—. "The Novel as Dramatic Poem (VII): *The Rainbow(I)*," *Scrutiny*, XVIII (1951-1952), 197-210.

—. "The Novel as Dramatic Poem (VII): *The Rainbow* (II)," *Scrutiny*, XVIII (1951-1952), 273-287.

—. "The Novel as Dramatic Poem (VII): *The Rainbow(III)*," *Scrutiny*, XIX (1952-1953), 15-30.

Le Breton, Georges. "D.H. Lawrence et l'architecture du roman," *Preuves*, No. 189 (1966), 70-73.

Ledoux, Larry V. "Christ and Isis: The Function of the Dying and Reviving God in *The Man Who Died*," *D.H. Lawrence Review*, V (1972), 132-148.

Lee, Brian. "America, My America," In *Renaissance and Modern Studies*, ed. G.R. Hibbard (London: Routledge and Kegan Paul, 1966), 181-188.

Lee, Robert H. "D.H. Lawrence and the Australian Ethos," *Southerly,* XXXIII (1973), 144-151. On *Kangaroo.*

—. "Morality and Tradition in the Novel, as Seen in the Relationship Between George Eliot and D.H. Lawrence," Dissertation, University of Witwatersrand (South Africa), 1965.

—. "A True Relatedness: Lawrence's View of Mortality," *English Studies in Africa,* X (1967), 178-185.

Lee, Robin. "Darkness and 'A Heavy Gold Glamour': Lawrence's *Women in Love,*" *Theoria,* XLII (1974), 57-64.

—. "Irony and Attitude in George Eliot and D. H. Lawrence," *English Studies in Africa,* XVI (1973), 15-21.

Lendon, Kenneth H. "The Early Novels of D.H. Lawrence," *Doctoral Dissertations,* XXI (1954), 609A-610A (John Hopkins University).

Lerner, Laurence. "How Beastly the Bourgeoisie Is," *Critical Survey,* I (1963), 87-89. Views of Lawrence's poetry.

—. "Lawrence's 'Carbon,'" In *Twentieth Century Interpretations of The Rainbow,* ed. Mark Kinkaid-Weekes, 91-95.

—. "Two Views of D.H. Lawrence's Poetry," *The Critical Survey,* I (1963), 87-89

Levin, Gerald. "The Symbolism of Lawrence's *The Fox,*" *College Language Association Journal,* XI (1967), 135-141.

Levy, Mervyn and Colin Wilson. "The Paintings of D.H. Lawrence," *Studio* (October, 1962), 130-135.

Levy, Raphael. "Lawrence's *Song of a Man Who Has Come Through,*" *Explicator,* XXII (1964), item 44.

Liddell, Robert. "Lawrence and Dr. Leavis: The Case of *St. Mawr,*" *Essays in Criticism,* IV (1954), 321-327.

Liddy, James. "The Figure of Christ in D.H. Lawrence and Edwin Muir," *University Review* (Dublin), I (n.d.), 26-33.

Lindenberger, Herbert. "Lawrence and the Romantic Tradition," In *A D.H. Lawrence Miscellany,* ed. Harry T. Moore, 326-341.

Lindsay, Jack. "The Impact of Modernism on Lawrence," In *The Paintings of D.H. Lawrence,* ed. Mervyn Levy (New York: Viking Press, 1964).

Littlewood, J.C. "Lawrence," *Essays in Criticism,* XXV (1975), 245-255. Review of Spender's *D.H. Lawrence: Novelist, Poet, Prophet.*

—. "Lawrence Old and New," *Essays in Criticism,* XXI (1971), 195-204. Review article on Draper's *D.H. Lawrence: The Critical Heritage* and Cavitch's *D.H. Lawrence and the New World.*

—. "D.H. Lawrence's Early Tales," *Cambridge Quarterly,* I (1966), 107-124.

—. "Son and Lover," *Cambridge Quarterly,* IV (1969), 323-361.

Locke, Raymond F. "Anais Nin and the Paintings of D.H. Lawrence," with 'A D.H. Lawrence Postscript" By Anais Nin, *Mankind: The Magazine of Popular History,* III (August, 1971), 18-21.

Lowell, Amy. "The Poetry of D.H. Lawrence," In *Poetry and Poets* (Boston: Houghton Mifflin and Company, 1930), 161-174.

Lucas, Barbara. "Apropos of 'England, My England,'" *Twentieth Century,* CLXIX (March, 1961), 288-393.

Lucie-Smith, Edward. "The Poetry of D.H. Lawrence with a Glance at Shelley," *D.H. Lawrence,* ed. Stephen Spender, 224-233.

MacDonald, Dwight. "London Letter," *Partisan Review,* XXVII (1961), 248-259. Comments on the trial of *Lady Chatterley's Lover.*

MacDonald, Edward D. "Introduction," *The Centaur Letters* (University of Texas Press, 1970).

MacLeish, Archibald. "Letter from Archibald MacLeish," In *Lady Chatterley's Lover* (New York: Grove Press, 1959), v-vii.

MacLennan, Hugh. "The Defence of Lady Chatterley," *Canadian Literature,* VI (1960), 18-23.

Magalaner, Marvin. "D.H. Lawrence Today," *Commonweal,* LXX (June 12, 1959), 275-276. Lawrence's reputation.

Mahnken, Harry E. "The Plays of D.H. Lawrence: Addenda," *Modern Drama,* VII (1965), 431-432.

Mailer, Norman. "The Prisoner of Sex," *Harper's,* March, 1971, 70-79. Millett's *Sexual Politics* in relation to Lawrence.

Major, Mabel. "On a September Sunday—'38," *Descant,* X (1966), 13-16. A visit to Frieda Lawrence.

Malafry, Hugh D. "The World and the Flesh: A Study of the Cosmological Interests in D.H. Lawrence," Dissertation, University of Denver, 1973.

Malraux, Andre. "D.H. Lawrence and Eroticism," In *From the N.R.F.: An Image of the Twentieth Century From the Pages of the Nouvelle Revue Francaise,* ed. Justin O' Brien (New York: Farrar, Straus, and Cudahy, (1958), 194-198. See also "L'Amant de Lady Chatterleys," *Criterion,* XII (January, 1933), 215-219. Review of *Lady Chatterley's Lover* (incidentally) and a discussion of Women.

Manchester, John. "From What to Where? Notes from the Life of Dorothy E. Brett," *Nimrod,* XVII (1973), 4-11. Illustrations include Brett's portrait of Lawrence.

Mandel, Oscar. "Ignorance and Privacy," *American Scholar,* XXIX (1960), 509-519. On *Lady Chatterley's Lover.*

Mann, Charles W. "D.H. Lawrence: Notes on Reading Hawthorne's *The Scarlet Letter,*" *Nathaniel Hawthorne Journal,* I (1973), 8-25.

Mansfield, Katherine. "A Letter About the Lawrences," In *A D.H. Lawrence Miscellany,* ed. Harry T. Moore, 131-133. Lawrence's Cornwall period during World War I.

Marks, W.S., III. "D.H. Lawrence and His Rabbit Adolph: Three Symbolic Permutations," *Criticism,* X (1968), 200-216. *Sons and Lovers* and *Women in Love.*

—. "The Novel as Puritan Romance: A Comparative Study of Samuel Richardson, the Brontes, Thomas Hardy, and D.H. Lawrence," *Dissertation Abstracts,* XXV (1964), 1214 (Stanford University).

—. "The Psychology of Regression in D.H. Lawrence's 'The Blind Man,'" *Literature and Psychology,* XVII (1967), 177-192.

—. "The Psychology of the Uncanny in Lawrence's 'The Rocking-Horse Winner,'" *Modern Fiction Studies,* XI (1966), 381-392.

Martin, Dexter. "D.H. Lawrence and Pueblo Religion: An Inquiry into Accuracy," *Arizona Quarterly,* IX (1953), 219-234.

Martin, Richard. "Abgeschiedenheit und Auferstehung: Die Entfaltung eines Motives in D.H. Lawrence' Letzten Kurgeschichten," *Poetica*, II (1968), 70-78.

Martin, W.B. "Significant Modern Writers: D.H. Lawrence," *Expository Times* (Edinburgh), LXXI (1960), 174-176.

Martin, W.R. "Fancy or Imagination?: 'The Rocking-Horse Winner,'" *College English*, XXIV (1962), 64-65.

—. "'Freedom Together' in D.H. Lawrence's *Women in Love*," *English Studies in Africa* (Johannesburg), VIII (1965), 111-120.

Martz, Louis L. "Portrait of Miriam: A Study in the Design of *Sons and Lovers*," In *Imagined Worlds*, ed. Maynard Mack and Ian Gregor (London: Methuen, 1968), 243-269.

Mason, H.A. "Lawrence in Love," *Cambridge Quarterly*, IV (1969), 181-200. Review of *Lawrence in Love: Letters to Louie Burrows*, ed. James T. Boulton (Nottingham: University of Nottingham, 1968).

Masugi, Tadashi. "Dai Niki ni D.H. Lawrence" ("D.H. Lawrence in His Second Period"), *Bulletin of Yamagata University*, I (1958), 31-46.

—. "Dai Sanki no D.H. Lawrence" ("D.H. Lawrence in His Third Period"), *Studies in English Language and Literature* (Yamagata University), IV (February, 1959), 1-26.

—. "Dai Yonki no D.H. Lawrence" ("D.H. Lawrence in His Fourth Period"), *Shiron* (Tohoku University), I (August, 1958), 14-42.

—. "D.H. Lawrence no Kaikyukan — Dai Sanki no Baai" ("D.H. Lawrence's View of Social Class, Especially in His Third Period"), *Shiron*, V (March, 1963), 44-52.

—. "D.H. Lawrence no Shi: *The Ship of Death*" ("On D.H. Lawrence's Poem 'The Ship of Death'"), *Studies in English Language and Literature*, V (March, 1960),1-15.

—. "*The Plumed Serpent* no Syocho" ("Symbolism in *The Plumed Serpent*"), *English and American Literature* (Tohoku University), IV (February, 1957), 13-24.

—. "*The White Peacock* — Tsuki to Kujaku" ("The *White Peacock: The Moon* and the Peacock"), *Shiron*, III (May, 1961), 41-59.

Mather, Rodney. "Patrick White and Lawrence: A Contrast," *Connecticut Review,* XIII (1970), 34-50.

Matsudaira, Yoko. "Lawrence ni Kansuru Ichi Kenkyu (O)" ("A Study of Lawrence(I)"), *Sonoda Women's College Studies,* No.2 (November, 1967), 1-27.

Matsumoto, Jun. "D.H. Lawrence no Bunsho" ("On The English of D.H. Lawrence"), *Joshidai Bungaku,* No. 3 (March, 1952), 38-52.

—. "D.H. Lawrence no Eigo to Seimei no Hyogen" ("D.H. Lawrence and Expressions of Vitality"), *Anglica* (Kansai University), III (1958), 28-40.

Maud, Ralph N. "D.H. Lawrence: True Emotion as the Ethical Control in Art," *Western Humanities Review,* IX (1955), 233-240.

—. "The Politics in *Kangaroo,*" *Southerly* (Australia), XVII (1956), 67-71.

Maxwell, J.C. *"Lady Chatterley's Lover:* A Correction," *Notes and Queries,* VII (1961),110.

Mayer, Elizabeth. "An Afternoon with D.H. Lawrence," In *A D.H. Lawrence Miscellany,* ed. Harry T. Moore, 141-143.

Mayhall, Jane. "D.H. Lawrence: The Triumph of Texture," *Western Humanities Review,* XIX (1965), 161-174.

McCabe, Thomas H. "Rhythm as Form in Lawrence: 'The Horse-Dealer's Daughter,'" *Publications of the Modern Language Association,* LXXXVII (1972), 64-68.

—. "Rhythm in D.H. Lawrence's Short Stories," *Dissertation Abstracts,* XXIX (1968), 609A-610A (University of Wisconsin).

McCurdy, Harold G. "Literature and Personality: Analysis of the Novels of D.H. Lawrence," *Character and Personality,* VIII (1940), 181-203, 311-322.

McDonald, Marguerite B. "An Evening with the Lawrences," *D.H. Lawrence Review,* V (1972), 63-66. Lawrence in New York, September 18, 1925.

Mck., Henry. "Carrying on: *Lady Chatterley's Lover,*" *Critical Review,* X (1967), 46-52.

McMillian, Douglas J. "The Phoenix in the Western World from Herdootus to Shakespeare," *D.H. Lawrence Review,* V (1972), 238-267.

McWilliam, G.H. "Verga and 'Verisimo,'" *Hermathena,* XCV (July, 1961), 3-20. Lawrence as a superior translator of Verga.

Meckier, Jerome. "Huxley's Lawrentian Interlude," In *Aldous Huxley: Satire and Structure* (London: Chatto & Windus, 1969), 78-123.

Megata, Morikimi. "D.H. Lawrence no 'Shinda Otoko' no Seisa-kujiki" ("The Date of D.H. Lawrence's *The Man Who Died"-, Kobe City University Journal,* IV (1953), 55-77.

Megroz, Louis R. "D.H. Lawrence," In *Post Victorians,* ed. William Inge (London: Nicholson and Watson, 1933), 317-328.

Meinke, Norman D. "D.H. Lawrence: Vitalism and the Universal Indefinite," Dissertation, University of Oregon, 1972.

Melchiori, Barbara. "'Objects in the Powerful Light of Emotion," *Ariel: A Review of International English Literature,* I (1970), 21-30. Visual symbols in *Sons and Lovers.*

Mellen, Joan. "Morality in the Novel: A Study of Five English Novelsits, Henry Fielding, Jane Austen, George Eliot, Joseph Conrad, and D.H. Lawrence," *Dissertation Abstracts,* XXIX (1968), 1543A (City University of New York).

—. "Outfoxing Lawrence: Novel into Film," *Literature/Film Quarterly,* I (1973), 17-27.

Mendel, Sydney. "Shakespeare and D.H. Lawrence: Two Portraits of the Hero," *Wascana Review,* III (1968), 49-60.

Merivale, Patricia. "D.H. Lawrence and the Modern Pan Myth," *Texas Studies in Literature and Langugage,* VI (1964), 297-305.

Mesnil, Jacques. "A Prophet: D.H. Lawrence," trans. Freida Lawrence. *Southwest Review,* XXXI (1946), 257-259.

Meyer, Horst. "An Addendum to the D.H. Lawrence Canon," *Publications of the Bibliographic Society of America,* LXVII (1973), 458-459.

Meyer, Kurt. R. "D.H. Lawrence: Zur Erlebten Rede im Englischen Roman des Zwanzigsten Jahrhunderts," Dissertation, Bern, 1957. Published as Swiss Studies in English, No. 43, Bern, 1957. 44-65.

Meyers, Jeffrey. "D.H. Lawrence and Homosexuality," London *Magazine*, XIII (November, 1973), 68-98. Also included in *D.H. Lawrence; Novelsit, Poet, Prophet*, ed. Stphen Spender.

—. *"The Plumed Serpent* and the Mexican Revolution," *Journal of Modern Literature*, IV (1974), 55-72.

—. "'The Voice of Water': *The Virgin and The Gypsy" English Miscellany*, XXI (1970), 199-207.

Mibu, Ikuo. "Birkin ni Tsuite" ("On Birkin"—Women *in Love), English Studies* (Nihon Technical University), No. 12 (March, 1964), 79-91.

—. "Lawrence no Buntai" ("The Style of Lawrence"—*The Man Who Died), English Studies, No.* 12 (March, 1962), 21-40.

—. "Zenki Sakulin no Josei" ("Women in the Early Works"), *English Studies, No.* 15 (November, 1964), 199-224.

Michaels, Jennifer. "The Polarity of North and South: Germany and Italy in the Prose Works of D.H. Lawrence," Dissertation, McGill University, 1974.

Michener, Richard L. "Apocalyptic Mexico: *The Plumed Serpent* and *The Power and the Glory," University Review* (Kansas City), XXXIV (1968), 313-316.

Michot, Paulette. "D.H. Lawrence. A Belated Apology," *Revue des Langues Vivantes*, XXVII (1961), 290-305. On the trial of *Lady Chatterley's Lover.*

Mickelson, Anne Z. "Vital Life Versus Sterile Denial: A Study of Family and Sexual Relationships in the Works of Thomas Hardy and D.H. Lawrence," Dissertation, Rutgers University, 1971.

Miko, Stephen. "D.H. Lawrence: His Development as a Novelist,' *Dissertation Abstracts*, XXVIII (1967), 236A-237A (Yale University).

Miller, Henry. "The Apocalyptic Lawrence," *Southwest Review*, XXXI (1946), 254-256.

Miller, Hillis. "D.H. Lawrence: The Fox and the Perspective Glass," *Harvard Advocate*, CXXXVI (December, 1952), 14-16, 26-28.

Miller, James E., Jr. "Four Cosmic Poets," *University of Kansas City Review,* XXIII (1957), 312-320. Lawrence and the Whitman tradition.

Miller, Milton. "Definition by Comparison: Chaucer, Lawrence, and Joyce," *Essays in Criticism,* III (1953), 369-381.

Miller, Nolan. "The 'Success' and 'Failure' of D.H. Lawrence," *Antioch Review,* XXII (1962), 380-392. Review article on Vivas, Nehls, *Collected Letters,* and Frieda Lawrence's Memoirs.

Millett, Robert. "Great Expectations: D.H. Lawrence's 'The Trespasser,'" *Festschriften,* XLVII (1970), 125-132.

—. "The Question of the Relationships Between the Painting and Written Works of D.H. Lawrence," Dissertation, University of Ottawa, 1965.

Milley, Frederick G. "The Ritual of Becoming: A Study of the Short Stories of D.H. Lawrence," Dissertation, Purdue University, 1973.

Misawa, Susumu. "D.H. Lawrence no Sei to Shi ('Shinda Otoko' o Chushin to Shi Te)" ("The Life and Death of D.H. Lawrence: An Interpretation of *The Man Who Died"*), *Kyoyo Ronso* (Keio University), No. 1 (December, 1956), 12-21.

Mitchell, George B. "D.H. Lawrence: Literary Critic," *Doctoral Dissertations,* XX (1953), 259 (New York University.

Mitchell, Giles, "Feeling and Will in the Modern Novel," *D.H. Lawrence Review,* IV (1971), 183-196. Review of Friedman's *The Turn of the Novel,* Hall's *The Lunatic Giant,* Kaplan's *The Passive Voice,* and Rabinovitz's *The Reaction Against Experiment in the English Novel.*

—. "Lawrence, Others, and the Self," *D.H. Lawrence Review,* VII (1974), 309-320. Review of Bedient's *Architects of the Self,* Paterson's *The Novel as Faith,* and Swigg's *Lawrence, Hardy, and American Literature.*

Mitchell, Peter T. "Lawrence's *Sea and Sardinia* Revisited," *Texas Quarterly,* VIII (1965), 67-72.

Mitra, A.K. "Revision in Lawrence's 'Wedding Morn,'" *Notes and Queries,* XVI (1969), 260.

Mittleman, Leslie B. "Lawrence's 'Snake' Not 'Sweet Georgia Brown,'" *English Literature in Transition,* IX (1966), 45-46.

Montgomery, Lyna Lee. "The Phoenix: Its Use as a Literary Device in English from the Seventeenth to the Twentieth Century," *D.H. Lawrence Review,* V (1972), 268-323.

Moody, H.L.B. "African Sculpture Symbols in a Novel by D.H. Lawrence," *Ibadan,* XXVI (1969), 73-77. *Women in Love.*

Moore, Everett T. "D.H. Lawrence and the 'Censor-Morons,'" *Bulletin of the American Library Association,* LIV (1960), 731-732.

Moore, Harry T. "Afterword: *Lady Chatterley's Lover:* The Novel as Ritual," In *Lady Chatterley.s Lover* (New York: Signet Books, 1962), 285-299.

—. "Comment on Leavis," In *Age of the Modern* (Carbondale: Southern Illinois University Press, 1971), 70-72. Response to Leavis's criticism of Moore's edition of *The Collected Letters.* Reprinted from *Sewanne Review,* LXXI (1963), 347-348.

—. "'The Fox,'" In *A D.H. Lawrence Miscellany,* ed. Harry T. Morre, 28-48.

—. "The Great Unread," In *Age of the Modern,* 9-12. Reprinted from *Saturday Review,* March 2, 1940. Lawrence in 1940, the 10th anniversary of his death.

—. *"Lady Chatterley's Lover* as Romance," In *A D.H. Lawrence Miscellany,* ed. Harry T. Moore (Carbondale: Southern Illinois University Press, 1959), 262-264.

—. "D.H. Lawrence," London *Times Literary Supplement,* December 19, 1963, 1038. On the setting of "The Woman Who Rode Away."

—. D.H. Lawrence and the Flicks," *Literature/Film Quarterly,* I (1973), 3-11.

—. "A Lawrence Budget," *Nation,* CXLII (October 24, 1936), 492-493. Review of *Phoenix: The Posthumous Papers of D.H. Lawrence,* but also an early prognostication of Lawrence's fame.

—. "Lawrence from All Sides," *Kenyon Review,* XXV (1963), 555-558.

—. "D.H. Lawrence: Love as a Serious and Sacred Theme," In *Age of the Modern,* 28-31. Reprinted from the *New York Times Book Review,* May 3, 1959.

—. "D.H. Lawrence to Henry Savage: An Introductory Note," *Yale Literary Gazette,* XXXIII (1959), 24-33.

—. "The Life and Works of D.H. Lawrence," *Doctoral Dissertations,* XVIII (1951), 222 (Boston University).

—. "The Prose Style of D.H. Lawrence," In *Langue et Litterature* (Paris: Societe d'Edition "Les Belles Lettres," 1961), 317-318.

—. "Some New Volumes of Lawrence's Letters," *D.H. Lawrence Review,* IV (1971), 61-73.

—. "The Status of D.H. Lawrence," *New Republic,* LXXXXVII (December 21,1938), 210-211. Review of Hugh Kingmill's derogatory biography of Lawrence, defending Lawrence.

Moorer, Clarence A. "The Poetry of D.H. Lawrence," Dissertation, University of Virginia, 1971.

Mori, Haruhide. "Articles on D.H. Lawrence: A Bibliography, 1916-1965," *Kobe Miscellany* (Kobe University), No. 5 (March, 1968), 105-141.

—. "Geijutsu no Hokai —*Aaron's Rod* to *Kangaroo* no Shisho Hyogen" ("Failure of Art: Ideas and Expression in *Aaron's Rod* and *Kangaroo"*) *Osaka Literary Review* (Osaka University), No. 2 (July, 1963), 51-61.

—. "Lawrence no Gikyoku ni Kansuru Oboegaki: *Mrs. Holroyd, Touch and Go, David"* ("Notes on Lawrence's Plays"), *Prelude* (Osaka University), No. 7 (November, 1963), 26-36.

—. "D.H. Lawrence no Hyogen Keishiki" ("Pattern in the Style of D.H. Lawrence"), *Kobe Miscellany,* No. 3 (February, 1965), 27-40.

—. "D.H. Lawrence: *The Plumed Serpent,"* Studies in Stylistics (Osaka Women's University), No. 6 (January, 1965), 27-40.

—. "Lawrence: *The Rainbow* no Buntai" ("The Style of *The Rainbow"*), *Gakuen Review* (Kobe University), No. 1 (June, 1956), 59-68.

—. "Lawrence's Imagistic Development in *The Rainbow* and *Women in Love,"* Journal of English Literary History, XXXI (1964), 460-481.

—. "Mujun to Shoso no Hyogen: *Women in Love,* Jinbutsu to Imeji" ("Expressions of Irritation and Contradiction: Characterization and Imagery in *Women in Love), Prelude* (Osaka University), No. 6 (September, 1962), 26-35.

—. *The Rainbow* no Kozo —Imeiji no Hasso Oyobi Sakuso to Tenkai" ("The Structure of *The Rainbow* and a Study of Its Imagery"), *Osaka Literary Review,* No. 1 (April, 1962), 57-69.

Morland, Michael. "Introduction," In *The Widowing of Mrs. Holroyd* and *The Daughter-in-Law* (London: Heinemann, 1968).

Morrill, Claire. "Taos Echoes of D.H. Lawrence," *Southwest Review,* XLVII (1962), 150-156.

—. "Taos in D.H. Lawrence," In *A Taos Mosaic: Portrait of a New Mexico Village* (Albuquerque: University of New Mexico Press, 1973), 108-128.

Morris, Tom. "On Etruscan Places." *Punch,* No. 40-41 (April, 1975), 8-39.

Morris, Wright. "Lawrence and the Immediate Present," In *The Territory Ahead* (New York: Harcourt, Brace, and Company, 1957). See also *A D.H. Lawrence Miscellany,* 7-12.

Morse, Stearns. "The Phoenix and the Desert Places," *Massachusetts Review,* IX (1968), 773-784. D.H. Lawrence and Robert Frost.

Mortland, Donald E. "The Conclusion of *Sons and Lovers:* A Reconsideration," *Studies in the Novel,* III (1971), 305-315.

Mosely, Edwin M. "Christ as Artist and Lover: D.H. Lawrence's *Sons and Lovers,"* In *Pseudonyms of Christ in the Modern Novel* (Pittsburgh: University of Pittsburgh Press, 1963), 69-83.

Moynahan, Julian. *"Lady Chatterley's Lover:* The Deed of Life," *Journal of English Literary History,* XXVI (1959), 66-90. See also Moynahan's *The Deed of Life* (Princeton: Princeton University Press, 1965).

—. "Lawrence's 'The Man Who Loved Islands': A Modern Fable," *Modern Fiction Studies,* V (1959), 57-64.

—. "Symbolism and Meaning in the Fiction of D.H. Lawrence," Dissertation, Harvard University, 1957.

Mudrick, Marvin. "Lawrence," *Hudson Review,* XXVII (1974), 424-442.

—. "The Originality of *The Rainbow,*" In *A D.H. Lawrence Miscellany,* 56-82.

Muggeridge, Malcolm. "Lawrence's *Sons and Lovers,*" *New Statesman and Nation,* XLIX (April 23, 1955), 581-582.

— and Helen Cork. "The Dreaming Woman —Helen Corke, in Conversation with Malcolm Muggeridge Tells of Her Relationship with D.H. Lawrence," *Listener,* LXXX (July 25, 1968), 104-107.

Muir, Edwin. "D.H. Lawrence," *Nation,* CXX (February, 1925), 148-150. Review of *The Boy in the Bush* and a perceptive understanding of the struggle in Lawrence, as well as of the underlying formal problems.

—. "Some Letters of Edwin Muir," *Encounter,* XXVI (January, 1966), 3-10. Lawrence discussed in one of the letters.

Muir, Kenneth. "The Three Lady Chatterleys," *Literary Half-Yearly,* II (1961), 18-25.

Muller, John A. "D.H. Lawrence's New World: The Place of America in His World View and Fiction," Dissertation, Indiana University, 1975.

Murphy, Richard M. "The Structure of Authorial Control in the Travel Books of D.H. Lawrence," Dissertation, University of Texas, Austin, 1970.

Murray, W. "Why Did the S.A. (South African) Censors Ban *Lady Chatterley's Lover?,*" *Forum* (South Africa), IX (1961).

Murry, John Middleton. "The Escaped Cock," *Criterion,* X (October, 1930), 183-188.

—. "D.H. Lawrence: Creative Iconoclast," In *A D.H. Lawrence Miscellany,* ed. Harry T. Moore, 3-6.

—. "The Living Dead —I. D.H. Lawrence," *London Magazine,* III (1956), 57-63.

Myers, Neil. "Lawrence and the War," *Criticism,* IV (1962), 44-58. Justification of Lawrence's response.

Nahal, Chaman. "The Colour Ambience of Lawrence's Early and Later Poetry," *D.H. Lawrence Review,* VIII (1975), 147-154.

Nakamura, Yoshio. "Chatterley Fujin no Ichiya" ("A Night Spent by Lady Chatterley"), *Focus* (Aichi University), No. 1 (December, 1964), 43-51.

—. *"Kangaroo* no Mondai" ("A Problem Raised by *Kangaroo"*), *Literary Symposium* (Aichi University), No. 15 (December, 1957), 27-51.

—. *"Lady Chatterley's Lover* ni Tsuite" ("On *Lady Chatterley.s Lover"*), *Literary Symposium,* No. 31 (January, 1966), 237-257.

—. "The *Lost Girl* Oboegaki" ("Notes on *The Lost Girl"*), *Literary Symposium,* No. 24 (February, 1963), 81-103.

—. *"The Rainbow* ni Tsuite" ("On *The Rainbow"*), *Literary Symposium,* No. 21 (February, 1961), 157-181

—. *"The Virgin and the Gypsy* Ron" ("On *The Virgin and the Gypsy"*), *Literary Symposium,* Special Number (March, 1957), 469-489.

Nakano, Kimiko. *"Lady Chatterley's Lover* ni Okeru Connie" ("Connie in *Lady Chatterley's Lover"*), *Englsih Literature in Hokkaido* (Hokkaido University), No. 10 (July, 1965), 53-62.

—. *"The Rainbow* ni Okeru D.H. Lawrence no Shiso" ("D.H. Lawrence's Attitude to Love and Religion in *The Rainbow"*), *Konan's Women's College Studies in English Literature,* No. 1 (December, 1964), 118-135.

—. *"Sons and Lovers* ni Tsuite" ("On *Sons and Lovers"*), *Konan Women's College Studies in English Literature,* No. 2 (December, 1965), 75-90.

—. *"Women in Love* ni Okeru Gerald Crich" ("Gerald Crich in *Women in Love"*), *Konan Women's College Researches,* No. 1 (March, 1965), 179-194.

Nazareth, Peter. "D.H. Lawrence and Sex," *Transition,* II (October, 1962), 54-57. Also *Transition,* III (March, 1963), 38-43.

Nehls, Edward H. "D.H. Lawrence: The Spirit of Place," In *The Achievement of D.H. Lawrence,* ed. Frederick J. Hoffman and Harry T. Moore, 268-290.

—. "The Spirit of Place in D.H. Lawrence: A Study of Places in Which He Lived and of Their Meaning for His Work," *Dissertation Abstracts*, XIV (1953), 440-441 (University of Wisconsin).

New, William H. "Character as Symbol: Annie's Role in *Sons and Lovers,*" *D.H. Lawrence Review*, I (1968), 31-43.

Newby, Frank S. "Dialectical Form in *The Rainbow* and *Women in Love,*" *Dissertation Abstracts*, XXVII (1966), 1062A-1063A (University of California, Berkeley).

Newman, Paul B. "D.H. Lawrence and *The Golden Bough,*" *Kansas Magazine* (1962), 79-82.

—. "The Natural Aristocrat in Letters," *University Review* (Kansas City), XXXI (October, 1964), 23-31.

Newton, Frances J. "Venice, Pope, T.S. Eliot, and D.H. Lawrence," *Notes and Queries*, V (1958), 119-120.

Nicholes, E.L. "The Symbol of the Sparrow in *The Rainbow* by D.H. Lawrence," *Modern Language Notes*, LXIV (1949), 171-174.

Nichols, Ann E. "Syntax and Style: Ambiguities in Lawrence's *Twilight in Italy,*" *College Composition and Communication*, XVI (1965), 261-266.

Nicholson, Homer K. "O Altitudo: A Comparison of the Writings of Walt Whitman, D.H. Lawrence, and Henry Miller," *Dissertation Abstracts*, XVII (1956), 2614 (Vanderbilt University).

Ninomiya, Takamichi. "Futatsu no 'Hi -Gakkyuteki' Lawrence Ron (Anais Nin to Henry Miller")" ("Two Unprofessional Studies of D.H. Lawrence —Anais Nin's and Henry Miller's"), *Kobe Miscellany* (Kobe University), No. 2 (June, 1963), 43-69.

—. "Higeki no Keisho (Lawrence no Thomas Hardy)" ("Tragedy Bequeathed: Lawrence on Thomas Hardy"), *Tauros* (Kobe University), No. 7 (February, 1965), 2-12.

—. "Lawrence no Tolstoi Kan (I)" ("Lawrence's View of Tolstoy (I)"), *Tauros*, No. 4 (January, 1964), 47-55.

—. "Lawrence no Tolstoi Kan (II)" ("Lawrence's View of Tolstoy(II)"), *Tauros*, No. 5 (June, 1964), 33-44.

—. "Lawrence no Utopia" ("Lawrence's Utopia"), *Modern Age* (Kobe University), No. 1 (December, 1952), 22-26.

—. "Lawrence to Ko— Otoko" ("Lawrence and the Small Man"), *Klopes* (Kobe University), No. 5 (February, 1954), 2-10.

—. "Taii no Ningyo Ron" ("On *The Captain's Doll*"), *Klopes* (Kobe University), No. 25 (September, 1957), 33-41.

Nishikawa, Masaharu. "Annable no Sowa" ("On the Episode of Annable"), *English Literature* (Waseda University), No. 19 (January, 1961), 210-233.

—. "D.H. Lawrence ni Okeru Seimeitekina Mono to Shocho" ("The Vital and Its Symbolism in the Works of D.H. Lawrence"), *English Literature*, No. 14 (October, 1957), 71-85.

—. "D.H. Lawrence ni Okeru Shi Ishiki" ("On the Consciousness of Death in the Works of D.H. Lawrence"), *Yamato Bunka* (Tenri University), No. 41 (March, 1963), 28-40.

—. "D.H. Lawrence no Buntai" ("On the Style of D.H. Lawrence"), *English Literature*, No. 12 (November, 1956), 54-61.

—. "D.H. Lawrence no Shimpishugi" ("Mysticism in D.H. Lawrence"), *Studies in English Literature* (Tokyo University), No. 35 (1959), 266-277.

—. "D.H. Lawrence no Shukyoteki Yoso ("The Religious Element in D.H. Lawrence"), *Yamato Bunka*, No. 36 (May, 1956), 151-171.

—. "D.H. Lawrence Ron" ("On D.H. Lawrence"), *Yamato Bunka*, No. 35 (March, 1955), 139-153.

Nishimura, Koji. "Nigenron no Yukue," *Eigo Seinen* (The Rising Generation), No. 115 (1969), 624-626.

—. "'Shi no Fune'" ("'Ship of Death'"), *Studies in Literature* (Meiji University), No. 4 (March, 1957), 59-73.

Nishimuru, Toru. "Mekishiko no Lawrence" ("Lawrence in Mexico"), *Joshidai Bungaku* (Osaka Women's University), No. 10 (March, 1958), 77-98.

—. "'Shinda Otoko' to 'Etoruriya Kiko' ni Tsuite" ("On *The Man Who Died* and *Etruscan Places*"), *Joshidai Bungaku*, No. 8 (January, 1956), 60-72.

—. Niwa, Chitose. "Futatsu no Utopia—Lawrence to Huxley" ("Two Types of Utopia—Lawrence and Huxley"), *Studies in the Humanities* (Osaka City University), VII (1957), 133-146.

—. "Hardy to Lawrence" ("Hardy and Lawrence"), *Studies in the Humanities*, IV (1953), 72-88.

—. "Hardy to Lawrence—Hoi" ("Hardy and Lawrence: A Supplement"), *Studies in the Humanities*, XI (1960), 87-100.

—. "Lawrence to Huxley," *Studies in the Humanities*, VII (1956) 87-100.

Noguchi, Yosiko. "Miriam ni Tsuite" ("Miriam in *Sons and Lovers*"), *English Studies* (Nihon University), No. 18 (March, 1968), 53-56.

Nojiri, Kichinoshin. "D.H. Lawrence no Jiyu" ("D.H. Lawrence and Freedom"), *English Literature in Hokkaido* (Hokkaido University), I (March, 1954), 26-35.

Noon, William T. "God and Man in Twentieth-Century Fiction," *Thought*, XXXVII (1962), 35-56.

Nosaka, Tosaku. "D.H. Lawrence Dainiki ni Okeru Buntai no Ichimen" ("Some Features of D.H. Lawrence's Style in His Second Phase"), *Kenkyu Ronbun-Shu* (Miyagi Women's College), No. 27 (January, 1966), 22-31.

—. "D.H. Lawrence: 'Taiyo'" ("D.H. Lawrence: 'Sun'"), *Kenkyu Ronbun-Shu*, No. 27 (January, 1967), 42-60.

—. "*Sons and Lovers* ni Okeru Buntai" ("The Style of *Sons and Lovers*"), *Kenkyu Ronbun-Shu*, No. 24 (July, 1964), 18-38.

Nott, Kathleen. "Whose Culture?," *Listener*, LXVII (April 12 and 19, 1962), 631-632, 677-678. Lawrence as the wrong culture hero for F.R. Leavis.

Nulle, Stebelton H. "D.H. Lawrence and the Fascist Movement," *New Mexico Quarterly*, X (1940), 3-15.

Nuno, Antonio Gaya. "El lider fascista en la novela inglesa de nuestro tiempo," *Cuadernos Hispanoamericanos*, LXXII (1967), 632-640. On *Kangaroo* and Huxley's *Point Counter Point*.

Ober, William B., M.D. "Lady Chatterley's What?," *Academy of Medicine of New Jersey Bulletin*, XV (1969), 41-65. Lawrence's tuberculosis in relation to disguised homosexuality.

O'Hare, Charles B. "The Role of European Literature in the Prose Works of D.H. Lawrence," *Dissertation Abstracts*, XVII (1956), 634 (University of Wisconsin).

Ohashi, Yasuichiro. "D.H. Lawrence no Shakespeare —Kan" ("D.H. Lawrence's View of Shakespeare"), *Sekaibungaku* (Tokyo Toritsu University), No. 29 (October, 1967), 23-33.

—. "Lawrence no Shi ni Arawaretta Dobutsu ni Tsuite" ("Animals in Lawrence's Poetry"), *Studies in Foreign Literatures* (Ritsumeikan University), II (1959), 80-97.

—. "Lawrence no Shi Arawaretta Ganseki to Kobutsu ni Tsuite" ("Rocks and Minerals in Lawrence's Poetry"), *Studies in Foreign Literatures*, IV (1961), 52-68.

—"Lawrence no Shi ni Arawaretta Shokubutsu ni Tsuite" ("Plants in Lawrence's Poetry"), *Studies in Foreign Literatures*, III (1960), 53-68.

—. "Lawrence no Shi ni Okeru ni Tsuite" ("Lawrence's Use of Colors in His Poetry"), *Studies in Foreign Literatures*, I (1958), 77-98.

—. "Shijin Lawrence to Girisha Shinwa" ("Greek Mythology in Lawrence's Poetry"), *Memoirs of Humanistic and Social Sciences* (Kyoto Technical University, No. 11 (December, 1962), 63-95.

— "Shijin Lawrence to Shi (Chu)" ("Lawrence: Poet and Death (Part Two)"), *Memoirs of Humanistic and Social Sciences*, No. 15 (January, 1967), 115-144.

—. "Shijin Lawrence to Shi (Jo)" ("Lawrence: Poet and Death (Part One)"), *Memoirs of Humanistic and Social Sciences*, No. 14 (March, 1966), 35-60.

—. "Shijin Lawrence to Tsuki" ("The Moon in Lawrence's Poetry"), *Memoirs of Humanistic and Social Sciences*, No. 12 (March, 1964), 59-84.

Okada, Taiji. "Chiche no Ka Lawrence" ("D.H. Lawrence: Son of Father"), *Review of Kobe University of Mercantile Marine: Part I Studies in Humanistic and Social Science*, XIII (March, 1965), 108-130.

—. "D.H. Lawrence: Chatterley Fujin no Ai no Kaishin" ("D.H. Lawrence: Lady Chatterley's Conversion of Love"), *Studies in Humanistic and Social Science* (Kobe University), XVI (March, 1968), 1-22.

—. "D.H. Lawrence Kuroi Me no Hirameki" ("D.H. Lawrence: A Spark of Black Eyes"), *Studies in Humanistic and Social Science*, XV (March, 1967), 166-190.

—. "'D.H. Lawrence ni Okeru Chichukai Sekai Fukkatsu no Genso" ("On the Fantasy of the Revival of the Mediterranean World in D.H. Lawrence"), *Studies in Humanistic and Social Science,* VIII (February, 1960), 99-124.

—. "D.H. Lawrence no Mashin to Seirei" ("D.H. Lawrence's Demon and Holy Ghost"), *Studies in Humanistic and Social Science,* X (March, 1962), 157-180.

—. "D.H. Lawrence to India" ("D.H. Lawrence and India"), *Studies in Humanistic and Social Science,* X (March, 1962), 177-207.

—. "D.H. Lawrence to Senso" ("D.H. Lawrence and the War"), *Studies in Humanistic and Social Science,* VI (February, 1958), 71-92.

Okuma, Ryuzo. "Shosetsu Kosei no Icherei—Yo*u Touched Me* ni Tsuite" ("On 'You Touched Me': An Example of Story-Making"), *Eibungakushi* (Hosei University), No. 7 (December, 1959), 51-57.

Okumura, Osamu. "D.H. Lawrence as a Religious Thinker," *Aoyoma Journal of General Education* (Aoyoma Gakuin University), I (November, 1960), 201-218.

—. "D.H. Lawrence the Preacher," *Aoyoma Journal of General Education,* II (November, 1961), 63-84.

Okumura, Toru. "Ai to Kuno no Henreki 'Miyo Warera Wa Yatte Kita!'" ("Lawrence's Pilgrimage of Love and Agony: *Look! We Have Com Through!"), English Literary Review* (Kyoto Women's University), V(March, 1961), 12-38.

—. "Lawrence Shosetsu No Hitotsu no Imi 'Musuke to Koibita' kara 'Koisuru Onna Tachi' Made" ("A Meaning of D.H. Lawrence's Novels— from *Sons and Lovers* to *Women in Love"), Review of English Literature* (College of Liberal Arts, Kyoto University), No. 21 (August, 1967), 103-117.

—. Lawrence to Daiichiji Taisen" ("Lawrence and the First World War"), *English Literary Review* (Kyoto Women's University), VI (March, 1962), 1-21.

—. "Michinaru Sekai o Motomete— 'Niji'" ("In Search of the Unknown World: *The Rainbow"), Review of English Literature* (College of Liberal Arts, Kyoto University, No. 17 (March, 1965), 74-108.

—. "Paul no Higeki—'Musuko to Koibito'" ("The Tragedy of Paul Morel: *Sons and Lovers*"), *Review of English Literature*, No. 16 (October, 1964), 106-140.

Okunishi, Akira. "'Niji' no Ketsumatsu to Symbol to Shite no Niji" ("The Conclusion of *The Rainbow* and *The Rainbow* as Symbol"), *Attic Review* (Kyoto University), No. 5 (February, 1967), 24-33.

Oppel, Horst. "D.H. Lawrence: *St. Mawr*," *Der Moderne Englische Roman: Interpretationem*, ed. Horst Oppel (Berlin: E. Schmidt, 1965).

Orr, Christopher J. "D.H. Lawrence: The Evolution of His Political Thought 1914-1930," Dissertation, Pennsylvania State University, 1972.

Orrell, Herbert M. "D.H. Lawrence: Poet of Death and Resurrection," *Cresset*, XXXIV (1971), 10-13. The poem, "Ship of Death."

Ort, Daniel. "Lawrence's *Women in Love*," *Explicator*, XXVII (1969), item 38.

Osborne, Marianne M. "The Hero and the Heroine in the British Bildungsroman: *David Copperfield and A Portrait of the Artist as a Young Man, Jane Eyre* and *The Rainbow*," Dissertation, Tulane University, 1972.

Ota, Saburo. "D.H. Lawrence: 'Shojo to Jipshi Hihyo" ("D.H. Lawrence's *The Virgin and the Gypsy*"), *Gakuen* (Showa Women's University), No. 308 (August, 1965), 2-13.

Owen, Frederick I. "D.H. Lawrence and Max Mohr: A Late Friendship and Correspondence," *D.H. Lawrence Review*, IX (1976), 137-156.

— and David Lindley. "Lawrentian World," *Human World*, XI (1973), 39-54.

Pace, Bill J. "D.H. Lawrence's Use in His Novels of Germanic and Celtic Myth from the Music Dramas of Richard Wagner," Dissertation, University of Arkansas, 1973.

Pachmus, Temira. "Dostoevsky, D.H. Lawrence and Carson McCullers: Influences and Confluences," *Germano-Slavica* (University of Waterloo), IV (1974), 59-68.

Paik, Nack-Chung. "A Study of *The Rainbow* and *Women in Love* as Expressions of D.H. Lawrence's Thinking on Modern Civilization," Dissertation, Harvard University, 1972.

Panichas, George A. "F.M. Dostoevsky and D.H. Lawrence: Their Vision of Evil," *Renaissance and Modern Studies,* V (1961), 49-75.

—. "The End of the Lamplight," *Modern Age* (Chicago), XIV (1970), 65-74. Lawrence and Lady Cynthia Asquith.

—. "E.M. Forster and D.H. Lawrence: Their Views on Education," In *Renaissance and Modern Essays,* ed. G.R. Hibbard (London: Routledge and Kegan Paul, 1966), 199-213

—. "D.H. Lawrence and the Ancient Greeks," *English Miscellany,* XVI (1965), 195-214.

—. "D.H. Lawrence, Religious Seeker," *Index to Theses,* XII (1962), 12 (University of Nottingham).

—. "D.H. Lawrence's Biblical Play *David,*" *Modern Drama,* VI (1963), 164-176.

—. "D.H. Lawrence's Concept of the Risen Lord," *Christian Scholar,* XLVII (1964), 56-65.

—. "D.H. Lawrence's War Letters," *Texas Studies in Literature and Language,* V (1963), 398-409.

—. "Voyage of Oblivion: The Meaning of D.H. Lawrence's Death Poems," *English Miscellany,* XIII (1962), 135-164.

Parry, Albert. "D.H. Lawrence Through a Marxist Mirror," *Western Review,* XIX (1955), 85-100.

Pascal, Roy. "The Autobiographical Novel and the Autobiography," *Essays in Criticism,* IX (1959), 138-150. *Sons and Lovers,* Charlotte Bronte, James Joyce.

Paterson, John. "D.H. Lawrence: The One Bright Book of Life," *The Novel as Faith* (Boston: Gambit, 1973), 14-183.

Patmore, Brigit. "A Memoir of Frieda Lawrence," In *A D.H. Lawrence Miscellany,* ed. Harry T. Moore, 137-140.

Patmore, Derek. "A Child's Memories of D.H. Lawrence," In *A D.H. Lawrence Miscellany,* ed. Harry T. Moore, 134-136.

Pearce, T.M. "The Unpublished 'Lady Chatterley's Lover,'" *New Mexico Quarterly,* VIII (1938), 171-179.

Pearsall, Robert B. "The Second Art of D.H. Lawrence," *South Atlantic Quarterly,* LXIII (1964), 457-467.

Peerman, D. "D.H. Lawrence: Devout Heretic," *Christian Century*, LXXVIII (1961), 237-241.

Peter, John. "The Bottom of the Well," *Essays in Criticism*, XII (1962), 226-227. Answers Wilson Knight's assertions in "Lawrence, Joyce, and Powys," *Essays in Criticism*, XI (1961), 467-488.

—. "Lady Chatterley Again," *Essays in Criticism*, XII (1962), 445-447.

Peterson, L. "D.H. Lawrence's 'The Rocking-Horse Winner,'" *Horisont* (Vasa, Finland), XI (1964), 32ff.

Phillips, Gene D., S.J. "Sexual Ideas in the Films of D.H. Lawrence," *Sexual Behavior*, I (1971), 10-16.

Phillips, Steven R. "The Double Pattern of D.H. Lawrence's 'The Horse-Dealer's Daughter,'" *Studies in Short Fiction*, X (1973), 94-97.

—. "The Monomyth and Literary Criticism," *College Literature*, II (1975), 1-16. "The Horse-Dealer's Daughter."

Phipps, William E. "D.H. Lawrence's Appraisal of Jesus," *Christian Century*, LXXXVIII (1971), 521-524.

Piccolo, Anthony. "Strategies of Crisis in the Shorter Fiction of D.H. Lawrence," Dissertation, New York University, 1969.

Pierle, Robert C. "D.H. Lawrence's *Studies in Classic American Literature:* An Evaluation," *D.H. Lawrence Review*, I (1968), 31-43.

—. "D.H. Lawrence's *Studies in Classic American Literature:* An Evaluation," *Southern Quarterly*, VI (1968), 333-340.

Pilpel, Harriet F. and Nancy F. Wechler. "The Law and Lady Chatterley," *New World Writing*, XVI (1960), 231-240.

Pinto, Vivian de Sola. "The Burning Bush: D.H. Lawrence as Religious Poet," In *Mansions of the Spirit: Essays in Literature and Religion,* ed. George A. Panichas (New York: Hawthorne Press, 1967), 213-235.

—. "D.H. Lawrence," In *The Politics of Twentieth-Century Novelists,* ed. George A Panichas (New York: Hawthorne Books, 1971), 30-50.

—. "Lawrence and Frieda," *English*, XIV (1963), 135-139. Review of Frieda Lawrence's *Memoirs* and Lawrence's *Collected Letters.*

—. "Lawrence and the Nonconformist Hymns," In *A D.H. Lawrence Miscellany*, ed. Harry T. Moore, 103-113.

—. "D.H. Lawrence: Letter Writer and Craftsman in Verse," *Renaissance and Modern Studies*, I (1957), 5-34.

—. "Poet Without a Mask," *Critical Quarterly*, III (1961), 5-18. See also "Introduction" to *Complete Poems* (New York: Viking Press, 1964), 1-21.

— and Warren Roberts. "A Note on Editing *The Complete Poems*," *D.H. Lawrence Review*, I (1968), 213-214.

Pirenet, C. "La structure symbolique de *Women in Love*," *Etudes Anglaises*, XXII (1969), 137-151.

Pittock, Malcolm. "The the Editor," London *Times Literary Supplement*, August 20, 1971. Was Lawrence first in the 1904 King's Scholarship Exam? Replies by Moore, Delavenay, Sagar, London *Times Literary Supplement*, September 10, 1971; M.B. Mencher, London *Times Literary Supplement*, September 17, 1971; Moore, London *Times Literary Supplement*, October 1, 1971.

Poesch, Jessie. "The Phoenix Portrayed," *D.H. Lawrence Review*, V (1972), 200-237.

Pollak, Paulina S. "The Letters of D.H. Lawrence to Sallie and Willie Hopkin," *Journal of Modern Literature*, III (1973), 24-34.

Pollnitz, C.P. "The Poetry of D.H. Lawrence: Extending Romanticism," Dissertation, University of Leicester (England), 1974.

Porter, Katherine Anne. "A Wreath for the Gamekeeper," *Shenandoah*, XI (1959), 3-12. On *Lady Chatterley's Lover.*

Potts, Abbie F. "Piping of Pan: D.H. Lawrence as Elegist, *Look! We Have Come Through!*," In *The Elegaic Mode* (Ithaca: Cornell University Press, 1967), 395-432.

Poulsen, Bjorn. "D.H. Lawrence som moderne profet" ("D.H. Lawrence as a Modern Prophet"), *Dansk udsyn* (Copenhagen), XXXVIII (1958), 191-202.

Powell, Laurence C. "D.H. Lawrence and His Critics: A Chrono-
logical Excursion into Bio-Bibliography," *Colophon,* I
(1940), 63-74.

—. "The *Plumed Serpent,*" *Southwest Classics* (Los Angeles:
Ward Ritchie Press, 1974), 81-92.

—. "Southwest Classics Reread: *The Plumed Serpent* by D.H.
Lawrence," *Westways,* LXIII (1971), 18-20, 46-49.

Powell, S.W. "D.H. Lawrence as Poet," *Poetry Review,* Septem-
ber-October, 1934, 347-350.

Prasad, Madhusudan. "The Autobiographical Element in the
Novels of D.H. Lawrence," Dissertation, University of
Allahabad (India), 1974.

Prasad, Suman P. "The Tragic Vision in the Novels of Thomas
Hardy and D.H. Lawrence," Dissertation, University of
Leicester (England), 1971.

Pratt, Annis. "Women and Nature in Modern Fiction," *Contemporary Literature,* XIII (1972), 481-483.

Praz, Mario. In *Studi e Svaghi Inglesi* (Firenze: Sansoni, 1937.

Pritchard, William H. "Lawrence and [Wyndham] Lewis,"
Agenda, VII (1970), 140-147.

—. "Wyndham Lewis and Lawrence," *Iowa Review,* II (1971),
91-96.

Pritchett, V.S. "In Writing Nothing Fails Like Success," *New
York Times Book Review,* January 22, 1961. Hostile
environment necessary to Lawrence's creativity.

—. "Sons *and Lovers,*" In *The Living Novel* (New York: Reynal
and Hitchcock, 1947), 136-142.

Proctor, Margaret R. "E.M. Forster and D.H. Lawrence as Novelists of Ideas," Dissertation, University of Toronto, 1973.

Pryce-Jones, D. "Last Glowing Isolation: Countryside That
Inspired," *Reporter,* XXXIV (February 10, 1966), 49-50.

Purdy, Strother B. "On The Psychology of Erotic Literature,"
Literature and Psychology, XX (1970), 23-29. *Lady Chatterley's Lover.*

Quennell, Peter. "The Later Period of D.H. Lawrence," In
Scrutinies II, ed. Edgell Rickwood (London: Chatto &
Windus, 1936), 124-137.

—. "D.H. Lawrence and Aldoux Huxley," In *The English Novelist,* ed. Derek Virschoyle (London: Chatto & Windus, 1936), 267-278.

Quinn, Kerker. "D.H. Lawrence's *Phoenix,*" *Yale Review,* XXVI (1937), 847-848. Review article.

Rachman, Shalom. "Art and Value in D.H. Lawrence's *Women in Love,*" *D.H. Lawrence Review,* V (1972), 1-25.

Raddatz, Volher. "Lyrical Elements in D.H. Lawrence's *The Rainbow,*" *Revue des Langues Vivantes,* XL (1974), 235-242.

Ragussis, Michael. "The Double Perspective: A Study of D.H. Lawrence's Novels," Dissertation, John Hopkins University, 1970.

Rahv, Philip. "On Leavis and Lawrence," *New York Review of Books,* XI (September 26, 1968), 62-68.

Raina, M.L. "A Forster Parallel in Lawrence's *St. Mawr,*" *Notes and Queries,* XIII (1966), 96-97.

—. "The Use of Symbol by English Novelists 1900-1930, with Particular Reference to E.M. Forster, D.H. Lawrence, and Virginia Woolf," *Index to Theses,* XV (1965), 17 (University of Manchester).

Rajiva, Stanley F. "The Empathetic Vision," *Literary Half-Yearly,* IX (1968), 49-70. On *Birds, Beasts and Flowers.*

Raleigh, John H. "Victorian Morals and the Modern Novel," *Partisan Review,* XXV (1958), 241-264.

Ravilious, C.P. "Lawrence's 'Chladnix Figures,'" *Notes and Queries,* XX (1973), 331-332.

Rawlings, Donn. "Prophecy in the Novel," Dissertation, University of Washington, 1973.

Read, Herbert. "The Figure of Grammar: Whitman and Lawrence," In *The True Voice of Feeling: Studies in English Romantic Poetry* (London:Faber and Faber, 1953), 87-100.

—. "On D.H. Lawrence," *Twentieth Century,* CLXV (1959), 556-566.

Reddick, Bryan D. "Point of View and Narrative Tone in *Women in Love;* The Portrayal of Interpsychic Space," *D.H. Lawrence Review,* VII (1974), 156-171.

—. "Sons *and Lovers:* The Omniscient Narrator," *Thoth,* VII (1966), 68-75.

—. "Tone in Dramatic Narrative," Dissertation, University of California, Davis, 1969.

Rees, Marjorie. "Mollie Skinner and D.H. Lawrence," *Westerly,* I (1964), 41-49. *The Boy in the Bush.*

Rees, Richard. "Miss Jessel and Lady Chatterley," In *For Love or Money: Studies in Personality and Essence* (Carbondale: Southern Illinois University Press, 1961), 115-124.

—. "Politics of a Mystic," D.H. *Lawrence Review,* II (1969), 24-31. On John Middleton Murry.

Reeves, James. "Introduction," *Selected Poems of D.H. Lawrence* (New York: New Directions, 1947; London: William Heinemann, 1951).

Reichwagen, Wilhelm. "Der Expressionistiche Zug im Neusten Englischen Roman: Eine Weltanschaulich-Stilkritische Studie," Dissertation, Griefswald, 1935, 96.

Remsburg, Ann and John Remsburg. "D.H. Lawrence and art," *Revista da Faculaade de Letras* (University of Lisbon), III (1971), 5-33.

Remsburg, J.A. "D.H. Lawrence: Critic of Life," *Index to Theses,* XVI (1966), 16 (University of Exeter).

Remsburg, John. "'Real Thinking': Lawrence and Cezanne," *Cambridge Quarterly,* II (1967), 117-147. Lawrence's philosophy in his critical essays, "Study of Thomas Hardy" and "Introduction to These Paintings."

—. *"Women in Love* as a Novel of Change," *D.H. Lawrence Review,* VI (1973), 149-172.

Requardt, Egon. "D.H. Lawrence: Solipsist oder Prophet einer neuen Gemeinschaft?," *Die Neuren Sprachen,* XII (1963), 506-515.

—. "David Herbert Lawrence: *Sons and Lovers,*" *Die Neuren Sprachen,* X (1961), 230-234.

—. "Das Wesen und die Problematik der Zwischenmenschlichen Beziehungen bei D.H. Lawrence," Dissertation, University of Munster, 1950.

Reuter, Irmgard. "Studien Uber die Personlichkeit und die Kunstform von D.H. Lawrence," Dissertation, Marburg University, 1934.

Reynolds, Alan. "On Lawrence," *Bookman* (New York), LXXIII (July, 1931), 492-499. A plain man's view of Lawrence's work.

Rexforth, Kenneth. "Introduction," *Selected Poems of D.H. Lawrence* (New York: New Directions, 1947).

Rich, Adrienne. "Reflections on D.H. Lawrence," *Poetry*, CVI (1965), 218-225.

Richards, I.A. "Poem 8," In *Practical Criticism* (New York: Harcourt, Brace, and Company, 1966), 99-112. Student responses to Lawrence's poem "Piano."

Richardson, John A. and Jon I Ades. "D.H. Lawrence on Cezanne: A Study in the Psychology of Critical Intuition," *Journal of Aesthetics and Art Criticism*, XXVIII (1970), 441-453.

Ricks, Christopher. "Prophets," *New York Review of Books*, XX (January 24, 1974), 43-46. Review of Roger Sale's *Modern Heroes* and Frank Kermode's *d.h. lawrence.*

Rieff, Philip. "Introduction," *Psychoanalysis and the Unconscious and Fantasia of the Unconscious* (New York: Viking Press, 1960), vii-xxiii.

—. "A Modern Mythmaker," In *Myth and Mythmaking,* ed. Henry A. Murray (New York: George Braziller, 1960), 240-275.

—. "The Therapeutic as Mythmaker: Lawrence's True Christian Philosophy," In *The Triumph of the Therapeutic: Uses of Faith After Freud* (New York: Harper and Row, 1966), 189-231.

—. "Two Honest Men, Freud and Lawrence," *Listener*, LXII (May 5, 1960), 794-796.

Roberts, John H. "Huxley and Lawrence," *Virginia Quarterly*, XIII (1937), 546-557.

Roberts, Mark. "D.H. Lawrence and the Failure of Energy," In *The Tradition of Romantic Morality* (London: Macmillan, 1973), 322-348.

Roberts, Walter. "After the Prophet: The Reputation of D.H. Lawrence," *Month*, XXVII (April, 1962), 237-240. Primarily a review of Frieda Lawrence's *Memoirs*.

Roberts, Warren. "D.H. Lawrence, the Second 'Poetic Me': Some New Material," *Renaissance and Modern STudies*, XIV (1970), 5-25. Twelve unpublished poems.

—. "The Literary career of D.H. Lawrence, Materials for a Bibli-- ography," Dissertation, University of Texas, 1955.

—. "The MSS. of D.H. Lawrence," *Library Chronicle of the University of Texas*, V (1955), 36-43.

Robson, W.W. "D.H. Lawrence and *Women in Love*," *The Modern Age*, ed. Boris Ford (Baltimore:Penguin Books, 1961), 280-300.

Rose, Marilyn G. "If Proust Had Been British," *D.H. Lawrence Review*, I (1968), 63-71.

Rose, Shirley. "Physical Trauma in D.H. Lawrence's Short Fiction," *Contemporary Literature*, XVI (1975), 73-83.

Rosenburg, Judith. "Elements of Existentialism and Phenomenology in the Works of D.H. Lawrence," Dissertation, University of Illinois, 1973.

Rosenthal, T.G. "The Writer as Painter," *Listener*, LXIV (September 6, 1962), 349-350.

Ross, Charles L. "Art and 'Metaphysic' in D.H. Lawrence's Novels," *D.H. Lawrence Review*, VII (1974), 206-217. Review of R.E. Pritchard's *D.H. Lawrence: Body of Darkness* and Frank Kermode's *d.h. lawrence*.

—. "The Composition of *Women in Love*: A History, 1913-1919," *D.H. Lawrence Review*, VIII (1975), 198-212.

—. "A Problem of Textual Transmission in the Typewcript of *Women in Love*," *The Library*, Series 5, XXIX (1974), 197-205.

—. "Some Interpretations and Use of Myth, Symbol, and History in Selected Works of D.H. Lawrence," Dissertation, Oxford University, 1973.

— and George J. Zytaruk. "Goats and Compasses and/or *Women in Love*: An Exchange," *D.H. Lawrence Review*, VI *(1973), 33-46.*

Ross, Michael L. "Lawrence's Second 'Sun,'" D.H. Lawrence Review, VIII (1975), 1-18.

—. "Nature and Fate in the Early Novels of D.H. Lawrence," Dissertation, Harvard University, 1966.

Rossi, Patrizio. "Lawrence's Two Foxes: A Comparison of the Texts," *Essays in Criticism,* XXII (1972), 265-278.

Rossman, Charles. "Four Versions of D.H. Lawrence," *D.H. Lawrence Review,* VI (1973), 48-70. Review of books by Colin Clark, David Cavitch, Yudhistar, and Baruch Hochman.

—. "The Gospel According to D.H. Lawrence: Religion in Sons and Lovers," *D.H. Lawrence Review,* III (1970), 31-41.

—. "Lawrence on the Critics' Couch: Pervert or Prophet?," *D.H. Lawrence Review,* III (1970), 175-185.

—. "Organic Wholeness of Being in Selected Novels of D.H. Lawrence," *Dissertation Abstracts,* XXIX (1968), 3153-3154 (University of Southern California).

—. "Toward D.H. Lawrence and His Visual Bestiary," *D.H. Lawrence Review,* VII (1974), 295-308. Review article.

—. "'You Are the Call and I Am the Answer': D.H. Lawrence and Women," *D.H. Lawrence Review,* VIII (1975), 255-328.

Rowland, Paul G. "The Precarious Prophets, Thamas Carlyle and D.H. Lawrence," Dissertation, University of Sussex (England), 1972.

Rowley, Eugene G. "Individual Instinct and Societal Repression in the Writings of D.H. Lawrence," Dissertation, Tufts University, 1973.

Roy, Chitra. "D.H. Lawrence and E.M. Forster: A Study in Values," *Indian Journal of English Studies,* VII (1967), 46-58.

Roya, Gino. "Lawrence prefamesta," *Biologia Culturale, IV* (1969), 126-132.

Rudikoff, Sonya. "D.H. Lawrence and Our Life Today: Re-reading *Lady Chatterley's Lover,*" *Commentary,* XXVIII (1959), 408-413.

Rudrun, Alan. "Philosophical Implication in Lawrence's *Women in Love,*" *Dalhousie Review,* LI (1971), 88-92.

Ruggles, Alice M. "The Kinship of Blake, Vachel Lindsay, and D.H. Lawrence," *Poet Lore,* LXVI (1939), 88-92.

Runyan, Elizabeth. "Escape from the Self: An Interpretation of E.M. Forster, D.H. Lawrence, and Virginia Woolf," Dissertation, Kent State University, 1970.

Russell, John. "D.H. Lawrence and Painting," *D.H. Lawrence,* ed. Stephen Spender, 234-243. A sympathetic presentation in the context of the time.

Ruthven, K.K. "On the So-Called Fascism of Some Modernist Writers," *Southern Review,* V (1972), 225-230. Lawrence included.

—. "The Savage God: Conrad and Lawrence," *Critical Quarterly,* X (1968), 39-54.

Ryals, Clyde de. "D.H. Lawrence's 'The Horse-Dealer's Daughter': An Interpretation," *Literature and Psychology,* XII (1962), 39-43. Story as rebirth archetype.

Sagar, Keith. "'The Best I Have Known': D.H. Lawrence's 'A Modern Lover' and 'The Shades of Spring,'" *Studies in Short Fiction,* IV (1967), 143-151.

—. "Four Paintings by D.H. Lawrence," *D.H. Lawrence Review,* IV (1971), 42-43. Poems on Lawrence's paintings.

—. "The Genesis of 'Bavarian Gentians,'" *D.H. Lawrence Review,* VIII (1975), 47-53.

—. "The Genesis of *The Rainbow* and *Women in Love,*" *D.H. Lawrence Review,* I (1968), 179-199.

—. "Goats and Compasses and *Women in Love* Again," *D.H. Lawrence Review,* VI (1973), 303-308.

—. "'Little Living Myths': A Note on Lawrence's 'Tortoises,'" *D.H. Lawrence Review,* III (1970), 161-167.

—. "D.H. Lawrence: Dramatist," *D.H. Lawrence Review,* IV (1971), 154-182.

—. "Lawrence and Frieda: The Alternative Story," *D.H. Lawrence Review,* IX (1976), 117-125.

—. "The Lawrences and the Wilkinsons," *Review of English Literature* (Leeds), III (1962), 62-75. Italy, 1926-1928.

—. "Three Separate Ways: Unpublished D.H. Lawrence Letters to Francis Brett Young," *Review of English Literature,* VI (1965), 93-105.

—. "The Third Generation," In *Twentieth Century Interpretations of The Rainbow*, ed. Mark Kinkaid-Weekes, 58-72.

—. "To the Editor," London *Times Literary Supplement*, September 10, 1971. Textual problem in "The Red Wolf."

—. "Vision and Form in the Works of D.H. Lawrence," *Index to Theses*, V (1955), 12 (University of Leeds).

—. "What Mr. Williams Has Made of D.H. Lawrence," *Twentieth Century*, CLXVIII (July, 1960), 143-153.

Saibara, Sosumu. "Fukkatsu Joron— D.H. Lawrence no Fukkatsu ni Tsuite" ("On the Resurrection of D.H. Lawrence"), *Studies of Social Science* (Kochi Junior College), No. 4 (November, 1956), 1-38.

—. "D.H. Lawrence no Doku Shin Jidai (I)" ("The Early Life of D.H. Lawrence: His Life and World (I)"), *Studies of Social Science*, No. 14 (February, 1963), 1-20.

—. "D.H. Lawrence no Tampen— Shosetsu-Sono Keiko to Bunrui (I)" ("On the Short Stories of D.H. Lawrence: Their Tendency and Classification (I)"), *Studies of Social Science*, No. 8 (April, 1959), 48-71.

Sakamoto, Tadanobu, "D.H. Lawrence no Tampen—Shosetsu to Ai no Tema" ("A Study of the Short Stories of D. H. Lawrence and the Love Theme"—, *Memoirs of the Osaka Institute of Technology*, V (1960), 28-38.

—. "Mittsu no Shosetsu ni Tsuite" ("Essay on Three Novels": *Jacob's Room, Sons and Lovers, A Portrait of the Artist as a Young Man), Prelude* (Osaka University), No. 1 (January, 1958), 28-38.

Sale, Roger. "D.H. Lawrence, 1912-1916," *Massachusetts Review* VI (1965), 467-480. The psychological development of the early Lawrence.

—. "The Narrative Technique of *The Rainbow*," *Modern Fiction Studies*, V (1959), 29-38. The weak conclusion of *The Rainbow* accounted for by the nature of Lawrence's thematic materials. An analysis of the first order.

Salgado, Gamini. "D.H. Lawrence as Literary Critic," *London Magazine*, VII (1960), 49-57.

Salgado, R.G. "The Poetry of D.H. Lawrence," *Index to Theses*, V (1955), 12 (University of Nottingham).

Salter, K.W. "Lawrence, Hardy and 'The Great Tradition,'" *English* (London), XXII (1973), 60-65.

Samuels, Marilyn S. "Water, Ships, and the Sea: Unifying Symbols in Lawrence's *Kangaroo,*" *University Review*, XXXVII (1970), 46-57.

Sandoval, Patricia A. "D.H. Lawrence: A Study of His Poetic Theories," *Dissertation Abstracts*, XXIX (1968) 912A (University of Michigan).

San Juan, Epifanio, Jr. "Theme Versus Imitation: D.H. Lawrence's 'The Rocking-Horse Winner,'" *D.H. Lawrence Review*, III (1970), 136-140.

Sasaki, Hiroo. "D.H. Lawrence no 'Niji'" ("D.H. Lawrence's *The Rainbow*"), *Fukuoka University Review, Literature and Science*, V (1960), 173-198.

—. "D.H. Lawrence no Shuppatsu Ten (I)" ("D.H. Lawrence's Starting Point (I)"), *Fukuoka University Review*, III (1958), 315-348.

—. "D.H. Lawrence no Shuppatsu Ten (II)" ("D.H. Lawrence's Starting Point (II)"), *Fukuoka University Review*, III (1958), 449-534.

Savage, Derek S. "D.H. Lawrence: A Study in Dissolution," In *The Personal Principle: Studies in Modern Poetry* (London: Routledge, 1944), 134-154.

Sawamura, Kan. "Lawrence no Mother-Complex" ("Lawrence and the Mother-Complex"), *Jin-Bun Ronshu* (Waseda University), No. 5 (February, 1968), 91-100.

Sawyer, Paul W. "The Religious Vision of D.H. Lawrence," *Crane Review* (Tufts University, Theological School), III (1961).

Saxena, H.S. "The Critical Writings of D.H. Lawrence," *Indian Journal of English Studies* (Calcutta), II (1960), 130-137.

—. "D.H. Lawrence and the Impressionistic Technique," *Indian Journal of English Studies*, III (1961), 145-152.

Schmidt, Wolfgang. "Die Frau in der Romanen von D.H. Lawrence," Dissertation, University of Free Berlin, 1953.

Schneider, Daniel J. "The Symbolism of the Soul: D.H. Lawrence and Some Others," *D.H. Lawrence Review*, VII (1974), 107-126.

—. "Techniques of Cognition in Modern Fiction," *Journal of Aesthetics and Art Criticism,* XXVI (1968), 317-328. Includes a brief analysis of The *Rainbow.*

Schneidermann, Leo. "Notes on D.H. Lawrence's *Studies in Classic American Literature,*" *Connecticut Review,* I (1968), 57-71.

Schorer, Mark. "I Will Send Address: New Letters of D.H. Lawrence," *London Magazine,* III (1956), 44-67.

—. "Introduction," *Sons and Lovers* (New York: Harper's Modern Classics, 1956).

—. "D.H. Lawrence: Then, During, Now," *Atlantic Monthly,* CCXXXIII (March, 1974), 84-88.

—. "Lawrence and the Spirit of Place," In *A D.H. Lawrence Miscellany,* ed. Harry T. Moore, 280-294.

—. "Lawrence in the War Years," Stanford: Stanford University, 1968. 15 pp. Part of a brief lecture, a checklist of correspondence in Charlotte Ashley Felton Memorial Library at Stanford.

—. "On *Lady Chatterley's Lover,*" *Evergreen Review,* I (1957), 149-178. Excellent sturctural analysis of the story.

—. "Technique as Discovery," *Hudson Review,* I (1948), 67-87. The first major analysis of *Sons and Lovers* in which Schorer relates the narrative ambiguities of the novel to the nature of the experiences Lawrence presents, stopping short of complete Freudian commitment, but perceiving the gap between intention and performance.

—. "Two Houses, Two Ways: The Florentine Villas of Lewis and Lawrence, Respectively," *New World Writing,* No. 4 (October, 1953), 136-154.

—. *"Women in Love,"* In *The Achievement of D.H. Lawrence,* ed. Frederick J. Hoffman and Harry T. Moore, 163-177. Again, excellent structural analysis and the attempt to relate structural flaws to theme.

Schulman, Norma M. "D.H. Lawrence's *Birds, Beasts and Flowers:* Five Kinds of Poetry," Dissertation, Tufts University, 1972.

Scott, James. "The Emasculation of *Lady Chatterley's Lover,*" *Literature/Film Quarterly,* I (1973), 37-45.

Scott, Nathan A., Jr. "D.H. Lawrence: Chartist of the Via Mystica," In *Rehearsals of Discomposure: Alienation and Reconciliation in Modern Literature* (New York: King's Crown Press, 1952), 112-177, 247-260.

Secor, Robert. "Language and Movement in 'Fanny and Annie,'" *Studies in Short Fiction*, VI (1969), 395-400.

Seidl, Francis. "Lawrence's 'The Shadow in the Rose Garden,'" *Explicator*, XXXII (October, 1973), item 9.

Sellers, W.H. "New Light on Auden's *The Orators*," *Publications of the Modern Language Association*, LXXXII (1967), 455-464. Lawrence as a major influence on Auden.

Sepcic, Visnja. "The Category of Landscape in D.H. Lawrence's *Kangaroo*," *Studia Romanica et Anglica Zagrabiensia*, No. 28 (1969), 129-152. Landscape as psychic projection.

—. "The Dialogue of *Lady Chatterley's Lover*," *Studia Romanica et Anglica Zagrabiensia*, Nos. 29-32 (1970-1971), 461-480.

—. "Notes on the Structure of *Women in Love*," *Studia Romanica et Anglica Zagrabiensia*, No. 21-22 (1965), 289-304.

Shakir, Evelyn. "'New Blossoms of Me.' The Poetry of D.H. Lawrence," Dissertation, Boston University, 1972.

—. "'Secret Sin': Lawrence's Early Verse," *D.H. Lawrence Review*, VIII (1975), 155-175.

Shanks, Edward. "Mr. D.H. Lawrence: Some Characteristics," *London Mercury*, VIII (May, 1923), 64-75.

Shapiro, Karl. "The First White Aboriginal," *Walt Whitman Review*, V (1959), 43-52.

—. "The Unemployed Magician," In *A D.H. Lawrence Miscellany*, ed. Harry T. Moore, 378-395.

Sharpe, Michael C. "The Genesis of D.H. Lawrence's *The Trespasser*," *Essays in Criticism*, XI (1961), 34-39.

Sheed, Wilfrid. "The Trial of Lady Chatterley," *Jubilee*, IX (1961), 33-35.

Sheerin, John B. "Sane Censorship and Lady Chatterley," *Catholic World*, CLXXIX (1959), 412-416.

Shibata, Tikaji. "D.H. Lawrence no Shosetsuron" ("D.H. Lawrence's Theory of the Novel"), *Bulletin of the Department of General Education* (Nagoya City University), No. 5 (1959), 1-10.

—. "D.H. Lawrence to Bertrand Russell" ("D.H. Lawrence and Bertrand Russell"), *Bulletin of the Department of General Education*, No. 2 (1956), 13-22.

Shields, E.F. "Broken Vision in Lawrence's 'The Fox,'" *Studies in Short Fiction*, IX (1972), 353-363.

Shimizu, Kazuyoshi. "Lawrence no Bungaku Hiyo" ("Lawrence's Literary Criticism"), *Shiron* (Tohoku University), VI (June, 1964), 57-74.

—. "Lawrence no Rakuen (Riso Shakai 'Rananim' no Kosatsu)" ("The Utopian World of D.H. Lawrence: A Consideration of 'Rananim'"), *Literary Symposium* (Aichi University), No. 29 (February, 1965), 75-97.

Shimizu, Koya. "'There's a baby, but that is a side issue': The Discrepancy Between Creation and Procreation in D.H. Lawrence," *Studies in English Literature* (Japan), 1974, 228-230.

Shimpachiro, Mujata. "The Marquis on Trial," *Japan Quarterly*, VIII (1961), 494-496. Censorship of *Juliette* and *Lady Chatterley's Lover*.

Shirai, Toshitaka. "D.H. Lawrence no Imagery no Tenkou" ("The Development of D.H. Lawrence's Imagery"), *Studies in English Language and Literature*, (Yamagata University), IV (February, 1959), 27-43.

—. "D.H. Lawrence no Kaikyu Kan" ("D.H. Lawrence and Class"), *Shiron* (Tohoku University), V (March, 1963), 37-43.

—. "D.H. Lawrence no Working Method" ("D.H. Lawrence's Working Method"), *Shiron*, IV (February, 1962), 19-36.

—. "D.H. Lawrence to Freudianism" ("D.H. Lawrence and Freudianism"), *Studies in English Language and Literature* (Yamagata University), V (March, 1960), 35-62.

—. "D.H. Lawrence: *Women in Love* no Imeiji" ("Imagery in *Women in Love*"), *Studies in English Language and Literature*, II (January, 1956), 53-69.

—. "D.H. Lawrence: *Women in Love* no Kosei" ("The Structure of *Women in Love*"), *Bulletin of Yamagata University*, IV (1961), 57-80.

—. "D.H. Lawrence: *Women in Love*—Soundless Symphony," *Studies in English Language and Literature*, III (March, 1957), 25-37.

— and Takashi Fujita. "Word List of *The Rainbow*-A Study of D.H. Lawrence's Vocabulary," *Bulletin of Yamagata University,* V (1964), 31-165.

Shonfield, Andrew. "Lawrence's Other Censor," *Encounter,* XVII (1961), 63-64.

Sillitoe, Alan. "D.H. Lawrence and His District," *D.H. Lawrence,* ed. Stephen Spender, 42-70.

Simon, John I. "Women in Love," In *Movies into Film: Film Criticism 1967-1970* (New York: Dial Press, 1971), 57-62.

Simms, Theodore F. "Primitivistic Motifs in the Poetry of D.H. Lawrence," *Dissertation Abstracts,* XXIX (1968), 274A (New York University).

Sinclair, Stephen G. "Moralists and Mystics: Religion in the Modern British Novel," Dissertation, University of Michigan, 1974).

Singh, T.N. "D.H. Lawrence: The Evolution of a Genius," *Criticism and Research* (Banaras Hindu University), (1964), 69-83.

Singh, Vishnudat. "Lawrence's Use of 'Pecker,'" *Papers of the Bibliographical Society of America,* LXIV (1970), 355. The various connotations.

—. *"Women in Love:* A Textual Note," *Notes and Queries,* XVII (December, 1970), 466.

Sinha, R.K. "The Literary Influences on D.H. Lawrence's Poems and Novels," In *Oxford-Christ's Church,* 1950.

Sitesh, Aruna. "D.H. Lawrence as Literary Critic," Dissertation, University of Allahabad (India).

Sklar, Sylvia. "The Relationship Between Social Context and Individual Character in the Naturalist Drama, with Special Reference to Chekhov, D.H. Lawrence, and David Storey," Dissertation, University of London, 1974.

Skurnick, Blanche J. "D.H. Lawrence: A Study of His Shorter Fiction," Dissertation, Columbia University, 1972.

Smailes, T.A. "D.H. Lawrence: Poet," *Standpunte* (South Africa), LXXXV (1969), 24-36.

—. "Lawrence's *Birds, Beasts and Flowers,*" *Standpunte* (South Africa), LXXXIV (1968-1969), 26-40.

—. "Lawrence's Verse: More Editorial Lapses," *Notes and Queries,* XVII (1970), 465-466. "The Man of Tyre."

—. *"More Pansies* and *Last Poems:* Variant Readings Derived from M.S. Roberts E 192," *D.H. Lawrence Review,* I (1968), 200-213.

—. "The Mythical Bases of Women *in Love,*" *D.H. Lawrence Review,* I (1968) 129-136.

—. "The Verse of D.H. Lawrence," Dissertation, University of Port Elizabeth, South Africa, 1968.

—, ed. "D.H. Lawrence: Seven Hitherto Unpublished Poems," *D.H. Lawrence Review,* III (1970), 42-46.

Small, Michael. "The Tale the Critic Tells: D.H. Lawrence on Nathaniel Hawthorne," *Paunch,* No. 40-41 (April, 1975), 40-58.

Smith, Bob L. "D.H. Lawrence's *St. Mawr:* Transposition of Myth," *Arizona Quarterly,* XXIV (1968), 197-208.

Smith, Grover, Jr. "The Doll-Burners: D.H. Lawrence and Louisa Alcott," *Modern Language Queraterly,* XIX (1958), 28-32. *Sons and Lovers.*

Smith, Julian. "Vision and Revision: 'The Virgin and the Gypsy' as Film," *Literature/Film Quarterly,* I (1973), 28-36.

Smith, L.E. "Two Views of D.H. Lawrence's Poetry," *Critical Survey,* I (1963), 81-86.

Snodgrass, W.D. "A Rocking Horse: The Symbol, the Pattern, the Way to Live," *Hudson Review,* XI (1958), 191-200.

Sobchack, Thomas. "Social Criticism in the Novels of D.H. Lawrence," *Dissertation Abstracts,* XXIX (1968), 1235A-1236A (City University of New York).

—. *"The Fox:* The Film and the Novel," *Western Humanities Review,* XXIII (1969), 73-78.

Solecki, Sam. "D.H. Lawrence's View of Film," *Literature/ Film Quarterly,* I (1973), 12-16.

Solomon, Gerald. "The Banal, and the Poetry of D.H. Lawrence, *Essays in Criticism,* XXIII (1973), 254-267.

Southworth, James G. "D.H. Lawrence: Poet," In *Sowing the Spring: Studies in British Poetry from Hopkins to MacNiec* (Oxford: Basil Blackwell, 1940), 64-75.

Spano, Joseph. "A Study of Ursula and H.M. Daleski's Commentary," *Paunch,* No. 33 (December, 1968), 21-33. Ursula not an exemplary character.

Sparks, Richard. "Mural Words and Moral Theories," *New Republic,* CXLIII (December 12, 1960), 23-24. The trial of *Lady Chatterley's Lover.*

Sparrow, John. "After Thoughts on Regina v. Penguin Books, Ltd.," *Encounter,* XVIII (1962), 83-88.

—. "Regina v. Penguin Books, Ltd.," *Encounter,* XVIII (1962), 35-43. See Wilson Knight's "Lawrence, Joyce, Powys."

Spender, Stephen. "Laurentian Love-Hate for England," In *Love-Hate Relationships: English and American Sensibilities* (New York: Random House, 1974), 234-242.

—. "D.H. Lawrence, England, and the War," In *D.H. Lawrence: Novelist, Poet, Prophet* (New York: Harper and Row; London: Weidenfeld and Nicholson, 1973), ed. Stephen Spender, 71-76.

—. "Notes on D.H. Lawrence," In *The Destructive Element* (London: Jonathan Cape, 1935), 176-186. A natural sympathy and an almost intuitive understanding of Lawrence's point of view.

—. "Pioneering the Instinctive Life," In *The Creative Element* (London: Hamish Hamilton, 1953), 92-107.

Spiers, James G. "The Background to the Poetical Philosophy of Conrad and Lawrence," Dissertation, University of Toronto, 1970.

Spilka, Mark. "D.H. Lawrence," *Univeristy of Kansas City Review*, XXI (1955), 291-299.

—. "Lawrence Up-tight, or the Anal Phase Once Over," *Novel*, IV (1971), 252-267. Replies by George Ford, Frank Kermode, Colin Clark, *Novel*, V (1971), 54-70.

—. "Lawrence's Quarrel with Tenderness," *Critical Quarterly*, IX (1968), 363-377.

—. "Lessing and Lawrence: The Battle of the Sexes," *Contemporary Literature*, XVI (1975), 218-240.

—. "Post-Leavis Lawrence Critics," *Modern Language Quarterly*, XXV (1964), 212-217.

—. "The Shape of an Arch: A Study of Lawrence's *The Rainbow*," *Modern Fiction Studies*, I (1955), 30-38.

—. "Star-Equilibrium in *Women in Love*," *College English*, XVII (1955), 79-83. This and the previous essay are perhaps preliminaries to Spilka's *The Love Ethic of D.H. Lawrence* (Bloomington: University of Indiana Press, 1955), establishing him as the foremost vitalist critic of Lawrence.

—. "Was D.H. Lawrence a Symbolist?," *Accent*, XV (1955), 49-60.

Squires, Michael G. "Lawrence's *The White Peacock*: A Mutation of Pastoral," *Texas Studies in Literature and Language*, XII (1970), 263-283.

—. "The Pastoral Novel: Studies in George Eliot, Thomas Hardy, and D.H. Lawrence," Dissertation, University of Maryland, 1969.

—. "Pastoral Patterns and Pastoral Variants in *Lady Chatterley's Lover*," *English Literary History*, XXXIX (1972), 129-146.

—. "Recurrence as a Narrative Technique in *The Rainbow*," *Modern Fiction Studies*, XXI (1975), 230-236.

—. "Scenic Construction and Thetorical Signals in Hardy and Lawrence," *D.H. Lawrence Review,* VIII (1975), 125-146.

—. "Teaching a Story Thetorically: An Approach to a Short Story by D.H. Lawrence," *College Composition and Communication,* XXIV (1973), 150-156. "The Man Who Loved Islands."

Stacy, Paul H. "Lawrence and Movies: A Postscript," *Literature/ Film Quarterly,* II (1974), 93-95.

Stanford, Raney. "Thomas Hardy and Lawrence's *The White Peacock,*" *Modern Fiction Studies,* V (1959), 19-28. One of the earlier comparative studies illuminating the work.

Stanley, F.R. "The Artist as Pornographer," *Literary Half-Yearly,* IV (1963), 14-27. *Lady Chatterley's Lover.*

Stanzel, Franz. "G.M. Hopkins, W.B. Yeats, D.H. Lawrence, und die Spontaneitat Dichtung," In *Anglistische Studien,* ed. Brunner, Karl, *et al* (Vienna: W. Braumuller, 1958), 179-183.

Stavros, Constantine N. "William Blake and D.H. Lawrence," *University of Kansas City Review,* XXII (1956), 235-240.

—. "William Blake & D.H. Lawrence: A Comparative Study of the Similarity of Their Thought," *Dissertation Abstracts,* XII (1951), 430-431 (University of Buffalo).

—. "D.H. Lawrence's Psychology of Sex," *Literature and Psychology,* VI (1956), 90-95.

Steinhauer, H. "Eros and Psyche," *Modern Language Notes,* LXIV (1949), 217-228.

Stewart, J.E. "The Evolution and Source of Some Themes of Spontaneity in D.H. Lawrence's Writing until 1914," Dissertation, Cambridge University, 1968.

Stillert, Harriet. "D.H. Lawrence Kommer Tillbaka" ("The Return of D.H. Lawrence"), *Bokvannen* (Stockholm), XV (1960), 203-207.

Stilwell, Robert L. "The Multiplying of Entities: D.H. Lawrence and Five Other Poets," *Sewanee Review*, LXXVI (1968), 520-535. Includes a review of *Complete Poems.*

Stock, Noel. "Fragmentation and Uncertainty," *Poetry Australia*, XXXI (1969), 41-44. Lawrence and Romanticism.

Stoehr, Taylor. "Lawrence's 'Mentalized Sex,'" *Novel*, VIII (1975), 101-122.

Stohl, Johan. "D.H. Lawrence and the Religious Imagination: A Study of Sex, Rhetoric, and Ritual in the Major Novels, Dissertation, University of Chicago, 1972.

Stoker, Richard J. "Fiction: The Search for Friendship," Dissertation, State University of New York, Busffalo, 1973.

Stoll, John E. "Common Womb Imagery in Joyce and Lawrence," *Forum* (Ball State), XI (1970), 10-24. A basis for comparing and contrasting *The Rainbow, Women in Love, A Portrait of the Artist as a Young Man,* and *Ulysses.*

—. "Psychological Dissociation in the Victorian Novel," *Literature and Psychology*, XX (1970), 63-73. Imagery and character relationships culminating in Lawrence.

—. "Recent Lawrence Criticism," *Sewannee Review*, LXXXIII (1975), 191-203. The underlying assumptions and nature of recent criticism.

—. Review of David Cavitch's *D.H. Lawrence and the New World,* Stephen Miko's *Toward Women in Love,* and R.E. Pritchard's *Body of Darkness, Georgia Review,* XXVI (1972), 397-400.

—. Review of Emile Delavenay's *The Man and His Work. Georgia Review*, XXVIII (1974), 370-371.

—. Review of Sandra M. Gilbert's *Act of Attention: The Poems of D.H. Lawrence, Georgia Review*, XXVIII (1974), 173-175.

—. "The Search for Integration in the Novels of D.H. Lawrence," *Dissertation Abstracts*, XXVII (1966), 2547A (Wayne State University).

Stolpe, Herman. "'Lady Chatterley' Vann Processen," *Bokvanne* (Stockholm), XVI (1961), 168-169. The trial of *Lady Chatterley's Lover.*

Strickland, Geoffrey. "The First *Lady Chatterley's Lover,"* *Encounter*, XXXVI (1971), 44-52.

Stroupe, John S. "D.H. Lawrence's Portrait of Ben Franklin in *The Rainbow*," *Iowa English Yearbook*, No. 11 (1966), 64-68.

—. Ruskin, Lawrence, and Gothic Naturalism," *Forum* (Ball State), XI (1970), 3-9.

Sturm, Ralph D. "Lawrence: Critic of Christianity," *Catholic World*, CCVIII (1968), 75-79.

Suckow, Ruth. "Modern Figures of Destiny: D.H. Lawrence and Frieda Lawrence," *D.H. Lawrence Review*, III (1970), 1-30.

Suehiro, Yoshitaka. "D.H. Lawrence no Ai to Seimei no Rinri" ("The Love and Life Ethics of D.H. Lawrence"), *Journal of the Second College of Engineering Nihon University*, Series B, VI (March, 1965), 21-26.

—. "D.H. Lawrence no Shi ni Okeru Ai to Kodoku ni Tsuite no Kenkyu" ("A Study of Love and Solitude in the Poems of D.H. Lawrence"), *Journal of the Second College of Engineering Nihon University*, Series B, VII (1966), 25-35.

—. "D.H. Lawrence no Shokan ni Tsuite no Kenkyu" ("A Study of the Letters of D.H. Lawrence"), *Journal of the Second College of Engineering Nihon University*, Series B, VIII (1967), 25-33.

Sullivan, Alvin. "The Phoenix Riddle: Recent D.H. Lawrence Scholarship," *Papers on Language and Literature*, VII (1971), 203-221.

Sumimoto, Akiko. *"Women in Love* Ron: Shi to Sei" ("A Study of *Women in Love"), Mulberry* (Aichi Women's College), No. 12 (February, 1963), 19-25.

Swan, Michael. "D.H. Lawrence: Italy and Mexico," In *A Small Part of Time* (London: Jonathan Cape, 1957), 279-287.

—. "Lawrence the Traveller," *London Magazine,* IV (1957), 46-51.

Swarts, Donald C. "D.H. Lawrence's Literary Criticism: A Catalogue," Dissertation, University of Pittsburgh, 1953.

Swerdlow, Irwin. "The Vision of D.H. Lawrence," Dissertation, Harvard University, 1951.

Tannenbaum, Elizabeth B. "Concepts of the Self in the Modern Novel," Dissertation, Stanford University, 1972.

Tanner, Tony. "D.H. Lawrence and America," *D.H. Lawrence: Novelist, Poet, Prophet,* ed. Stephen Spender, 170-196.

Tao, Sadako. "'Musuke to Koibito' no Nakano Lawrence" (" Lawrence in His *Sons and Lovers"), English and American Studies* (Wayo Women's University), No. 5 (November, 1967), 73-83.

Tatsumiya, Sakae. "Hogen Oyobi Zokugo no Buntaika (D.H. Lawrence no Gengo Kozo)" ("Sylization of Dialect and Vulgarism: Linguistic Structure in D.H. Lawrence"), *Journal of Kumamoto Women's University,* V (1951), 1-5.

Tax, Meredith. "Sexual Politics," *Ramparts,* IX (1970), 50-58.

Taylor, John A. "The Greatness of *Sons and Lovers,*" *Modern Philology,* LXXI (1974), 380-387.

Taylor, Kim. "A Phoenix Out of the Ark," *Private Library,* Second Series (Middlesex, England), III (1970), 110-120. The contemporary relevance of Lawrence's social message.

Tedlock, Ernest W., Jr. "A Forgotten War Poem by D.H. Lawrence," *Modern Language Notes,* LXVII (1952), 410-413.

—. "D.H. Lawrence and America—A Biographical and Critical Study of the Influence of the United States and Mexico on the Thought and Writing of D.H. Lawrence," *Doctoral Dissertations,* XVII (1951), 229 (University of Southern California).

—. "D.H. Lawrence's Annotations of Ouspensky's *Tertium Organum*," *Texas Studies in Literature and Language*, II (1960), 206-218.

Tenenbaum, Louis. "Two Views of the Modern Italian: D.H. Lawrence and Sean O'Faolain," *Italica*, XXXVII (1960), 118-125.

Terada, Takehiko. "D.H. Lawrence 'Koisura Onnatachi'—Kaishaku to Bunseki" ("D.H. Lawrence's *Women in Love:* An Interpretation and Analysis"), *Kindai* (Kobe University), Nos. 16-17 (1956), 33-63, 1-28.

—. "D.H. Lawrence Mondai to Oto" ("D.H. Lawrence: Problems and Responses"), *Eikbungaku Hyoron* (Kyoto University), No. 7 (1960), 104-171.

—. "D.H. Lawrence ni Okeru Ketsugo no Mondai" ("D.H. Lawrence: Problem of Conjugation"), *Kindai* (Kobe University), No. 5 (1953), 1-39.

—. "D.H. Lawrence Rekishi Taiken" ("D.H. Lawrence's Vision of History"), *Eigaku* (Kansai University), I, No. 4 (1957), 60-115.

—. "D.H. Lawrence Rekishi Taiken" ("D.H. Lawrence's Vision of History"), *Eigaku* (Kansai University), I, No. 5 (1958), 1-28.

Terry, C.J. "Aspects of D.H. Lawrence's Struggle with Christianity," *Dalhousie Review*, CIV (1974), 112-129.

—. "F.W. Nietzsche and D.H. Lawrence: A Comparative Study," Dissertation, Kent University, Canterbury, 1972.

Tetsumura, Haruo. "*Aaron's Rod* Dansha (Sakuhin to Ningen Lawrence)" ("On *Aaron's Rod*"), *Hiroshima Studies in English Language and Literature*, XII (1966), 33-43.

—. "Ai no Shigan *The Rainbow*" ("On *The Rainbow* as It is to be Transcended"), *Shimonoseki Economic Review* (Shimonoseki Christian College), VII (1964), 53-74.

—. "D.H. Lawrence Kenkyu (II) (Sono Shinpi Shugi o Sasaeru Mono)" ("A Study of D.H. Lawrence (II): An Aspect of His Mysticism"), *Shimonoseki Economic Review*, VII (1963), 61-90.

—. "D.H. Lawrence's Mysticism: What the Moon Signifies," *Hiroshima Studies in Egnlish Language and Literature,* IX (1963), 51-65.

—. *"The Man Who Died* ni Tsuite (Shukyoteki de Arukoto to Sono Hyogen)" ("A Study of *The Man Who Died:* Religiousness as Lawrence's Quintescence"), *Hiroshima Studies in English Language and Literature* (University of Hiroshima), XIV (1967), 53-65.

—. *"Sons and Lovers* kara *Women in Love* e (Shi no Gutaitekina Kankaku ni Mukatte)" ("From *Sons and Lovers* to *Women in Love:* Towards a More Concrete Sense of Death"), *Shimonoseki Economic Review,* VII (1965), 81-104.

Teunissen, John J. and Evelyn Hinz. "The Attack on the Pieta: An Archetypal Analysis," *Journal of Aestetics and Art Criticism,* XXXIII (1974), 43-50.

Theobald, John R. "The Dionysian Strain in the Poems of D.H. Lawrence," *Programs Announcing Candidates for Higher Degrees* (University of Iowa), 1942.

—. "The Dionysian Strain in the Poems of D.H. Lawrence," *Doctoral Dissertation,* X (1943), 92 (University of Iowa).

Thody, Philip. *"Lady Chatterley's Lover:* A Pyrhhic Victory," *Threshold,* V (1961), 36-49.

Thomas, Helen. "Two Pieces of Advice from D.H. Lawrence," London *Times Literary Supplement,* March 22, 1963, 12.

Thomas, John. H. "The Perversity of D.H. Lawrence," *Criterion,* X (1930), 5-22.

Thompson, Leslie M. "The Christ Who Didn't Die: Analogues to D.H. Lawrence's *The Man Who Died," D.H. Lawrence Review,* VIII (1975), 19-30.

—. "A Lawrence-Huxley Parallel: *Women in Love* and *Point Counter Point," Notes and Queries,* XV (1968), 58-59.

—. "D.H. Lawrence and Judas," *D.H. Lawrence Review,* VIII (1975), 1-19.

Thulin, Richard L. "Men and Women in the Writings of David Herbert Lawrence and of Certain Contemporary Theologians: A Dialogue in Theology and Literature," Dissertation, Boston University School of Theology, 1972.

Thurber, James. "My Memories of D.H. Lawrence," In *The Achievement of D.H. Lawrence,* ed. Frederick J. Hoffman and Harry T. Moore, 88-90.

Tibbets, Robert A. "Addendum to Roberts: Another Piracy of *Lady Chatterley's Lover," Serif,* II (1974), 58.

Tiedje, Egon. "D.H. Lawrence's Early Poetry: The Composition-Dates of the Drafts in MS. E 317," *D.H. Lawrence Review,* IV (1971), 227-252;

Tindall, William York. "Introduction," *The Later D.H. Lawrence* (New York: Alfred A. Knopf, 1952).

—. "Introduction," *The Plumed Serpent* (New York: Alfred A. Knopf, 1951), v-xiv.

—. "D.H. Lawrence and the Primitive," *Sewanee Review,* XLV (1937), 198-211.

Tolchard, Clifford. "D.H. Lawrence in Australia," *Walkabout,* XXXIII, No. 11, 28-31.

Tomlinson, T.B. "Lawrence and Modern Life: *Sons and Lovers, Women in Love," Critical Review* (Melbourne), VIII (1965), 3-18.

—. "Literature and History—the Novel," *Critical Review,* IV (1961), 93-101. Lawrence included.

Toraiwa, Masuzumi. "Nikutai to Sono Kage: D.H. Lawrence Oboegaki" ("Body and Illusion: A Note on D.H. Lawrence"), *English Literature* (Waseda University), No. 22 (November, 1962), 45-56.

Toyokuni, Takashi. "A Modern Man Obsessed by Time: A Note on 'The Man Who Loved Islands,'" *D.H. Lawrence Review,* VII (1974), 78-82.

Trail, George Y. "A Prologomena to the Poetry of D.H. Lawrence," *Dissertation Abstracts International,* XXX (1969), 3479A (University of Missouri).

—. "Toward a Laurencian Poetic," *D.H. Lawrence Review,* V (1972), 67-82.

Traschen, Isadore. "Pure and Ironic Idealism," *South Atlantic Quarterly,* LIX (1960), 163-170. General essay, Lawrence included.

Traversi, Derek. "Dr. Leavis and the Case of D.H. Lawrence," *Month,* XV (March, 1956), 166-171. A review of Leavis's approach to Lawrence.

Travis, Clayton L. "A Wall of Fire, A Wall of Ice: Growth as an Aesthetic Criterion in the Fiction of D.H. Lawrence," Dissertation, University of Michigan, 1970.

Travis, Leigh. "D.H. Lawrence: The Blood-Conscious Artist," *American Imago,* XXV (1968), 163-190.

Trilling, Diana. "Introduction," *The Portable D.H. Lawrence* (New York: Viking Press, 1947).

—. "Lawrence: Creator and Dissenter," *Saturday Review of Literature,* XXIX (1946), 17-18, 82-84.

—. "D.H. Lawrence and the Movements of Modern Culture," In *D.H. Lawrence: Novelist, Poet, Prophet,* ed. Stephen Spender, 1-17.

—. "A Letter of Introduction to D.H. Lawrence," *Partisan Review,* XXV (1958), 32-48. See also *A D.H. Lawrence Miscellany,* ed. Harry T. Moore, 114-130.

Trilling, Lionel. "D.H. Lawrence: A Neglected Aspect," *Symposium,* I (1930), 361-370.

Troy, William. "D.H. Lawrence as Hero," In *William Troy: Selected Essays,* ed. Stanley Edgar Hyman (New Brunswick, New Jersey: Rutgers University Press, 1967), 110-119. Review of *Letters,* ed. Aldous Huxley.

—. "The D.H. Lawrence Myth," In *The Partisan Reader,* ed. Philip Rahv and William Phillips (New York: Dial Press, 1946), 336-347.

Truchlar, Lee. "Zur Spatlyrik von D.H. Lawrence," *Die Neueren Sprachen,* XVIII (1969), 600-606.

Tucker, Betty Jean. "An Archetypal Imagery Study of the Fall of the Family in the Nineteenth-Century English Novel," Dissertation, University of Alabama, 1971.

Tudor, Kathleen K. "The Androgynous Mind in W.B. Yeats, D.H. Lawrence, Virginia Woolf, and Dorothy Richardson," Dissertation, University of Toronto, 1972.

Tudsberry, M.T. *"Lady Chatterley's Lover,"* Notes and Queries, VIII (1961), 149.

Turner, G.R. "Princess on a Rocking Horse," *Studies in Short Fiction,* V (1967), 72.

Uchiki, Jotaro. "'Koisuru Onnatachi' ni Okeru Koseijo no Tokucho ni Tsuite" ("On the Characteristics in the Composition of *Women in Love"*), *Sylvan* (Tohoku University), X (May, 1965), 10-22.

—. "Lawrence no 'Niji' no Kosei ni Kansuru Ichi Kenkyu" ("A Study on the Composition of *The Rainbow"*), *Sylvan,* VIII (May, 1963), 14-24.

—. "'Shinda Otoko' ni Tsuite" ("On *The Man Who Died"*), *Sylvan,* XII (December, 1967), 15-24.

—. *"Sons and Lovers* ni Tsuite" ("On *Sons and Lovers"*), *Report of the Chiba Institute of Technology (Humane Studies),* VIII (December, 1966), 83-109.

—. "Tsubasa Aru Hebi Tsuite" ("On *The Plumed Serpent"*), *Report of Rikkyo University (Humane Studies),* No. 23 (May, 1968), 1-47.

Ueda, Teruo. "D.H. Lawrence no Shi Ichimen" ("An Aspect of D.H. Lawrence's Poetry"), *Studies in the Humanities* (Osaka City University), VII (1957), 68-81.

144

—. "Lawrence to Sei" ("Lawrence and Life"), *Studies in the Humanities* (Osaka City University), VIII (1957), 119-132.

Uehata, Yoshikazu. "D.H. Lawrence no 'Barazono no Kage' Ni Okeru Shukyu Teki Yoso" ("Religious Elements in D.H. Lawrence's 'The Shadow in the Rose Garden'"), *Bungaku-kai Ronshu* (Konan University), No. 33 (March, 1967), 67-83.

—. "D.H. Lawrence to Dento" ("D.H. Lawrence and Tradition"), *Kansai-Daigaku Bungaku* (Kansai University), No. 12 (January, 1963), 58-71.

—. *"St. Mawr* no Hyoka o Megutte" ("On Some Appreciations of *St. Mawr"), Bungaku-kai Ronshu* (Konan University), No. 36 (March, 1968), 125-148.

Ulmer, Gregory L. "D.H. Lawrence and the Rousseau Tradition," Dissertation, Brown University, 1972.

Undset, Sigrid. "D.H. Lawrence," In *Men, Women, and Places,* trans. Arthur C. Chater (New York: Alfred A. Knopf, 1939), 33-53. See also *The Achievement of D.H. Lawrence,* ed. Frederick J. Hoffman and Harry T. Moore, 49-62.

Unterecker, John. "Lawrence on a Low Budget," *New Leader,* November 9, 1959, 23-25. Lawrence in paperback.

Untermeyer, Louis. "Hot-Blood's Blindfold Art," *Saturday Review of Literature,* IX (1933), 523-524.

—. "D.H. Lawrence," *New Republic,* XXIII (August 11, 1920), 314-315. A review of all of Lawrence's work to date with the war and modern times as background.

Usui, Yoshitaka. "Lawrence to Hiyoda-Tachi" ("Lawrence and His Critics"), *English Literature* (Waseda University), No. 28 (March, 1963), 135-145.

Vacarelli, Mary M. "'Nostalgia for Sicily': The Fictional Modes of Giovanni Verga and D.H. Lawrence," Dissertation, Catholic University of America, 1972.

Vakeel, H.J. "D.H. Lawrence: Social Theorist and Mystic," *Visvabharati Quarterly,* XXVI (1960), 24-44.

Van Ghent, Dorothy. "On *Sons and Lovers*," In *D.H. Lawrence: A Collection of Critical Essays,* ed. Mark Spilka (Englewood Cliffs, New Jersey: Prentice-Hall, 1963), 15-28. In defense of the integrity and completeness of the work.

Van Time, James G. "Major Polarities in the Shorter Fiction of D.H. Lawrence," *Dissertation Abstracts,* XXIX (1968), 3160A-3161A (Claremont).

Vickery, John B. "James C. Cowan's *D.H. Lawrence's American Journey,* Sven Armen's *Archetypes of the Family in Literature,* and D.H. Lawrence's *The Rainbow,*" *Psychological Perspectives,* II (1971).

—. *"Golden Bough:* Impact and Archetype," *Virginia Quarterly,* XXXIX (1963), 37-57. Lawrence's use of Frazer.

—. *"The Golden Bough* and Modern Poetry," *Journal of Aesthetics and Art Criticism,* XV (1957), 271-288.

—. "D.H. Lawrence: The Evidence of Poetry," *The Literary Impact of the Golden Bough* (Princeton: Princeton University Press, 1973), 280-293.

—. "D.H. Lawrence: The Mythic Elements," *The Literary Impact of the Golden Bough,* 294-325.

—. "D.H. Lawrence's Poetry: Myth and Matter," *D.H. Lawrence Review,* VII (1974), 1-18.

—. "The Literary Impact of *The Golden Bough,* Dying Gods in Eliot, Lawrence, and Joyce," Dissertation, University of Wisconsin, 1955.

—. "Myth and Ritual in the Shorter Fictions of D.H. Lawrence," *Modern Fiction Studies,* V (1959), 65-82. Perceptive and anticipates the main direction of Lawrence Studies at the moment.

—. *"The Plumed Serpent* and the Eternal Paradox," *Criticism,* V (1963), 119-134. One of the few "archetypal" interpretations of this work that captures its spirit and structure.

—. *"The Plumed Serpent* and the Reviving God," *Journal of*

146

Modern Literature, II (1972), 505-532.

Vidas, Louise W. "The Single Green Light and the Splendid and Terrible Spectrum: A Study of the Secular Romance Quest in the Novels of Thomas Hardy and D.H. Lawrence," Dissertation, University of Illinois, 1974.

Vitoux, Pierre. "Aldous Huxley and D.H. Lawrence: An Attempt at Intellectual Sympathy," *Modern Language Review*, LXIX (1974), 501-522.

Vivas, Eliseo. "Lawrence's Problems," *Kenyon Review*, III (1941), 83-94. Vivas assumes that the case against Lawrence is proved because Lawrence is homosexual.

—. "Mr. Leavis on D.H. Lawrence," *Sewanee Review*, LXV (1957), 123-136. Too heavy-handed an attack on Leavis.

—. "The Substance of *Women in Love*," *Sewanee Review*, LXVI (1958), 588-632. The essential moralistic approach to Lawrence and a study incorporated into Vivas's *D.H. Lawrence: The Failure and the triumph of Art* (Evanston, Illinois: Northwestern University Press, 1960).

—. "The Two Lawrence," *Bucknell Review*, VII (1958), 113-132.

Vogelsang, John. "The Concept of Self in the Works of D.H. Lawrence and Virginia Woolf," Dissertation, State University of New York, Buffalo, 1974.

Vowles, Richard B. "Lawrence's *The Blind Man*," *Explicator*, XI (1952), item 14.

Vredenburgh, Joseph L. "Further Contributions to a Study of the Incest Object," *American Imago*, XVI (1959), 263-268. Miriam and Clara as incest objects for Paul Morel in *Sons and Lovers*.

Wada, Shizuo. "D.H. Lawrence oboegaki (I)" ("A Note on D.H. Lawrence (I)"), *Kyushu Shoka Daigaku Shokei Ronso* (Kyushu University), No. 3 (April, 1963), 111-135. On *The White Peacock*.

—. "D.H. Lawrence oboegaki (II)" ("A Note on D.H. Lawrence (II)"), *Kyushu Sangyo Daigaku Kyoyobu Kiyo* (Kyushu Sangyo University), No. 1 (1964), 27-62.

—. "D.H. Lawrence Oboegaki (III) ('Musuke to Koiboto' ni Tsuite)" ("A Note (III) on D.H. Lawrence's Oedipus Complex in *Sons and Lovers*"). *Kyushu Sangyo Daigaku Kyoyovu Kiyo*, No. 2 (1967), 75-93.

Wade, John S. "D.H. Lawrence in Cornwall: An Interview with Stanley Hocking," *D.H. Lawrence Review*, VI (1973), 237-283.

Wagner, Jeanie. "A Botanical Note on *Aaron's Rod*," *D.H. Lawrence Review*, IV (1971), 287-290.

Wagner, Robert D. and F.R. Leavis. "Lawrence and Eliot," *Scrutiny*, XVIII (1951), 136-144.

Wain, John. "The Teaching of D.H. Lawrence," *Twentieth Century*, CLXI (May, 1955), 464-465.

Waldron, Philip. "The Education of D.H. Lawrence," *Journal of the Australasian Universities Language and Literature Association*, No. 24 (November, 1965), 239-252.

Walker, Cynthia L. "Power and Isolation in the Political Novels of D.H. Lawrence," Dissertation, Purdue University, 1974.

Walker, Grady J. "The Influence of the Bible on D.H. Lawrence as Seen in His Novels," Dissertation, University of Tulsa, 1972.

Walker, Ronald G. "The Blood, Border, *Barranca:* The Role of Mexico in the Modern English Novel," Dissertation, University of Maryland, 1974.

Wallace, Mary E. "'Study of Thomas Hardy': D.H. Lawrence's 'Art-Speech' in the Light of Polanyi's *Personal Knowledge*," Dissertation, University of Kent at Canterbury, 1975.

Walsh, William. "The Childhood of Ursula," In *Twentieth Century Interpretations* of *The Rainbow*, ed. Mark Kinkaid-Weekes, 82-91.

—. "The Writer and the Child," In *The Use of the Imagination*, 163-174. Ursula of *The Rainbow*.

—. "The Writer as Teacher: The Educational Ideas of D.H. Lawrence," In *The Use of the Imagination: Educational Thought and the Literary Mind* (London: Chatto & Windus, 1959), 199-228.

Warschausky, Sidney. "'The Blind Man' and 'The Rocking-Horse Winner,'" In *Insight*, ed. John V. Hagopian and Martin Dolch (Frankfort, Germany: Verlag, 1964), 221-233.

Wasserman, Jerry. *"St. Mawr* and the Search for Community," *Mosaic: Sociological Perspectives on Literature*, II (1971-1972), 113-123.

Wasson, Richard. "Comedy and History in *The Rainbow*," *Modern Fiction Studies*, XIII (1967), 465-477.

Waterman, Arthur E. "The Plays of D.H. Lawrence," *Modern Drama*, II (1960), 349-357.

Waters, Frank. "Quetzalcoatl Versus D.H. Lawrence," *Western American Literature*, III (1968), 103-113.

Way, Brian. "Sex and Language," *New Left Review*, No. 27 (September, 1964), 66-80. Henry Miller and Lawrence.

Wayland, James W. "D.H. Lawrence: The Prose Style and Use of Dialect," Dissertation, University of California, Los Angeles, 1973.

Weatherby, H.L. "Atheological Symbolism in Modern Fiction," *Southern Humanities Review*, IV (1970), 81-91. Hardy's *Tess* and Lawrence.

—. "Old Fashioned Gods: Eliot on Lawrence and Hardy," *Sewanee Review*, LXXV (1967), 301-316.

Weathers, Winston. "Mythology in Modern Literature," *D.H. Lawrence Review*, VI (1973), 201-213.

Weaver, Robert. "Lady Chatterley and All That," *Tamarack Review*, No. 21 (Autumn, 1961), 49-57.

Weidner, Ingeborg. "Botschaft Verkundigung und Selbstausdruck in Prosawerk von D.H. Lawrence," Dissertation, Humboldt University, Berlin, 1938.

Weiner, Ronald S. "Irony and Symbolism in 'The Princess,'" In *A D.H. Lawrence Miscellany*, ed. Harry T. Moore, 221-238.

—. "The Rhetoric of Travel: The Example of *Sea and Sardinia*," *D.H. Lawrence Review*, II (1969), 230-244.

—. "The Two Worlds of D.H. Lawrence," Dissertation, Harvard University, 1960.

Weintraub, Stanley. Review of Emile Delavenay's *The Man and His Work*, Frank Kermode's *d.h. lawrence*, and Robert Lucas's *Frieda Lawrence*. In *New Republic* CLXIX (August 18, 1973), 26-28.

Weisberg, Edzia. "The Triumph and the Failure of D.H. Lawrence," *Partisan Review*, XXVII (1961), 309-314. Review of Vivas.

Weiss, Daniel A. "D.H. Lawrence's Great Circle: *From Sons and Lovers to Lady Chatterley*," *Psychoanalytic Review*, L (1963), 112-138.

—. "Oedipus in Nottinghamshire," *Literature and Psychology*, VII (1957), 33-42.

—. "The Thought-Adventures of D.H. Lawrence," *Dissertation Abstracts*, XV (1954), 2221 (Northwestern University).

Welch, Colin. "Black Magic, White Lies," *Encounter*, XVI (1961) 85.

— and E.L. Mascall. "Chatterley and the Law," *Encounter*, XVI (1961), 85.

Welker, Robert H. "Advocate for Eros," *American Scholar*, XXX (1961), 191-202.

Welland, D.S. "D.H. Lawrence: 'Studies in Classic American Literature," *British Association for American Studies Bulletin*, No. 5 (1957), 3-8.

Werner, Alfred. "Lawrence and Pascin," *Kenyon Review,* XXIII (1961), 217-228.

Weslau, Werner. "Der Pessimismus bei D.H. Lawrence," Dissertation, Greifswald University, 1931.

West, Geoffrey. "The Significance of D.H. Lawrence," *Yale Review,* XXII (1933), 392-395. Review of *Lorenzo in Taos, Son of Woman, Apocalypse,* and the *Letters* edited by Huxley.

West, Paul. "D.H. Lawrence: Mystical Critic," In The *Wine of Absurdity: Essays on Literature and Consolation* (University Park, Pa.: Pennsylvania State University Press, 1966), 19-38.

West, Ray B. "Point of View and Authority in 'The Blind Man,'" In *The Art of Writing Fiction* (New York: Crowell, 1968), 223-236.

West, Rebecca *et al. "Chatterley,* the Witnesses, and the Law," *Encounter,* XVI (1961), 52-56.

Westbrook, Max. "The Poetical Spirit, Sacrality, and the American West," *Western American Literature,* III (1968), 193-205. Lawrence's *Apocalypse* and folk practices of the American West.

Whitaker, Thomas R. "Lawrence's Western Path: 'Mornings in Mexico,'" *Criticism,* III (1961), 219-236.

White, Myron L. "The Early Primitivism of D.H. Lawrence," *Dissertation Abstracts,* XIX (1958), 3311 (University of Washington).

White, Victor. "Frieda and the Lawrence Legend," *Southwest Review,* L (1965), 388-397.

White, William. "Lawrence and Marquand," *D.H. Lawrence News and Notes,* II (1962).

—. "What is a Collector's Item: Emily Dickinson, E.A. Robinson, D.H. Lawrence? (An Essay in the Form of a Bibliography)," *American Book Collector,* VI (1956), 6-8.

Wickes, George. "The Art of Fiction XXVIII," *Paris Review,* VII (1962), 129-159. Henry Miller and his efforts to write about Lawrence.

Wickham, Anna. "The Spirit of the Lawrence Women: A Post humous Memoir," *Texas Quarterly,* IX (1966), 31-50.

Widmer, Kingsley. "Laurentian Maniacs: A Review of Recent Studies of D.H. Lawrence," *Studies in the Novel,* V (1973) 547-558. Review of books by Lucas, Delavenay, Swigg, Cowan, and Kermode.

—. "D.H. Lawrence and the Art of Nihilism," *Kenyon Review,* XX (1958), 604-616.

—. "D.H. Lawrence and Critical Mannerism," *Journal of Modern Literature,* III (1973), 1044-1050. Review of books by Gilbert, Miko, and Pritchard.

—. "Lawrence and the Fall of Modern Woman," *Modern Fiction Studies,* V (1959), 47-56.

—. "Lawrence as Abnormal Artist," *D.H. Lawrence Review,* VII (1975), 220-232.

—. "Notes on the Literary Institutionalization of D.H. Lawrence: An Anti-Review of the Current State of Lawrence Studies," *Punch,* No. 26 (1966), 5-13.

—. "Our Democratic Heritage: D.H. Lawrence," In *A D.H. Lawrence Miscellany,* ed. Harry T. Moore, 295-311.

—. "The Pertinence of Modern Pastoral: Three Versions of *Lady Chatterley's Lover,*" *Studies in the Novel,* V (1973), 547-558.

—. "The Perverse Art of D.H. Lawrence," *Dissertation Abstracts,* XVIII (1957), 238-239 (University of Washington).

—. "The Primitive Aesthetic: D.H. Lawrence," *Journal of Aesthetics and Art Criticism,* XVII (1959), 344-353.

—. "The Sacred Sun in Modern Literature," *Humanist* (Antioch), XIX (1959), 368-372.

Wiehe. R.E. "Lawrence's 'Tickets, Please,'" *Explicator*, XX (1961), item 12.

Wilbur, Richard. "Seven Poets," *Sewanee Review*, LVIII (1950), 130-143. Includes a review of *Selected Poems*.

Wilde, Alan. "The Illusion of *St. Mawr:* Technique and Vision in D.H. Lawrence's Novel," *Publications of the Modern Language Association*, LXXIX (1964), 164-170.

Wilder, Amos. "Primitivism of D.H. Lawrence," In *Spiritual Aspects of the New Poetry* (New York: Harper's, 1940), 153-165.

Wildi, Max. "The Birth of Expressionism in the Work of D.H. Lawrence," *English Studies*, XIX (1937), 241-259.

Wilding, Michael. "Between Scylla and Charybdis: *Kangaroo* and the Form of the Political Novel," *Australian Literary Studies*, IV (1970), 334-348.

—. "'A New Show': The Politics of *Kangaroo,"* *Southerly* (Sydney), XXX (1970), 20-40.

Wiley, Paul L. "D.H. Lawrence," *Contemporary Literature*, XIII (1972), 249-254. Review of books by Cowan, Hochman, and Cavitch.

Williams, Charles. "Sensuality and Substance," *Theology*, May, 1939, 352-369.

Williams, George C. "D.H. Lawrence's Philosophy as Expressed in His Poetry," *Rice Institute Pamphlet*, XXXVIII (1951), 73-94.

Williams, Hubertein H. "D.H. Lawrence: The Making of a Poet," *Dissertation Abstracts*, XXIX (1968), 4028A (Bowling Green State University).

Williams, Raymond. "Introduction," *D.H. Lawrence's Three Plays* (Harmondsworth and Baltimore: Penguin Books, 1969).

—. "The Law and Literary Merit," *Encounter*, XVII (1961), 66-69. On *Lady Chatterley's Lover*.

—. "Lawrence and Tolstoy," *Critical Quarterly,* II (1960), 33-39.

—. "Our Debt to Dr. Leavis," *Critical Quarterly,* I (1959), 245-247.

—. "The Social Thinking of D.H. Lawrence," In *A D.H. Lawrence Miscellany,* ed. Harry T. Moore, 295-311.

—. "Tolstoy, Lawrence, and Tragedy," *Kenyon Review,* XXV (1963), 632-650.

Williams, Tennessee. "I Rise in Flame, Cried the Phoenix," *Ramparts,* VI (1968), 14-19. A play about Lawrence and Freida.

Wilson, Angus. "At the Heart of Lawrence," *Encounter,* V (1955), 81-83. Review article.

Wilson, Colin. "Existential Criticism," *Chicago Review,* XIII (1959), 152-181. Includes Lawrence.

Wilson, Edmund. "Signs of Life: *Lady Chatterley's Lover,*" In *The Shores of Light* (New York: Farrar, Straus, and Young, 1952), 403-407. See also *The Achievement of D.H. Lawrence,* ed. Frederick J. Hoffman and Harry T. Moore, 185-188. A fine appreciation and recognition of the work.

Wise, James N. "Emerson's 'Experience' and *Sons and Lovers,*" *Costerus,* VI (1972), 179-221.

Woerner, Robert F. "D.H. Lawrence and Herman Hesse: A Comparative Study of Two Critics of Modern Culture," *Dissertation Abstracts,* XXIV (1963), 306-307 (Indiana University).

Wolf, Howard B. "British Fathers and Sons: From Filial Submissiveness to Creativity," *Psychoanalytic Review,* LII (1965), 53-70.

Wood, Frank. "Rilke and D.H. Lawrence," *Germanic Review,* XV (1939), 213-223.

Wood, Paul A. "The Primitive Element in the Fiction of D.H. Lawrence," Dissertation, New York University, 1969.

Woodcock, George. "Mexico and the English Novelists," *Western Review*, XXI (1956), 27-29.

Woodward, A.G. "The Artist and the Modern World," *English Studies in Africa*, XVI (1973), 9-14.

Woolf, Virginia. "Notes on D.H. Lawrence," In *The Moment and Other Essays* (New York: Harcourt, Brace, 1948), 193-198

Woolwich, the Bishop of. "The Christian and Lady Chatterley," *Time and Tide*, XLI (1960), 1320-1321. Defends Lawrence.

Worthen, John. "D.H. Lawrence and Louie Burrows," *D.H. Lawrence Review*, IV (1971), 253-262.

—. "The Reception in England of D.H. Lawrence from *The White Peacock* to *Women in Love*," Dissertation, University of Kent, England, 1967.

Wright, Raymond. "Lawrence's Non-Human Analogues," *Modern Language Notes*, LXXVI (1961), 426-432.

—. "The Novels of D.H. Lawrence," *Index to Theses*, X (1960), 12 (University of Liverpool).

Yamaguchi, Keizabro. "Chijo no Shinwa" ("D.H. Lawrence's *The Plumed Serpent*"), *Bulletin of the Faculty of Liberal Arts* (Hosei University), IX (April, 1965), 85-104.

—. "D.H. Lawrence Kenkyu ni Okeru Jidenteki (I)" ("D.H. Lawrence: Biographical Elements in His Literature (I)"), *Review of Arts and Sciences* (Shibaura Institue of Technology), III (February, 1966), 54-60.

—. "D.H. Lawrence Kenkyu ni Okeru Jidenteki (II)" ("D.H. Lawrence: Biographical Elements in His Literature (II)"), *Review of Arts and Sciences* (Shibaura Institue), IV (February, 1967), 114-120.

—. "D.H. Lawrence Niji no Higeki" ("D.H. Larence: Double Tragedy in 'Odour of Chrysanthemums' and *The Widowing of Mrs. Holroyd"*), *Studies in English Literature* (Hosei University), IX (February, 1966), 51-62.

—. "D.H. Lawrence no Ikyosei" ("Paganism in Lawrence's Literature"), *Studies in English Literature* (Hosei University), V (December, 1962).

—. "D.H. Lawrence no Shukyoteki Tsuikyo (*David* ni Tsuite)" ("D..H. Lawrence's Religious Quest: The Biblical Play *David"*), *Bulletin of the Faculty of Liberal Arts* (Hosei University), XI (April, 1967), 93-114.

—. "D.H. Lawrence no Tampen Shosetsu no Giho to Stairu" ("Technique and Style of D.H. Lawrence's Short Stories"), *Studies in English Literature*, VIII (December, 1965), 69-83.

Yamaji, Kutsuyuki. "Bungaku—Seiji Rekishi (Lawrence Bungaku Josetsu)" ("Literature, Politics, and History: A Preface to the Study of D.H. Lawrence"), *Cultural Science Reports* (Kagoshima University), VII (August, 1958), 143-164.

—. "Lawrence Bungaku ni Okeru Shizen" ("Nature in D.H. Lawrence's Works"), *Volcano* (Kagoshima University), No. 2 (March, 1966), 20-27.

—. "On the Oriental Esthetic Stasis and the Occidental Creative Dynamics in Literature," *Cultural Science Reports* (Kogoshima University), VIII (July, 1959), 35-75.

—. "On the Sun(II): Three Types of Love in D.H. Lawrence's Literature," *Cultural Science Reports*, X (July, 1961), 47-64.

Yamasaki, Susumu. "Lawrence ni Okeru 'Nirvana' no Mondai" ("On Lawrence's 'Nirvana'"), *Reports of Himeji Institute of Technology*, II (1953), 1-27.

—. "*Women in Love* ni Nagareru San Shicho (I)" ("Three Central Thoughts in *Women in Love* (I)"), *Reports of Himeji Institute of Technology*, XVI B (October, 1966), 10-22.

—. *"Women in Love* ni Nagareru San Shicho (II)" ("Three Central Thoughts in *Women in Love* (II)"), *Reports of Himeji Institute of Technology,* XVII B (October, 1967), 12-29.

Yasukawa, Akira. "D.H. Lawrence no *David"* ("On D.H. Lawrence's *David"*), *Essays and Studies* (Kansai University), XIV (1967), 1-16.

—. "D.H. Lawrence no 'Shinda Otoko' ni Tsuite" ("On D.H. Lawrence's *The Man Who Died"*), *Essays and Studies* (Kansai University), IX (1959), 26-37.

Yoshida, Tetsuo. "The Broken Balance and the Negative Victory in *Lady Chatterley's Lover,"* *Studies in English Literature,* XXIV (1974), 117-129.

Young, Archibald M. "Rhythm and Meaning in Poetry: D.H. Lawrence's 'Snake,'" *English,* XVII (1968), 41-47.

Youngblood, Sarah. "Substance and Shadow: The Self in Lawrence's Poetry," *D.H. Lawrence Review,* I (1968), 114-128.

Yudhishtar, M. "The Depiction of Conflict in the Novels of D.H. Lawrence," *Index to Theses,* X (1960), 12 (University of Leeds).

Zambrano, Ana L. *"Women in Love:* Counterpoint on Film," *Literature/Film Quarterly,* I (1973), 46-54.

Zanger, Jules. "D.H. Lawrence's Three Strange Angels," *Papers on English Language and Literature,* I (1965), 184-187.

Zuckerman, Elliott. "Wagnerizing on the Isle of Wight," In *The First Hundred Years of Wagner's Tristan* (New York: Columbia University Press, 1964), 124-127. *The Trespasser.*

Zytaruk, George J. "The Chambers Memoirs of D.H. Lawrence—Which Chambers?," *Renaissance and Modern Studies,* XVII (1973), 5-37.

—. "Introduction," In *The Quest for Rananim: D.H. Lawrence's Letter to S.S. Koteliansky, 1914-1930* (Montreal and London: McGill-Queen's University Press, 1970), xiv-xxi.

—. "D.H. Lawrence's Hand in the Translation of Maxim Gorki's 'Reminiscences of Leonid Andreyev,'" *Yale University Library Gazette,* XLVI (July, 1971), 29-34.

—. "D.H. Lawrence's Reading of Russian Literature," *D.H. Lawrence Review,* II (1969), 120-137.

—. "D.H. Lawrence's Response to Russian Literature," *Dissertation Abstracts,* XXVI (1965), 4678-4679 (University of Washington).

—. "The Phallic Vision of D.H. Lawrence and V.V. Rozanov," *Comparative Literature Studies,* IV (1968), 283-297.

—. "'The Undying Man': D.H. Lawrence's Yiddish Story," *D.H. Lawrence Review,* IV (1971), 20-27.

—. "What Happened to D.H. Lawrence's *Goats and Compasses?,*" *D.H. Lawrence Review,* IV (1971), 280-286. Earliest version of *Women in Love.*

—, ed. "Dorothy Brett's Letters to S.S. Koteliansky," *D.H. Lawrence Review,* VII (1974), 240-274.

—, ed. "The Last Days of D.H. Lawrence: Hitherto Unpublished Letters of Dr. Andrew Morland," *D.H. Lawrence Review,* I (1968), 44-50.

—, ed. "D.H. Lawrence: Letters to Koteliansky," *Malahat Review,* I (1967), 17-40. Twenty unpublished letters.

SELECTED REVIEW:
LAWRENCE IN AND OUT OF HIS TIME

A.,L. (Abercrombie, Lascelles). Review of *Sons and Lovers*, *Manchester Guardian*, July 2, 1913, p.7. Calls the "constant juxtaposition of love and hatred" obsessive, points out other defects, but agrees that the novel is "an achievement of the first quality."

Aiken, Conrad. "The Disintegration of Modern Poetry," *Dial*, June, 1924. Review of *Birds, Beast and Flowers*.

—. "The Melodic Line," *Dial* August 9, 1919. Review of *Look! We Have Come Through!*

—. "Mr. Lawrence, Sensationalist," *Nation and Athenaeum*, July 12, 1924. Review of Studies *in Classic American Literature*.

—. "Review of *Birds, Beasts and Flower*, In *A Reviewers ABC* (New York: Meridian Books, 1958), 256-261.

—. Review of *Collected Poems*, *New York Evening Post*, July 20, 1929.

—. Review of *Mornings in Mexico*, *Dial*, October 15, 1927.

Aldington, Richard. "An Estimate of Lawrence," *Sunday Referee*, April 15, 1930.

—. "D.H. Lawrence," *Everyman*, March 13, 1930. Lawrence's death.

—. "D.H. Lawrence as Poet," *Saturday Review of Literature,II* (May 1, 1926), 749-750. Lawrence's poetry often a very successful revolt against a "Non-human scale of values."

159

Alpert, Hollis. "Up the Rebels," *Saturday Review,* July 25, 1970. Film version of *The Virgin and the Gypsy.*

Anderson, Sherwood. "A Man's Mind," *New Republic,* May 21, 1930. Includes a review of *Assorted Articles.*

Anonymous. "Famous Novelist's Shameful Book," *John Bull,* XLIV (October 20, 1928), 11. Review of *Lady Chatterley's Lover,* "The foulest book in English literature."

Anon. "Fine and Imprisonment for Selling Lawrence's book *Lady Chatterley's Lover,* " *Publishers' Weekly,* November 30, 1929.

Anon. "Frustrate Ladies," *Nation* (New York), September 7, 1921. Review of *The Lost Girl.*

Anon. "A Genius Pain-Obsessed," *Manchester Guardian,* March 4, 1930, 12. Obituary.

Anon. "D.H. Lawrence and Louis Burrows," London *Times Literary Supplement,* May 1, 1969, 465.

Anon. "Lawrence the Poet: Achievement and Irrelevance," London *Times Literary Supplement,* August 26, 1965, 725-727.

Anon. "D.H. Lawrence's Dark and Vehement Genius," *Current Opinion,* February, 1922.

Anon. "Mr. D.H. Lawrence and Lord Brentford," *Nation and Athenaeum,* January 11, 1930. Review of *Pornography and Obscenity.*

Anon. "Mr. Lawrence's American Studies," London Times Literary Supplement, July 24, 1924.

Anon. "Magistrate Order Prints of D.H. Lawrence's Paintings to be Destroyed," London *Daily Express,* August 5, 1929.

Anon. Obituary, *The Times* (London), March 4, 1930, 11.

Anon. "Paintings Seized by London Police as Indecent," *New York Times,* July 6, 1929.

Anon. "Poetry of Fear," *Saturday Review*, September, 1933. Review of *Collected Poems*.

Anon. "Pornography and the Censorship," *New Statesman*, November 23, 1929. Review of *Pornography and Obscenity*.

Anon. "Recent Verse," *New Statesman*, X (1918), 406-407.

Anon. "Search for Atlantis," London *Times Literary Supplement*, May 12, 1961, 292.

Anon. "Some Books of the Week," *Spectator*, September 29, 1928, 403.

Anon. "Suppression of Lawrence's *Rainbow*," *Current Opinion*, February, 1916.

Anon. "The Theme of Decline Again," *Glasgow Herald*, March 4, 1930, 5 Obituary.

Anon. "Two Realists: Russian English," *Athenaeum*, IV (June 1, 1912), 613-614. Review of *The Trespasser*.

Anon. "Who's Obsene," *Nation* (New York), February 26, 1930.

Anon. Review of *Amores:* London *Times Literary Supplement*, August 10, 1916; *New York Times Book Review*, November 26, 1916; *Review of Reviews*, December, 1916.

Anon. Review of *Birds, Beasts and Flowers:* London *Times Literary Supplement*, December 13, 1923, 864.

Anon. Reviews of *Collected Poems: Spectator*, September 29, 1928; *New Statesman*, October 20, 1928; *Nation and Athenaeum*, November 10, 1928; London *Times Literary Supplement*, November 15, 1928, 852; London *Times Literary Supplement*, September 29, 1932, 673-674.

Anon. Review of *England, My England: New York Times Book Review*, November 19, 1922, 13-14.

Anon. Reviews of *Kangaroo:* London *Times Literary Supplement,* September 20, 1923, 617. A fine book in spite of its flaws—"experimental, masterful, challenging the rules and his reader." Also, *New York Times Book Review,* October 24, 1923.

Anon. Review of *The Ladybird* and *The Captain's Doll:* London *Times Literary Supplement,* March 22, 1923, 195; *Spectator,* April 14, 1923; *New York Times Book Review,* April 22, 1923.

Anon. Review of *Lady Chatterley's Lover* (expurgated edition of 1932 in England and America: London *Times Literary Supplement,* February 25, 1932, 130. Novel emasculated but still the work of genius.

Anon. Review of *Letters to Bertrand Russell:* New Yorker, March 12, 1949.

Anon. Reviews of *Look! We Have Come Through!:* London *Times Literary Supplement,* November 22, 1917, 571; *New Statesman,* January 26,1918; Athen*aeum,* February, 1918; *New York Times Book Review,* April 20, 1919.

Anon. Review of *The Lost Girl:* London *Times Literary Supplement,* December 2, 1920; *Nation and Athenaeum,* January, 1921; *Spectator,* January 19, 1921.

Anon. Review of *Love Poems and Others: Nation,* XVI (November 14, 1914), 220-221. Lawrence's poetry decidedly new, imagistic, captures the spirit of the age.

Anon. Reviews of *Mornings in Mexico:* London *Times Literary Supplement,* July 7, 1927; *New York Book Review,* August 7, 1927; *Nation and Athenaeum,* August 13, 1927; *Saturday Review,* August 27, 1927.

Anon. Review of *New Poems: Athenaeum,* February, 1919; London *Times Literary supplement,* February 6, 1919; *Nation* (New York), Supplement No. 414, October 13, 1920; *New Statesman,* December 14, 1918.

Anon. Review of *Pansies:* London *Times Literary Supplement,* July 4, 1929, 532.

Anon. Review of *A Prelude:* London *Times Literary Supplement,* April 28, 1950.

Anon. Reviews of *The Plumed Serpent:* London *Times Literary Supplement,* January 21, 1926; *Spectator,* January 30, 1926; *New Republic,* February 19, 1926; *Boston Evening Transcript,* February 24, 1926; *Living Age,* April 3, 1926; *Dial,* June, 1926.

Anon. Reviews of *The Prussian Officer: Outlook,* XXXIV (December 19, 1914), 795-796; *Saturday Review,* January 9, 1915; *Athenaeum,* January 23, 1915; *Bookman* (New York), February, 1917; *Nation* (New York), March 15, 1917.

Anon. Review of *The Rainbow: Standard,* October 1, 1913, 3. The novel defies all the conventions, may cause offense and be condemned, but "there is no flaw in its construction."

Anon. Reviews of *Sons and Lovers: Standard,* May 30, 1913, 5— Lawrence returns to Nottinghamshire and arrives at full maturity; *Westminster Gazette,* XLI (June 14, 1913); *Saturday Review,* CXV (June 21, 1913), 780-781; *Athenaeum,* June 21, 1913; *Saturday Review,* June 21, 1913; *Nation,* XIII (July 12, 1913), 577—a boring, sexually morbid work; *New York Times Book Review,* September 21, 1913; *Independent,* October 9, 1913; *Outlook,* December 6, 1913; *Nation* (New York), December 11, 1913; *New Republic,* April 10, 1915.

Anon. Review of *St. Mawr: New York Times Book Review,* June 14, 1925; *Boston Evening Transcript,* June 20, 1925; *Dial* November, 1925.

Anon. Review of *Touch and Go:* London *Times Literary Supplement,* May 13, 1920; *Survey,* August 20, 1920; *Spectator,* August 28, 1920.

Anon. Reviews of *The Trespasser: Athenaeum,* June 1, 1912; *Saturday Review,* June 22, 1912; *New York Times Book Review,* November 17, 1912, Also, *Morning Post* (London) June 17, 1912, 2: An "interesting and ugly piece of work" dealing with "abnormal persons," with some fine passages. And *New York Times Book Review,* November 17, 1912, 677: One of the frankest and best of contemporary novels on the castrating woman.

Anon. Review of *Twilight in Italy:* London *Times Literary Supplement,* June 15, 1916; *Review of Reviews,* February, 1917; *Nation* (New York), March 15, 1917.

Anon. Reviews of *The White Peacock:* London *Times Literary Supplement,* January 21, 1911, 35— Lawrence's feeling for nature on the "pathetic side"; *Morning Post,* February 9, 1911, 2— Lawrence here to stay defects and all; *Daily News* (London), February 14, 1911, 3— a sick book by a sick author; *Athenaeum,* February 25, 2911; *Saturday Review,* May 15, 1911.

Anon. Reviews of *The Widowing of Mrs. Holroyd: Independent,* May 25, 1914; *Nation* (New York), July 23, 1914; *New York Times Book Review,* October 4, 1914; *Outlook* (London), December 24, 1926 (on the production of the play).

Anon. Reviews of *The Woman Who Rode Away:* London *Times Literary Supplement.* May 13, 1920 *Survey,* August 20, 1920, *Spectator,* August 28, 1920.

Anon. Review of *Women in Love: Saturday Westminster Gazette,* LVIII (July 2, 1921), 14-15.

Arnold, M. "D.H. Lawrence and the Book of the Spinster," *Bookman* (New York), April, 1922.

Arvin, Newton. "Mr. D.H. Lawrence's Criticism," *Freeman,* October 31, 1923. Review of *Studies in Classic American Literature.*

Auden, W.H. "Some Notes on D.H. Lawrence," *Nation,* April 26, 1947. Includes a review of *The Portable Lawrence* (New York: Viking, 1947).

B., E. "What Are Those Golden Builders Doing," *Athenaeum,* XLIV (1928), 216

Bates, E.S. Review of *Apocalypse, Saturday Review of Literature,* February 13, 1932.

Beals, Carleton. "Acknowledge the Wonder," *Nation* (New York) September 14, 1927. Review of *Mornings in Mexico.*

—. Review of *Mornings in Mexico, Saturday Review of Literature,* August 27, 1927.

Bennett, Arnold. "D.H. Lawrence's Delusion," *Evening Standard* (London), April 10, 1930.

Beresford, J.D. "Some Autumn Novels," *Nation and Athenaeum,* December 8, 1923.

Bickley, Francis. Review of *Amores* and *Twilight in Italy, Bookman* (London), LI (October, 1916), 26-27. Lawrence a true poet even in his novels, and the poems contain a perfect relation of opposites.

Blunden, Edmund. Review of *Cavalleria Rusticana, Nation and Athenaeum,* March 10, 1928. D.H. Lawrence, trans.

Bogan, Louise. Review of *Selected Poems, New Yorker,* March 20, 1048, 102-106.

Boynton, H.W. Review of *Aaron's Rod, Independent,* May 27, 1922.

—. Review of *Kangaroo, Independent,* November 10, 1923.

—. Review of *The Ladybird* and *The Captain's Doll, Independent,* May 26, 1923.

—. Review of *The Prussian Officer, Bookman* (New York), February, 1917.

Breit, Harvey. Review of *Letters to Bertrand Russell, New York Times Book Review,* January 23, 1949.

(Brentford, Viscount). Review of *Pornography and Obscenity, New Statesman,* XXXIV (November 23, 1929), 219-220. The Home Secretary versus Lawrence.

Brickell, Herschel. Review of *Cavalleria Rusticana, New York Herald-Tribune Books,* October, 1928.

—. Review of *The Woman Who Rode Away, North American Review,* July, 1928.

Brock, I. Review of *Studies in Classic American Literature, New York Times Book Review,* September 16, 1923.

Brooks, W.R. Review of *Apocalypse, Outlook,* March, 1932.

Broun, Heywood. "A First-Class Writing Man is Dead," *New York Evening Telegram,* March 4, 1930.

—. Review of *The Ladybird* and *The Captain's Doll, New York World,* April 22, 1923.

Brown, I. Review of the Production of *The Widowing of Mrs. Holroyd, Saturday Review,* December 18, 1926.

Buermeyer, L.L. Review of *Psychoanalysis and the Unconscious, Nation, July 27, 1921.*

Bullett, Gerald. Review of *St. Mawr, Saturday Review,* May 23, 1925.

Burdett, Osbert. Review of *A Collier's Friday Night, London Mercury,* September, 1934.

—. Review of *Apocalypse, Saturday Review,* July 11, 1931.

Burgum, Edwin B. "Brass Impregnable," *Sewanee Review,* XLI (1933), 112-116. Review of *Letters* (New York: Viking Press, 1932).

Burman, R.L. Review of *England, My England, Fantasia of the Unconscious,* and *Women in Love, Nation,* January 17, 1923.

Bynner, Witter. "Pen Portrait of D.H. Lawrence," *Laughing Horse,* April, 1926.

Cabot, Currie. Review of *A Modern Lover, Saturday Review of Literature,* November 10, 1934.

Campkin, D. Review of *Apocalypse, Week-End Review*, May 7, 1932.

Canaan, Gilbert. "A Defense of D.H. Lawrence," *New York Tribune*, January 10, 1920.

Canby, H.S. "Critics from Abroad," *New York Evening Post Literary Review*, October 13, 1923. *Studies in Classic American Literature.*

—. Review of *Kangaroo, New York Evening Post Literary Review* November 17, 1923.

—. "Too Soon, and Too Late," *Saturday Review of Literature*, June 2, 1928. Review of *The Woman Who Rode Away.*

Cantwell, Robert. Review of *The Virgin and the Gypsy, New Republic*, December 24, 1930.

Carew, Dudley. Review of *Reflections on the Death of a Porcupine, London Mercury*, April, 1926.

Carswell, Catherine. "D.H. Lawrence," *Time and Tide*, March 14, 1930. Lawrence's death.

—. "D.H. Lawrence in His Letters," *Nineteenth Century*, November, 1932.

—. Review of *Phoenix, Spectator*, November 27, 1936.

—. Review of *The Rainbow, Glasgow Herald*, November 4, 1915, 4. Almost the only positive view of *The Rainbow* during the war. But Lawrence's defects, particularly his increasing "tendency to the repetition of certain words and a curiously vicious rhythm into which he constantly falls," are also noted.

Carter, Frederick. Letter with Reference to Lawrence's Introduction to *The Revellations of St. John the Divine, London Mercury*, September, 1930.

Carter, John. "*The Rainbow* Prosecution," London *Times Literary Supplement*, February 27, 1969, 216.

Cavender, Kenneth. *"Sons and Lovers," Sight and Sound*, XXIX (1960), 145. Review of the film version.

Cecil, Lord David. "Lawrence in His Poems," *Spectator*, August 4, 1933, 163.

—. Review of *Letters, Spectator*, November 18, 1932.

Chamberlain, J.R. Review of *The Woman Who Rode Away, New York Times Book Review*, June 3, 1928.

Chance, R. "Love and Mr. Lawrence," *Fortnightly*, October, 1929.

Chesterton, G.K. "The End of the Moderns," *London Mercury*, January, 1933.

—. "The Spirit of Modern Literature," *Bookman*, October, 1930.

Chew, S.C. Review of *Phoenix, Christian Science Monitor*, November 4, 1936.

Christian, Moe. "Playwright Lawrence Takes the Stage in London," *D.H. Lawrence Review*, II (1969), 93-97. Review of the Royal Court's 1968 production of *The Daughter-in-Law* and *The Widowing of Mrs. Holroyd*.

Church, R. "D.H. Lawrence," *Spectator*, April 13, 1930. Lawrence's death.

—. Review of *Pansies, Spectator*, August 3, 1929.

Colton, Arthur W. "English Types and Settings," *New York Evening Post Literary Review*, February 10, 1923. Review of *England, My England*.

—. "D.H. Lawrence," *Saturday Review of Literature*, May 17, 1930. Review of *Assorted Articles*.

—. Review of *The Ladybird* and *The Captain's Doll, New York Evening Post Literary Review*, June 2, 1923.

Colum, Mary M. "The Quality of D.H. Lawrence," *Freeman,* June 22, 1921. Review of *The Lost Girl.*

Colum, Padraic. Review of *Sea and Sardinia, Dial,* February, 1921.

Comerford, Anthony. "Women in Love," London *Times Literary Supplement,* December 11, 1969, 1426. Review of film version.

Cooper, Frederic T. Review of *The White Peacock, Bookman* (New York), April, 1911.

Cournos, John. Review of *David, Literary Digest,* November, 1926.

Crawford, J.W. Review of *St. Mawr, New York World,* July 5, 1925.

Crawford, N.A. Review of *New Poems, Poetry,* September, 1921.

Crehan, Hubert. "Lady Chatterley's Painter," *Art News,* February, 1957.

Crichton, Kyle S. Review of *Letters, Scribners,* November, 1932.

Crump, G.B. "The Fox on Film," *D.H. Lawernce Review,* I (1968), 238-244.

Cuppy, Will. Review of *Fantasia of the Unconscious, New York Herald-Tribune Books,* January 14, 1923.

D., C.V. "Hungry," *Nation* (New York), January 26, 1921. Review of *Women in Love.*

D., R. Review of *Last Poems, Christian Science Monitor,* March 25, 1933.

Daniels, K.L. "Mr. Lawrence on American Literature," *New Republic,* October 24, 1923. Review of *Studies in Classic American Literature.*

Davenport, Basil. Review of *The Man Who Died, Saturday Review of Literature,* August 1, 1931.

—. Review of *The Virgin and the Gypsy, Saturday Review of Literature,* May 16, 1931.

Davis, Lord Cecil. "Lawrence in His Poems," *Spectator,* August 4, 1933.

Davis, H.J. "New Writers," *Canadian Forum,* Februaury, 1930.

—. Review of *A Modern Lover, Canadian Forum,* January, 1935.

Davis, Robert H. "D.H. Lawrence, Shy Genius, Sits for Two Camera Studies," *New York Times Book Review,* December 23, 1928.

Deutsch, Babette. Review of *New Poems, Dial,* January, 1920.

Dobree, Bonamy. "D.H. Lawernce: An Introduction," *Exchanges* December, 1929.

—. "Mr. Lawrence's *David,"* *Nation and Athenaeum,* April 24, 1926.

Douglas, Donald. Review of *Reflections on the Death of a Porcupine, Nation* (New York), March 17, 1926.

—. Review of *St. Mawr, New York Evening Post Literary Review,* June 27, 1925.

Douglas, James. Review of *The Rainbow, Star* (London), October 22, 1915, 4. A hideous book that "has no right to exist."

Dupee, Frederick W. Review of The *Man Who Died, Bookman* (New York), July, 1931.

—. Review of Selected *Poems, New York Times Book Review,* March 7, 1948, 4.

Eagle, Solomon (J.C. Squire). "Books in General," *New Statesman,* VI (November 20, 1915), 161. Discusses the banning of *The Rainbow.*

Earp, T.W. "Mr. Lawrence on Painting," *New Statesman*, XXXIII (August 17, 1929), 578. The paintings bad art.

Edgett, E.F. Review of The Lost Girl, Boston Evening Transcript, February 16, 1921.

Edwards, G.B. "Lawrence and the Young Men," *New Adelphi*, June-August, 1930.

Egan, Maurice. Review of *Studies in Classic American Literature, Literary Digest International Book Review*, September, 1923.

Eliot, T.S. "Son of Woman," *Criterion*, July, 1931.

Empson, William. "Swinburne and D.H. Lawrence," London *Times Literary Supplement*, February 20, 1969, 185.

Field, L.M. Review of *Aaron's Rod, New York Times Book Review*, April 30, 1022.

—. Review of *The Lost Girl, New York Times Book Review*, March 27, 1921.

—. Review of *Sons and Lovers, New York Times Book Review*, September 21, 1913, 479. Miriam's character alone " makes this book one of rare excellence."

Fletcher, John Gold. "Lawrence's *Last Poems*," *Poetry*, June, 1933.

—. "Night-Haunted Lover," *New York Herald-Tribune Books*, July 14, 1929. 1, 6.

—. Review of *Collected Poems, New York Herald-Tribune Books*, July, 14, 1929.

—. Review of *Look! We Have Come Through!, Poetry*, XII (August, 1918), 269-274. Lawrence has arrived at maturity, "is able to grasp a subject through its external aspect and internal meaning simultaneously."

—. Review of *New Poems, Freeman*, July 21, 1920.

Fletcher, Stuart. Review of *The Paintings of D.H. Lawrence, Sackbut*, October, 1929.

Fluchere, Henri. Review of *Letters* (London: Heinemann, 1932), *Cahiers du Sud*, November, 1932.

Forman, H.J. "With D.H. Lawrence in Sicily," *New York Times Book Review*, August 27, 1922.

Forster, E.M. "D.H. Lawrence: A Letter," *Nation and Athenaeum*, March 29, 1930. Lawrence's death.

—. Review of *Pornography and Obscenity, Nation and Athenaeum*, LXVI (January 11, 1930), 508-509.

Frank, Waldo. "A Note on D.H. Lawrence," *New Adelphi*, June-August, 1930.

Franklin, John. Review of *The Boy in the Bush, New Statesman*, XXIII (September 27, 1924), 706-707.

French, Philip. "Major Miner Dramatist," *New Statesmam*. March 22, 1968, 390. Review of *A Collier's Friday Night, The Daughter-in-Law,* and *The Widowing of Mrs. Holroyd.*

French, Yvonne. Review of *Last Poems, London Mercury*, XXVIII (1933), 262-264.

Fuller, H.B. "Sardinia Days," *Freeman*, March 1, 1922. Review of *Sea and Sardinia.*

Furst, H. "The Paintings of D.H. Lawrence," *Apollo*, July, 1929.

G., P. "A Novel of Qualtiy," *Bookman* (London), August, 1913. Review of *Sons and Lovers.*

Garnett, David. Review of *Phoenix, New Statesman and Nation*, November 21, 1936.

—. "The Whole Hive of Genius," *Saturday Review of Literature*, October, 1932. Review of *Letters* (London: Heinemann, 1932).

Garnett, Edward. "Art and the Moralists: Mr. D.H. Lawrence's Work," *Dial*, November 16, 1916.

—. "D.H. Lawrence, His Posthumous Papers," *London Mercury*, December, 1936. Review of *Phoenix*.

—. Review of *The Lost Girl, Manchester Guardian*, December 10, 1905, 5. Novel compares with Arnold Bennett's "pictures of the *Five Towns.*"

Gates, Barrington. Review of *Pansies, Nation and Athenaeum*, July 27, 1929.

Gerhardi, William. "Mr Lawrence and the Wreck of the Love Service," *Adelphi*, November, 1923.

Gillet, Louis. "D.H. Lawrence d'apres sa Correspondence," *Revue des Deux Mondes*, December 1, 1932.

Gillette, J. "Sons and Lovers," *Film Quarterly*, XIV (1960), 41-42. Review of film version.

Gilliat, Penelope. "This England, This Past," *New Yorker*, July 4, 1970. Film review of *The Virgin and the Gypsy*.

Gilman, Richard. "What's Left of Lawrence?," New Republic, March 23, 1968, 31-36. Review of *Phoenix* and *Phoenix II* (New York: Viking Press, 1968).

Goldberg, Isaac. "In the World of Books," *Freeman*, April 5, 1930. Lawrence's death.

Gorman, H.S. Review of *Birds, Beasts and Flowers, New York Times Book Review*, December 9, 1923.

—. Review of *New Poems, New York Times Book Review*, July 4, 1920.

Gould, Gerald. Review of *Aaron's Rod, Saturday Review*, July 15, 1922.

—. Review of *The Boy in the Bush, Saturday Review*, September 6, 1924.

—. Review of *The Ladybird, New Statesman*, March 31, 1923.

Gregory, Alyse. "Artist Turned Prophet," *Dial,* LXXVI (January, 1924), 66-72.

—. Review of *Psychoanalysis and the Unconscious, Fantasia of the Unconscious, Studies in Classic American Literature,* and *Kangaroo.* Lawrence driven to dogmatism in his later works by sex. *Kangaroo* is bad art, and Lawrence has sacrificed his gifts.

Gregory, Horace. Review of *Etruscan Places, New Republic,* December 14, 1932.

—. Review of *Lady Chatterley's Lover, New Republic,* December 14, 1932.

—. Review of *Letters, New Republic,* December, 1932.

Gwynn, Stephen. "Mr. D.H. Lawrence," *Fortnightly,* CXXVII (April, 1930), 553-556.

H., J.E. "Mr. Lawrence's Criticsim," *New Statesman,* August 2, 1924. Review of *Studies in Classic American Literature.*

Hackett, Francis. "A Week in D.H. Lawrence," *New Republic,* January 11, 1922. Review of *Sea and Sardinia.*

—. Review of *The Lost Girl, New Republic,* March 16, 1921, 77-78.

—. Review of *Psychoanalysis and the Unconscious, New Republic,* August 17. 1921.

—. Review of *Sea and Sardinia, New Republic,* January 11, 1922, 184-185.

—. "The Surplus Woman," *New Republic,* March 16, 1921. Review of *The Lost Girl.*

Hale, E.E., Jr. "New Realists," *Independent,* August 30, 1915.

Hall, Arthur. "Lawrence in Etruria," *Bookman* (London), October, 1932.

Hall, E.B. Review of *Collected Poems, Boston Evening Transcript,* July 20, 1929.

Hansen, Harry. "D.H. Lawrence," *New York World,* March 4, 1930. Lawrence's death.

Harding, D.W. "Lawrence's Evils," *Spectator*, November 11, 1960, 735-736.

Hartley, L.P. Review of *The Boy in the Bush, Spectator,* CXXX-III (September 13, 1924), 264-266.

—. Review of *The Plumed Serpent, Saturday Review,* CXLI (January 30, 1926), 129-130.

—. Review of *The Woman Who Rode Away, Saturday Review,* June 2, 1928.

Harwood, H.C. Review of *The Plumed Serpent, Outlook,* April, 1926.

Haslip, Joan. Review of *Apocalypse, London Mercury,* November, 1931.

—. Review of *The Man Who Died, London Mercury,* November, 1930.

Hawk, Affable (Desmond MacCarthy). "Books in General," *New Statesman,* XXXII (1928), 51.

—. Review of The *Collected Poems, New Statesman,* October 20, 1928.

Hawkins. A.D. Review of *Phoenix, New Criterion,* July, 1937.

Hazlitt, Henry. "Bowdlerized Lawrence," *Nation* (New York), CXXXV (September 7, 1932), 214-215. Review of *Lady Chatterley's Lover.*

—. "Last Testament," *Nation* (New York), April 30, 1930. Review of *Assorted Articles.*

Herbert, Sir Alan. "Thoughts on Lady Chatterley," *Listener* (November 10, 1960), 834-835. The trial of *Lady Chatterley's Lover.*

Hersch, Virginia. "The Last Days of D.H. Lawrence," *New York World,* September 28, 1930.

Hervey, G.M. "The Genius of Mr. Lawrence," *Nation and Athenaeum,* August 21, 1926.

Hicks, Granville. "D.H. Lawrence as Messiah," *New Republic,* October 28, 1936. Review of *Phoenix.*

Higgins, Bertram. Review of "Memoirs of the Foreign Legion by M.M.," *The Calendar*, March, 1925.

Hoggart, Richard. "The Voice of Lawrence," *New Statesman*, June 14, 1968, 796-797. Review of *Phoenix II*.

Hughes, Richard. Review of *Birds, Beasts and Flowers*, *Nation and Athenaeum*, XXXIV (January 5, 1924), 519-520.

Hunt, Violet. Review of *The White Peacock*, *Daily Chronicle* (London), February 10, 1911, 6. An important contribution to literature by an author "unconscious of class," a book of great merits and defects.

Hutchinson, Percy. Review of *Apocalypse*, *New York Times Book Review*, February 28, 1932.

—. Review of *Collected Poems*, *New York Times Book Review*, July 7, 1929.

—. Review of *The Lovely Lady*, *New York Times Book Review*, February 12, 1933.

—. Review of *The Plumed Serpent*, *New York Times Book Review*, February 7, 1926.

Huxley, Aldous. "The Censor," *Vanity Fair*, November, 1929. On Lawrence's paintings.

—. Review of *Etruscan Places*, *Spectator*, November 4, 1932.

Jacks, P.M. Review of *A Modern Lover*, *New York Times Book Review*, November 4, 1934.

James, Henry. "The Younger Generation," London *Times Literary Supplement*, Spring, 1914.

Jennings, R. Review of *David*, *Spectator*, May 28, 1927.

Jones, Alan-Pryce. Review of *Last Poems*, *London Mercury*, November, 1932.

Jones, E.B. Review of *England, My England*, *Nation and Athenaeum*, February 23, 1924.

Josephson, Matthew. "Precocious Superman," *Saturday Review of Literature*, November 29, 1924. Review of *The Boy in The Bush*.

Kael, Pauline. "Lust for 'Art,'" *New Yorker,* March 28, 1970, 97-101. Film review of *Women in Love.*

Kain, Richard M. "Lady *Chatterley's Lover,*" London *Times Literary Supplement,* VIII (January 8, 1970), 34.

Kantor, L. Review of *England, My England, New York Herald-Tribune Books,* December 24, 1922.

Kauffman, Stanley. "Lady Chatterley at Last," *New Republic,* CLV (May 25, 1959), 13-16.

—. "Three Cities," *New Republic,* CLXIX (December 15, 1973)), 22, 33-34.

—. "The *Virgin and the Gypsy,*" *New Republic,* CXLVI (August 1, 1950). film review.

—. *"Women in Love,*" *New Republic,* CLXVI (April 18, 1970; August 1, 1970). film review.

Kennedy, G.W. Review of *The Woman Who Rode Away,*" *New Statesman,* June 2, 1928.

Kennedy, P.C. Review of *The Plumed Serpent, New Statesman,* January 30, 1926.

—. Review of *St. Mawr, New Statesman,* June 20, 1925.

Kermode, Frank. "Lawrence in His Letters," *New Statesman and Nation,* March 23, 1962, 422-423. Review of *Collected Letters of D.H. Lawrence,* ed. Harry T. Moore.

Kimpel, Ben D. and T.C. Duncan Eaves. "The Fight for Barbara on Stage," *D.H. Lawrence Review,* I (1968), 72-74. Review of the Mermaid Theatre production, 1967.

Knight, Arthur. "Liberated Classics," *Saturday Review,* March 21, 1970, 50. Film review of *Women in Love.*

Kronenberger, L. Review of *St. Mawr, Saturday Review of Literature,* August 1, 1925. See also *Dial,* November, 1925.

Krutch, Joseph Wood. "D.H. Lawrence," *Nation* (New York), March 19, 1930. Lawrence's death.

—. "Love's Exasperations," *Nation* (New York), June 7, 1922. Review of *Aaron's Rod*.

—. "A Nietzschean Novel," *Nation* (New York), November 24, 1924. Review of *The Boy in the Bush*.

—. "Wasteland," *Nation* (New York), November 7, 1923. Review of *Kangaroo*.

Kuttner, Alfred. Review of *Sons and Lovers, New Republic*, II (April 10, 1915), 255-257. Notes the alteration in Lawrence from the poorly motivated "mis-matings" of the earlier work to the "radical inability to mate." Novel full of unrecognized distortion.

Lane, J.W. Review of *Etruscan Places, Bookman* (New York), January, 1933.

Latimer, Margery. Review of *Assorted Articles, New York World*, April 27, 1930.

Leavis, F.R. "Genius as Critic," *Spectator,* March 24, 1961, 412, 414. Review of *Phoenix.*

—. Review of *Phoenix, Scrutiny,* December, 1937.

Leighton, F.W. "The Bite of Mr. Lawrence," *The Laughing Horse,* April, 1926.

Lesemann, M. "D.H. Lawrence in New Mexico," *Bookman* (London), March, 1924.

Lewis, Wyndham. "'Paleface' or Love? What ho! Smelling Strangeness," *The Enemy,* No. 2, September, 1927.

Lewisohn, Ludwig. Review of *Touch and Go, Nation* (New York), September 11, 1920.

Lippmann, Walter. "Apropos of Mr. Lawrence: The Crude Barbarian and the Noble Savage," *New Republic, December 15, 1920.

Littell, R. Review of *St. Mawr, New Republic,* July 8, 1925.

Lowell, Amy. "A New English Poet," *New York Times Review of Books,* April 20, 1919, 205, 210-211, 217.

—. Review of *Look! We Have Come Through!, New York Times Book Review,* April 20, 1919.

—. Review of *Touch and Go. New York Times Book Review,* August 22, 1926.

Lowenfels, W. "D.H. Lawrence," *The Irish Statesman,* April 12, 1930. Lawrence's death.

Lucas, F.L. Review of *Birds, Beasts and Flowers, New Statesman,* March 8, 1924.

—. "Sense and Sensibility," *New Statesman,* XXII (1924), 634-635.

Luhan, Mabel Dodge. Review of *The Plumed Serpent, The Laughing Horse,* April, 1926.

—. Review of *The Portable D.H. Lawrence* (New York: Viking Press, 1947), *Chicago Sun Book Week,* February, 1947.

Lynd, Robert. "D.H. Lawrence," London *Daily News,* March 4, 1930. Lawrence's death.

—. Review of *The Rainbow,* London *Daily News,* October 5, 1915, 6. An indecent book lacking the "marks of good literature" that must cause Lawrence's reputation to suffer.

M. (John Middleton Murry). Review of *The Lost Girl, Athenaeum,* December 17, 1920, 836. Novel betrays Lawrence's loss of imaginative power.

M., A. (Allan Monkhouse). Review of *The White Peacock, Manchester Guardian,* February 8, 1911.

M., C. (Charles Marriott). Review of *The Ladybird, The Fox, The Captain's Doll, Manchester Guardian,* April 6, 1923, 7.

—. Review of *The Plumed Serpent, Manchester Guardian,* January 29, 1926, 9.

M., O. "D.H. Lawernce," London *Times Literary Supplement,* March 13, 1930. Lawrence's death. See also *Nation and Athenaeum, March 22, 1930.*

Macauley, J. "For D.H. Lawrence," *American Freeman,* July 5, 1930. A poem.

MacCarthy, Desmond. "Notes on D.H. Lawrence," *Life and Letters,* May, 1930.

—. Review of the Production of *The Widowing of Mrs. Holroyd, New Statesman,* December 18, 1926.

Macy, John. "The American Spirit," *Nation* (New York), October 10, 1923. Review of *Studies in Classic American Literature.*

—. Review of *The Ladybird* and *The Captain's Doll, Nation* (New York, June 6, 1923.

—. Review of *The Lost Girl* and *Women in Love, New York Evening Post Literary Review,* March 19, 1921, 3-4.

Malcolm, Donald. "Books: The Prophet and the Poet," *New Yorker,* XXXV (September 12, 1959), 193-194, 196-198. Review of *Lady Chatterley's Lover.*

Mansfield, Katherine. Review of *The Lost Girl,* from *The Scrapbook of Katherine* Mansfield, ed. John Middleton Murry (London: Constable, 1939), 156-157. Lawrence denies life and has "blasphemed against the spirit of reverence."

Markum, Leo. Review of *The Ladybird* and *The Captain's Doll, Literary Digest International Book Review,* July, 1923.

Massingham, H.J. "Personal Estimate of D.H. Lawrence," *Nation and Athenaeum,* April 5, 1930.

—. Review of *Sons and Lovers, Daily Chronicle* (London), June 17, 1913, 3.

Mayne, Richard. *"Sea and Sardinia* Revisited," *New Statesman and Nation,* LIX (1960), 899-900.

McDowell, Elizabeth. Review of *The Boy in the Bush, Literary Digest International,* June, 1925. See also *Dial,* June,1925.

McFee, William. Review of *The Woman Who Rode Away, Bookman* (New York), July, 1928.

McHugh, Vincent. Review of *Cavalleria Rusticana, New York Evening Post Literary Review,* October 20, 1928.

McIntyre, R. "The Exhibition at the Warren Gallery," *Architectural Review,* August, 1929. Review of *The Paintings of D.H. Lawrence.*

Mera, Harry. "Caricature of D.H. Lawrence," *The Laughing Horse,* April, 1926.

Monroe, Harriet. "D.H. Lawrence," *Poetry,* May, 1930. Lawrence's death.

—. "D.H. Lawrence Up-to-Date," *Poetry,* February, 1930.

Moore, Harry T. "John Thomas and Lady Jane," *New York Times Book Review,* August 27, 1972, 7. Review of the Viking Press edition of the second version of *Lady Chatterley's Lover.*

—. "A Lawrence Budget," *Nation* (New York), October 24, 1936. Review of *Phoenix.*

—. Review of *The Later D.H. Lawrence, New York Times Book Review,* March 9, 1952.

Moore, L. "D.H. Lawrence Revives Mexico's Ancient Gods," *Literary Digest International Book Review,* March, 1926. Review of *The Plumed Serpent.*

Moore, Ruth F. "Spades and D.H. Lawrence," *Bookman* (New York), October, 1930.

Morrell, Ottoline (M.O.). "D.H. Lawrence, 1885-1930," *Nation and Athenaeum,* XLVI (March 22, 1930).

Morris, Lloyd. "Mr Lawrence on the Frontiers of Civilization," *Philadelphia Public Ledger Literary Review*, November 9, 1924. Review of *The Boy in the Bush* and *The Rainbow*.

—. Review of *The Boy in the Bush, New York Times Book Review,* October 26, 1924, 9, 17.

Morrison, Theodore. Review of *Last Poems, Atlantic Monthly,* July, 1933.

Mortimer, Raymond. Review of *Kangaroo, New Statesman,* September 19, 1923.

—. Review of *The Ladybird* and *The Captain's Doll, New Statesman,* March 31, 1923.

—. Review of *The Woman Who Rode Away, Nation and Athenaeum,* June 9, 1928.

Moult, T. "Mr. Lawrence and the People," *Athenaeum,* June 11, 1920. Review of *Touch and Go.*

Muir, Edwin. "D.H. Lawrence," *Nation and Athenaeum,* July 4, 1925.

—. "Mr. Lawrence Speeded Up," *Nation and Athenaeum,* September 20, 1924. Review of *The Boy in the Bush.*

—. "Poetry in Becoming," *Freeman* VIII (January 2, 1924), 404-405. Review of *Birds, Beasts and Flowers.* Lawrence wasting his ability. Many "astonishing strokes of natural genius" in the volume, but "not a single good poem."

—. Review of *The Plumed Serpent, Nation and Athenaeum,* February 20, 1926.

—. Review of *St. Mawr, Nation and Athenaeum,* May 30, 1925.

Murry, John Middleton. "The Decay of Mr. D.H. Lawrence," *Athenaeum,* December 17, 1920. Review of *The Lost Girl.*

—. Letter Concerning His Review of *Women in Love, Nation and Athenaeum,* August 27, 1921.

—. "The Nostalgia of Mr. Lawrence," *Nation and Athenaeum*, August 13, 1921. Review of *Women in Love.*

—. "Relevancy," *Nation and Athenaeum*, March 31, 1923. Review of *Fantasia of the Unconscious.* Lawrence has arrived, the only writer on the scene with something to say.

—. "Reminiscences of D.H. Lawrence," *New Adelphi'* June-August, 1930.

—. "Reminiscences of D.H. Lawrence" (ii), *New Adelphi,* October, 1930.

—. "Reminiscences of D.H. Lawernce" (iii), *New Adelphi,* November, 1930.

—. "Reminiscences of D.H. Lawrence" (iv), *New Adelphi,* December, 1930.

—. "Reminiscences of D.H. Lawrence" (v), *New Adelphi,* January, 1931.

—. "Reminiscences of D.H. Lawrence" (vi), *New Adelphi,* February, 1931.

—. "Reminiscences of D.H. Lawrence" (vii), *New Adelphi,* March, 1931.

—. Review of *Aaron's Rod, Nation and Athenaeum,* XXXI (August 12, 1922), 655-656. Novel "the most important thing that has happened to English literature since the war," "more important than *Ulysses.*"

—. Review of *Collected Poems, Adelphi,* II (December, 1928), 165-167.

—. Review of *Lady Chatterley's Lover, Adelphi,* II (June, 1929), 367-370. An appreciative critical estimate.

—. Review of *The Man Who Died, Criterion,* 1930.

—. Review of *Women in Love, Nation and Athenaeum,* XXIX (August 13, 1921), 713-714. *Women in Love* "five hundred pages of vehemence," Lawrence no longer an artist, crisis of novel occurs in "Excurse."

Neville, George H. "The Early Days of D.H. Lawrence," *London Mercury*, XXIIII (No. 137, March, 1931).

Nicholson, Harold. Review of *Letters* (London: Heinemann, 1932), *New Statesman and Nation*, October 1, 1932.

Nuhn, Ferner. "Lawrence and the Short Story," *Nation* (New York), March 24, 1933. Review of *The Lovely Lady*.

—. Review of *Letters, Nation* (New York), October 19, 1932.

—. Review of *A Modern Lover, Nation*, October 24, 1934.

Oates, Joyce Carol. "Candid Revelations: On *The Complete Poems of D.H. Lawrence*," *American Poetry Review*, I (November-December, 1972), 11-13.

O'Casey, Sean. Review of *A Collier's Friday Night, New Statesman*, July 28, 1934.

Ogden, Dorothy. Review of *Aaron's Rod, New York Evening Post Literary Review*, June 3, 1922.

Omicron. Review of the Stage Production of *David, Nation and Athenaeum*, May 28, 1927.

Oppenheim, E.C. Review of *Etruscan Places, Spectator*, December 23, 1932.

P., D.L. "To D.H. Lawrence," *New Adelphi*, June-August, 1930.

P.,R. "Dragging in Mr. Pound," *Christian Science Monitor*, March 25, 1933, 8.

Panter-Downes, Mollie. "Letter from London," *New Yorker*, May 11, 1968, 102. Review of *A Collier's Friday Night, The Daughter-in-Law*, and *The Widowing of Mrs. Holroyd*.

Parsons, M. Review of *Apocalypse, Spectator*, may 14, 1932.

Patten, Mercury (David Garnett). Review of *The Lovely Lady, New Statesman and Nation*, January 21, 1933.

Patterson, Isabel. "Many Mysteries," *Bookman* (New York), March, 1926. Review of *The Plumed Serpent.*

Pickthorn, Kenneth. Review of *Movements in European History, London Mercury,* August, 1926.

Pittock, Malcolm. "To the Editor," *Times Literary Supplement,* August 20, 1971. Was Lawrence first in the 1904 King's Scholarship exams? Replies by Moore, Delavenay, Sagar, *Times Literary Supplement,* September 10, 1971; Moore, *Times Literary Supplement,* October 1, 1971.

Plowman, Max. Review of *Etruscan Places. New Adelphi,* February, 1933.

—. "The Significance of D.H. Lawrence," *New Adelphi,* June-August, 1930.

Porter, Katherine Anne. Review of *The Plumed Serpent, New York Herald-Tribune Books,* March 9, 1926, 1-2. Reprinted in *The Days Before.*

Pound, Ezra. "Review of *Love Poems and Others,*" *Poetry,* II (July, 1913), 149-151. Pound views Lawrence's poetry with distaste, but calls it "the most important book of the season." See also *New Freewoman,* I (September, 1913), 113.

Powell, Dilys. "Lawrence's Last Book," *London Mercury,* February, 1935. Review of *A Modern Lover.*

Priestly, J.B. Review of *England, My England, London Mercury,* March, 1924.

—. Review of *Kangaroo, London Mercury,* November, 1923.

—. Review of *The Ladybird and The Captain's Doll, London Mercury,* May, 1923.

Pritchett, V.S. "Lawrence's Laughter," *New Statesman,* July 1, 1966, 18-19. Review of *Complete Plays.*

—. Review of *Collected Poems, Fornightly Review,* October 1, 1932, 534-535.

—. Review of *Lady Chatterley's Lover, Fortnightly Review,* CXXXI (April 1, 1932), 536-537. Better unpublished than expurgated, a crime against Lawrence.

—. Review of *The Man Who Died, Fortnightly Review,* November, 1931.

Pruette, Lorine. "He Who Asked 'Why?,'" *New York Herald-tribune Books,* April 27, 1930. Review of *Assorted Articles.*

—. Review of *Apocalypse, New York Herald-Tribune Books,* February 14, 1932.

—. Review of *Etruscan Places, New York Herald-Tribune Books,* November 13, 1932.

—. Review of *The Man Who Died, New York Herald-Tribune Books,* March 24, 1931.

Purnell, Idella. "Black Magic," *The Laughing Horse,* April, 1926.

Quennell, Peter. Review of *Letters* (London: Heinemann, 1932), *Life and Letters,* December, 1932.

—. Review of *Mornings in Mexico, New Statesman,* July 23, 1927.

—. Review of *Pansies, New Statesman,* July 27, 1929.

Rascoe, Burton. Review of *The Ladybird* and *The Captain's Doll, New York Herald-Tribune Books,* May 27, 1923.

Rauh, Ida. "Bust of D.H. Lawrence," *The Laughing Horse,* April, 1926.

Redman, Ben Ray. Review of *The Lovely Lady, Saturday Review of Literature,* March 11, 1933.

Rees, Richard. "Lawrence and Britannia," *New Adelphi,* June-August, 1930. Review of *Pornography and Obscenity* and *Nettles.*

Rexroth, Kenneth. "Poet in a Fugitive Cause," *Nation,* CXCIX (November 23, 1964), 382-383. Review of *Complete Plays.*

Roberts, R. Ellis. "D.H. Lawrence," *New Statesman*, March 8, 1930. Lawrence's death.

Robinson, Landon M. Review of *The Lost Girl, Publishers' Weekly*, February 19, 1921.

—. Review of *The Plumed Serpent, New York Evening Post Literary Review*, February 20, 1926.

Rosenfeld, Paul. "D.H. Lawrence," *New Republic*, LXII (March 26, 1930), 155-156. Lawrence's death and an assessment of his work.

Ross, Mary. Review of *The Woman Who Rode Away, New York Herald-Tribune Books*, June 10, 1928.

S., B. (Basil de Selincourt). Review of *The Trespasser, Manchester Guardian*, June 5, 1912, 5. Lawrence's objectivity and lack of compassion, incisive poetical style, convincing psychological motivation.

S., C.K. (Clement Shorter). "A Literary Letter," *Sphere*, LXIII (October 23, 1915), 104. Review of The *Rainbow*. Zola child's play compared to Lawrence.

S., H.M. (H.M. Swanwick). Review of *The Rainbow, Manchester Guardian*, October 28, 1915, 5. A boring novel with fine things to be said about it nevertheless.

Sackville-West, Edward. Review of *David* and *Reflections on the Death of a Porcupine, New Statesman* XXVII (July 10, 1926), 360-361.

Salgado, R.G.N. Review of *Complete Poems, Critical Quarterly*, VII (1965), 389-392.

Savage, Henry. Review of *The White Peacock, English Review*, May, 1911. See also Academy, LXXX (March 18, 1911), 328. An astonishing book of uncommon merit with George Saxton as the greatest achievement.

Schaffner, Halle. Review of *Mornings in Mexico, Survey*, November, 1927.

Schneider, Isidor. Review of *Last Poems, New Republic*, June 7, 1933.

—. Review of *The Lovely Lady, New Republic*, June 7, 1933.

—. "Salvation Through Sex," *Book League Monthly*, October, 1929. Review of *Collected Poems*.

Schorer, Mark. Review of *The Later D.H. Lawrence (Phoenix II), New Republic*, April 7, 1952.

Scott, Evelyn. "Philosophy of the Erotic," *Dial*, LXX (April, 1921), 458-461. *Women in Love* the last word of an age in revolt, *The Lost Girl* a new beginning.

Secker, Martin. "D.H. Lawrence," London *Times Literary Supplement*, November 3, 1966, 1012.

Seldes, Gilbert. Review of *Touch and Go, Dial*, August, 1920.

Seligman, H.G. Review of *Kangaroo, New York Herald-Tribune Books*, October 14, 1923.

—. Review of *Lady Chatterley's Lover, New York Sun*, September 1, 1928.

Sergeant, E.S. Review of *The Plumed Serpent, Saturday Review of Literature*, April 24, 1926.

Shakespear, Olivia. "The Poetry of D.H. Lawrence," *Egoist*, May 1, 1915, 81.

Shanks, Edward. "D.H. Lawrence," *John o'London's Weekly*, March 22, 1930. Lawrence's death.

—. "Mr. D.H. Lawrence: Some Characteristics," *London Mercury* May, 1923.

—. Review of *Aaron's Rod, London Mercury*, October, 1922, 655-657.

—. Review of *Collected Poems of D.H. Lawrence, Saturday Review*, October 6, 1928.

—. Review of *The Lost Girl, London Mercury*, December, 1920.

—. Review of *The Plumed Serpent, London Mercury,* April, 1926. See also *Dial,* June, 1926.

—. Review of *Studies in Classic American Literature, London Mercury,* October, 1924.

—. Review of *Women in Love, London Mercury,* August, 1921.

—. Review of *The Woman Who Rode Away, London Mercury,* August, 1928. See also Dial, August, 1928.

Sheaver, Edwin. Review of Assorted *Articles, New York Evening Post Literary Review,* April 26, 1930.

Sherman, Stuart P. "America is Discovered," *New York Evening Post Literary Review,* IV (October 20, 1923), 143-144. Review of *Studies in Classic American Literature.* Lawrence a mere impressionist, justifying his "instincts."

—. "Lawrence Cultivates His Beard," *New York Herald-Tribune of Books,* June 14, 1925, 1-3. Review of *St. Mawr.*

Ship, H. Review of the Production of *The Widowing of Mrs. Holroyd, English Review,* Janaury, 1927.

Shorey, Paul. Review of *Fantasia of the Unconscious, Independent,* December 23, 1922.

Shorter, Clement. "Literary Letter," *Sphere,* October 23, 1915. Includes a review of *The Rainbow.*

Slesinger, Tess. Review of *The Woman Who Rode Away, New York Evening Post Literary Review,* June 22, 1928.

Soskin, William. "D.H. Lawrence," *New York Evening Post Literary Review,* July 16, 1930.

—. Review of *Letters, New York Evening Post Literary Review,* September 24, 1932.

Soule, George. "A Novelist as Psychoanalyst," *Nation* (New York), July 27, 1921. Review of *Psychoanalysis and the Unconscious.*

189

Spencer, Theordore. "Is Lawrence Neglected?," *Saturday Review of Literature*, October 31, 1936. Review of *Phoenix*.

—. Review of *Letters, Atlantic Monthly*, March, 1933.

Spurling, Hilary. "Old Folk at Home," *Spectator, March 22,* 1966, 378-379. Review of *A Collier's Firday Night, The Daughter-in-Law*, and *The Widowing of Mrs. Holroyd*.

Squire, J.C. "D.H. Lawrence," London *Observer,* March 9, 1930. Lawrence's death.

—. "The Precious Residuum," *Observer* (London), March 9, 1930, 6. Lawrence's death.

—. Review of *Birds, Beasts and Flowers, London Mercury*, IX (1924), 317-318.

Stephen, Adrian. "The Science of the Unconscious," *Nation and Athenaeum*, August 25, 1921. Review of *Psychoanalysis and the Unconscious*.

Stokes, F.W. "An Australian Reformer and an English Vicar," *Nation and Athenaeum*, October 13, 1923. Review of *Kangaroo*.

Strickland, Geoffrey. "The Poems of D.H. Lawrence," London *Times Literary Supplement*, March 24, 1961, 185.

Strong, L.A. Review of *The Lovely Lady, Spectator*, January 27, 1933.

Suckow, Ruth. Review of *The Woman Who Rode Away, Outlook* (New York), August 29, 1928.

Sunne, Richard. Review of *The Man Who Died, New Statesman and Nation*, March 28, 1931.

T., E. (Eunice Tietjens). Review of *Amores, Poetry,* IX (February, 1917), 264-266.

Taggard, Genevieve. Review of *Mornings in Mexico, New York Herald-Tribune Books*, August 7, 1927.

Taylor, R.A. Review of *The Woman Who Rode Away, Spectator,* June 2, 1928.

Thomas, Edward. "More Georgian Poetry," *Bookman* (London), XLIV (April, 1913), 47. Review of *Love Poems,* Notes Lawrence's absolute concentration and lack of conventional rhythm and rhyme.

Thompson, Alan R. "D.H. Lawrence," *Bookman* (London), LXXII (1931), 492-499.

Tomlinson, H.M. "D.H. Lawrence and Norman Douglas," *Weekly Westminster,* February 14, 1925.

Towse, J.R. Review of *Touch and Go, New York Evening Post Literary Review,* November 27, 1920.

Trilling, Diana. "Rainbow's End," *New Statesman,* June 15, 1973, 894-896.

—. Review of *The First Lady Chatterley, Nation* (New York), April 22, 1944.

Trilling, Lionel, "D.H. Lawrence: A Neglected Aspect," *Symposium,* July, 1930.

—. Review of *The Virgin and the Bypsy, Nation* (New York), December 24, 1930.

Tunstill, Robert. "D.H. Lawrence," *London Mercury,* April, 1930. Lawrence's death.

Tunzelmann, G.W. Review of *The Rainbow, Athenaeum,* November 20, 1915.

Twitchett, G.E. Review of *Collected Poems, London Mercury,* February, 1929.

Untermeyer, Jean S. "Poet-Prophet Problem," *Saturday Review of Literature,* March 20, 1948. Review of *Selected Poems.*

Untermeyeer, Louis. "Hot Blood's Blindfold Art," *Saturday Review of Literature,* August 3, 1929. Review of *Collected Poems.*

—. Review of Last *Poems, Saturday Review of Literature,* April 8, 1933.

—. "Strained Intensities," *Bookman* (New York), LIX (April, 1924), 219-222. Review of *Birds, Beast and Flowers.*

Van Doren, Carl. Review of *Pansies, New York Herald-Tribune Books,* December 15, 1929, 15.

—. Review of *Sea and Sardinia, Nation* (New York), January 4, 1922.

Van Doren, Mark. "In the Image of Bigness," *Nation* (New York), December 5, 1923. Review of *Birds, Beasts and Flowers.*

—. Review of *Pansies, New York Herald-Tribune Books,* December 15, 1929.

—. "Two English Poets," *Nation* (New York), January 15, 1930. Includes a review of *Collected Poems.*

W., P.B. Review of *Kangaroo, Boston Evening Transcript,* October 13, 1923.

Wadman, Milton. Review of *St. Mawr, London Mercury,* June, 1925.

Walpole, Hugh. London Letter, *New York Herald-Tribune Books,* April 27, 1930. Lawrence's death.

Walsh, Thomas. Review of *Mornings in Mexico, Commonweal,* September 28, 1927.

Walton, Eda Lou. Review of *Last Poems, New York Herald-Tribune Books,* March 26, 1933.

Warner, R.E. "D.H. Lawrence," *Saturday Review,* April 26, 1930. Lawrence's death.

Warren, C.H. "The Greed of D.H. Lawrence," *Fortnightly Review,* November, 1932.

—. Review of *Last Poems, Fortnightly Review,* December, 1932.

Watson, E.L. "On Hell and Mr. Lawrence," *English Review,* March, 1924.

Weaver, R.M. Review of *New Poems, Bookman* (New York), September, 1920.

—. Review of *Studies in Classic American Literature, Bookman* (New York), November, 1923.

Welby, T.E. Review of *Etruscan Places, Observer,* October 23, 1923.

West, Geoffrey. Review of *Last Poems, New Criterion,* April, 1933.

—. Review of *Letters* (London: Heinemann, 1932), *New Criterion,* April, 1933.

—. Review of *The Lovely Lady, New Criterion,* April, 1933.

West, Rebecca. "Elegy," *New Adelphi,* June-August, 1930. Lawrence's death.

—. "Letter from Abroad: D.H. Lawrence as Painter," *Bookman* (London), September, 1929.

—. Review of *Aaron's Rod, New Statesman,* July 8, 1922.

—. Review of *Women in Love, New Statesman,* July 9, 1921.

Whicher, G.F. Review of *The Later D.H. Lawrence (Phoenix II), New York Herald-Tribune Books,* April 27, 1952.

White, Kenneth. Review of *Apocalypse, New Republic,* June 1, 1932.

Wiggington, W. "Animals and Ideas," *The Laughing Horse,* April, 1926.

Wilkinson, Clennell. "Mr. Lawrence's Spiritual Home," *London Mercury,* October, 1923. Review of *Sea and Sardinia.*

—. Review of *Mornings in Mexico, London Mercury,* December, 1927.

Williams-Ellis, A. "Mr Lawrence's Work," *Spectator,* October 1, 1921.

Wilson, Edmund. *"Lady Chatterley's Lover:* A Review," *New Republic,* July 3, 1929.

Wolfe, Humbert. "D.H. Lawrence," *Nineteenth Century,* April, 1930. Lawrence's death.

—. "D.H. Lawrence in the Wilderness," *Weekly Westminster,* September 27, 1924. Review of *The Boy in the Bush.*

—. Review of *Apocalypse, Observer* (London), July 3, 1932.

—. Review of *Collected Poems, Observer,* August 13, 1932, 6.

Woodbridge, H.E. Review of *The Widowing of Mrs. Holroyd, Dial,* January 16, 1915.

Woolf, Virginia (unsigned). Review of *The Lost Girl,* London *Times Literary Supplement,* December 2, 1920, 795. Novel a disappointment, "either a postscript or a prelude."

Woolsey, D.B. Review of *The* Woman *Who Rode Away, New Republic,* August 29, 1928.